*Advanced Techniques
of Population Analysis*

The Plenum Series on Demographic Methods and Population Analysis

Series Editor: Kenneth C. Land, *Duke University, Durham, North Carolina*

ADVANCED TECHNIQUES OF POPULATION ANALYSIS
Shiva S. Halli and K. Vaninadha Rao

THE DEMOGRAPHY OF HEALTH AND HEALTH CARE
Louis G. Pol and Richard K. Thomas

FORMAL DEMOGRAPHY
David P. Smith

MODELING MULTIGROUP POPULATIONS
Robert Schoen

A Continuation Order Plan is available for this series. A continuation order will bring delivery of each new volume immediately upon publication. Volumes are billed only upon actual shipment. For further information please contact the publisher.

Advanced Techniques of Population Analysis

Shiva S. Halli

University of Manitoba
Winnipeg, Manitoba, Canada

K. Vaninadha Rao

Bowling Green State University
Bowling Green, Ohio

Plenum Press • New York and London

Library of Congress Cataloging-in-Publication Data

Halli, Shivalingappa S., 1952-
    Advanced techniques of population analysis / Shiva S. Halli, K.
Vaninadha Rao.
        p.   cm. -- (The Plenum series on demographic methods and
population analysis)
    Includes bibliographical references and index.
    ISBN 0-306-43997-2
    1. Demography--Methodology.   I. Vaninadha Rao, K.   II. Title.
III. Series.
HB849.4.H35   1992
304.6'072--dc20   91-48135
                                                               CIP

18467385

ISBN 0-306-43997-2

© 1992 Plenum Press, New York
A Division of Plenum Publishing Corporation
233 Spring Street, New York, N.Y. 10013

Printed in the United States of America

To Rohini and Rama

Foreword

Although I feel honored to write a foreword for this important book, it is a task that I approach with some trepidation. The topics covered in the book summarize the current state of the art in technical demography. However, my knowledge and expertise with respect to technical demography are limited to the most fundamental and intermediate-level methods; hence, critical commentary on the contents of this volume is beyond my scope in this foreword. Since I have some understanding of the logic and substantive aspects of the methods rather than the complicated mathematics used in describing them, my comments will necessarily be restricted to the book's general organization and content.

To date, most texts published on technical demography have been limited to traditional demographic methods: sources and limitations of data, life table construction and applications, standardization techniques, various methods for preparing population estimates and forecasts, etc. However, population specialists have in recent years been developing and successfully applying a variety of sophisticated techniques not covered in the more standard introductory texts. In addition, many traditional methods that are unique to the demographic discipline have been improved and extended. Yet, to my knowledge, no one has made an attempt to bring these many new developments in population data analysis together in a single volume such as this; and a book such as this one, which summarizes several of the more widely used sophisticated techniques in social science data analysis for the benefit of practicing demographers, population data analysts, graduate students, and others who want a systematic but condensed overview of the nature and purpose of the population data analysis techniques in current use, is long overdue. For this reason alone, the effort undertaken by Professors Halli and Rao in preparing this book is commendable, and I congratulate them on its successful completion.

No book could possibly include all of the methods ever proposed as useful for population data analysis, and this book makes no such claim. Rather, it attempts to include and functionally distinguish some of the emerging demographic methods and statistical techniques that are in fairly common use but not now generally included in an introductory text on demographic methods. Like many ambitious young researchers, the authors may have tried to do too much. On the one hand, they have tried to expose the reader to a variety of methodological techniques without any in-depth discussion or emphasis on theory; and the book lacks discussion of the mathematical and statistical derivations behind the methods. On the other hand, appropriate communication in a technical book is always a difficult problem: If one writes at too low a level, one is not able to explain many important points; and if one writes at too advanced a level, then one runs the risk of losing most of one's audience. However, although the authors may have sometimes been too cryptic in their discussion of the logic of scientific enquiry, theory, and multivariate thinking in population analysis, and have not fully exposed the student to cogent uses of the advanced methods, a number of other texts are available to supplement this weakness.

The strength of the book, as indicated earlier, lies in its nature as a collection of the most up-to-date techniques developed in population-related research. As the authors state in the Preface, they have not invented any new techniques or made original contributions to the theory of statistical techniques. Nevertheless, the application and interpretation of the topics included in the text [such as decomposition of aggregate indices, age–period–cohort analysis, an introduction to linear structural relations (LISREL), logit and probit models, proportional hazards models, and multiregional analysis] make this book an extremely useful source for students of population studies as well as others—such as teachers, government officials, and a variety of private business organizations interested in population projections and forecasting. There is urgent need for a book of this kind, and I thank the authors for giving me this opportunity to comment on their efforts.

Edward G. Stockwell

Bowling Green State University

Preface

This book brings together the most recent developments in statistical modeling and their applications in population studies. We try to provide the necessary details of each statistical model and an application to demography wherever possible. There are several variations of any given statistical model, but we restrict our discussion to the most popular versions of a particular model as witnessed in recent demographic literature. In addition, we try to provide an easy-to-follow application, discussion of available software, and interpretation of results obtained from software packages. Illustrative examples are drawn from all population processes such as fertility, mortality, migration, nuptiality, family and household relationships, and labor force participation. The emphasis is on the application to substantive research issues involved and the interpretation of statistical results obtained, rather than on research design and theory development.

The idea of writing a volume of this persuasion was in our minds, but we received the moral commendation after reading a book review by Diamond on *Technical Demography* in *Population Studies* (Diamond, 1987). Our contemplation was similar to that of Diamond regarding the current state of population data analysis and we candidly agree with his conclusion that "a text in technical demography bringing together statistical and mathematical models for demographic analysis would be most welcome" (p. 523). In developing this volume, we have considered Diamond's comments. However, we do not claim to have completely filled the gap that he outlines.

There are many introductory texts available for demographic data analysis, but they are not necessarily geared toward sophisticated data analysis. Except for the first two chapters, the material covered in this book is not found in any text on demographic methods. One of the earlier texts of population techniques by Barclay (1958) discusses rates and ratios. Shryock and Siegel's (1976) volumes *The Methods and Materials of Demography* discuss direct and indirect standardization procedures. These topics are briefly explained in Chapter 1. We introduce basic formulation of life table procedures in Chapter 2. Most of the material covered in Chapter 2 is already available from textbook and non-textbook sources. This is partly due to ongoing research in this area and the evolution of new models and methods. Chapter 3 is devoted to age, period, and cohort effects. A substantive example of the age, period, and cohort model to the study of the Canadian labor force from 1950 to 1982 is provided. We try to balance our discussion on the merits and problems with the age, period, and cohort model and the usefulness of such a model in the study of demographic processes.

The multiple regression model is introduced in Chapter 4. Some of the issues in multiple regression such as the problem of outliers, multicollinearity, and the like are discussed and references are provided for continued discussion of these issues. Path analysis, factor analysis, and LISREL modeling are introduced as a natural extension of regression philosophy. Obviously, more detailed coverage of these models in one chapter is not possible, and mathematically inclined readers are advised to consult the references for technical modalities.

Logistic and probit models for binary dependent variables are the subject of Chapter 5 and log-linear analysis is elaborated in Chapter 6. Here again, our mission is to convey the main theme of each of these models and provide an illustrative demographic application and interpretation of results. Chapters 7 and 8 provide a thorough development of the proportional hazards and the parametric failure time models, respectively. Detailed examples with the Canadian Fertility Survey data for each of the models covered are presented. Often the nonavailability of proper computer software or ignorance of their modalities scares away potential researchers from these models. It is in this context that we discuss at great length all aspects of the proportional hazards model, its assumptions, data requirements, and computer programs to fit these models. While summarizing the methods covered here, wherever possible we discuss their limitations. We hope demographers and others concerned with event history analysis and the application of hazard models will benefit from our exposition of issues in a simple and straightforward manner. Most of Chapter 9 is based on Willekens and Rogers's contribution to multiregional demography.

The point we are trying to stress is that the material covered in this book is not original and generally has been published in one form or another. The multivariate statistical techniques considered in this book have been developed over the years. It is not possible to cover all statistical models in a single volume and thus we have included those that are most popular with demographers and most easily adaptable to demographic applications. In a way this is a limitation of this book. On the other hand, a foundation has been laid to a new area of development in demographic analysis. We neither propose new statistical models nor do we make original contributions to the theory of social science research methods in this volume. However, never before have so many well-established techniques for demographic methods been brought together in a single text.

Initially we planned to provide computer packages for all of the applications of the techniques, but realized that they would soon become obsolete as the computer packages are continuously revised, expanded, and corrected. During the four-year development of this book, several revisions in the programs have occurred. We include the computer programs for some important models in Chapters 7 and 8.

As stated earlier, the material covered in this book is not original. Hence, we would like to acknowledge and express our deepest appreciation and gratitude to all those responsible for the development of the techniques discussed in this book. Many people have made a direct contribution. They deserve special recognition. The method of decomposition of the index of overall headship in Chapter 1 was developed by S. S. Halli under the direction of T. K. Burch. Without his guidance and insights, it would not have been possible to formulate this procedure. All of Section 3.5 is from an article by F. T. Evers and S. S. Halli. It is unfair to Professor Evers to mention his name in the acknowledgments; he deserves to be the main author of this section. Similarly, Section 4.3.2 is from an article by B. C. Sutradhar and S. S. Halli. Some sections of Chapter 5 were taken from articles by Alfred DeMaris and K. V. Rao, and by James Trussell and K. V. Rao. We are grateful to Drs. Sutradhar, DeMaris, and Trussell for their contributions to these sections. D. Rondeau was instrumental in the completion of Chapter 6. We have greatly benefited from his tabular construction. Chapters 7 and 8 were drawn from the doctoral dissertation of K. V. Rao at the University of Western Ontario. We are thankful to T. R. Balakrishnan for his guidance and support in preparing the dissertation. We are grateful to Edward Stockwell for reading the entire manuscript and agreeing to write a foreword to the book. Also, David Smith, Frans Willekens, and D. Rennie read the manuscript and offered valuable suggestions. We very much appreciate their comments.

A book of this nature could not have been completed without the support of esteemed colleagues in the Departments of Sociology at Bowling Green State University and at the University of Manitoba. We acknowledge with thanks the generous secretarial assistance, computer resources, and other help received by K. V. Rao from the Department of Sociology, Bowling Green State University, and by S. S. Halli from the Department of Sociology, University of Manitoba. Initial work on this book was started when K. V. Rao was a Notestein Fellow at the Office of Population Research, Princeton University. We are grateful to the Office of Population Research and the Population Council for providing necessary facilities and support to K. V. Rao during the foundation stages of this volume. Diane Bulback and Kathy Olafson of the University of Manitoba, and Deb Fentress, Kathy Hill, and Patricia Kane of Bowling Green State University typed parts of the manuscript. Jiang Yunan, graduate student at Bowling Green State University, spent a considerable amount of time typesetting the mathematical formulas and cross-checking references. We are thankful to them.

We would like to thank Eliot Werner, Christopher Curioli, Kenneth Schubach, and other editorial and production staff at Plenum for their patience and help in bringing this volume to successful completion.

Finally, we would like to acknowledge the very special people in our lives—Rohini and Rama—for their understanding, cooperation, and support. Dedicating this book to them is a small token of our love and appreciation.

Shiva S. Halli
K. Vaninadha Rao

Winnipeg and Bowling Green

Contents

CHAPTER 1

Basic Demographic Methods

1.1. INTRODUCTION

The purpose of this volume is to introduce the latest developments in demographic analysis that are not covered in any introductory texts of population data analysis, the exception being those methods that are covered in the first two chapters. This chapter includes the most basic conventional methods of demography such as rates and ratios and the measures derived from these concepts, standardization and decomposition procedures, and mathematical modeling. The computational formulas, rules, and procedures that facilitate an understanding of their general nature are discussed in detail in many introductory texts on demographic methods. Hence, we will not discuss these methods in great detail but we will attempt to explain some of the limitations of these methods and also suggest possible further improvements, especially in decomposing the aggregate rates in terms of their component parts. The exercise of decomposition is useful because many vital events in demography depend upon various risk factors. For instance, the annual number of births that occur in a population depend upon biological determinants and factors such as age of the couple, their marital status (especially in societies where births occur predominantly to married women), duration of marriage, past fertility experience, practice of birth control methods, and other intermediate variables. This chapter also includes a brief presentation of the mathematical models of demography, as model-building is becoming increasingly important.

1.2. RATIOS AND RATES

The terms *ratio* and *rate* are not well defined in demography. There are conceptual distinctions between the two, but these distinctions are not consistently observed. For instance, survival rate, frequently used in demography and actuarial science, is the ratio of the number of persons in a cohort at one date to the number at an earlier date. It simply implies survival from a given age to a subsequent age. It is usually calculated from two age distributions of different censuses, or from a life table population. Survival rate fits the definition of a ratio, in situations where one number is related to another number, to provide comparison or relation between these two numbers. However, there are many types of ratios. One kind of ratio is a/b where both the numerator, a, and the denominator, b, come from the same "universe." "Universe" may comprise a group of people, houses, records, legislators, and so on. The specific nature of the universe depends on the research problem. For instance, births, and females in the reproductive ages may belong to two different universes. The universe has to be defined in terms of content and extent. With the second type of ratio, $a/(a + b)$, though both the numerator and the denominator come from the same universe, the numerator is included in the denominator. Examples of this type are proportions, because the numerator is a part of the denominator. The third type of ratio is that which describes two numbers from different universes, i.e., a ratio a/b indicates that a is from one universe and b from another. An example of this type is a sex ratio, M/F, where M is the number of males recorded in some statistical universe of persons, and F is the number of females in another universe.

Rates are computed in the same manner as ratios. Conceptually, a rate may be considered as a special case of a ratio. The difference between the two is the kind of source material used for the two numbers, numerator and denominator. In demography, the term *rate* implies a relationship between the numerator and the denominator. The numerator refers to the events and the denominator is the population at risk. The precision of a rate depends upon how closely we relate events in the numerator to the population at risk in the denominator. For instance, the incidence of divorce is often measured by the Crude Divorce Rate, which is defined as the number of divorces in a given year per 1000 (or 100,000) midyear population. This is not a refined measure because it is based on a population (denominator) which includes never married, widowed, and divorced persons who are not at risk of being divorced. A more appropriate measure is one which is based on the number of existing marriages which are at risk of being dissolved by divorce. This is not the "purest" measure of divorce incidence because it is a product not only of divorce risks, but also of death rates. The higher the mortality among the married population, the lower will be the proportion of marriages that end in divorce (Preston, 1975). Other factors which may affect the proportion of marriages ending in divorce are duration of marriage and the age distribution of the married population. In order to account for these factors, age-specific and duration-specific divorce rates need to be calculated.

The use of rates and ratios is clear to most population specialists. Ratios are used for descriptive purposes, and rates are used in the analysis of change (Shryock and Siegel, 1976). However, ratios of the third type, discussed earlier, may be used to measure relative change. For instance, a change in the population size may be measured as the difference between population at time 2 (P_2) and population at time 1 (P_1). The relative change is computed by the ratio $(P_2 - P_1)/P_1$. This ratio indicates the degree of growth of a population, but it is not a "rate of growth." A rate of growth should express growth as a relative change in population size per year (Barclay, 1958). Further usefulness and application of ratios and rates are discussed in the following section.

1.3. FERTILITY, MORTALITY, AND MIGRATION SUMMARY INDICES

The most commonly used measures in the study of fertility, mortality, and migration are based on the above-discussed concepts, rates and ratios. The understanding of rates and ratios will be useful to identify the strengths and weaknesses of the measures that we will discuss in this section. These are not the only measures of fertility, mortality, and migration. Moreover, the discussion of these measures is brief and one should consult the basic demography books for a thorough discussion of these measures.

1.3.1. Fertility Indices

The measurement of fertility is a complex problem and has been receiving the particular attention of demographers and social scientists. Various indices have been proposed for the measurement of the fertility levels of a population, each being considered to be relatively more sensitive than the other, on the basis of its ability to detect even small changes in fertility levels.

The simplest measure of the fertility level of a population is the Crude Birth Rate. This is usually calculated for a calendar year. This is a ratio of annual births in a population for a particular year based on vital statistics to the total midyear population. It is a crude indicator of fertility because the denominator (midyear population) is not really the population at risk as it includes children, women who are not in the reproductive ages, etc. It does not account for differential population structures by age, sex, marital status, etc. An improvement over this rate is the General Fertility Rate (also referred to as the "fertility rate" as opposed to the "birth rate") which relates the number of annual births to the total midyear population of females in reproductive ages. However, better measures are those that take into account population age structures, and duration of marriage, if births occur only among married women. Such rates are called age- or duration-specific rates. These are usually computed for females in the reproductive age groups for each age or duration interval, relating births occurring in a year to a group of women of the same age. Furthermore, the sum of age-specific fertility rates will provide an idea of the completed fertility of a woman and this is known as the Total Fertility Rate (TFR). Note that it is based on the fictitious cohort approach. Instead of relating all births in the numerator to the total female population of reproductive age, if the numerator is restricted to only female births, then the sum of these female age-specific fertility rates would represent the average number of girls born per woman. This is known as the Gross Reproduction Rate (GRR). If one takes into account mortality among female births, subtracting those who do not survive to their respective mothers' age, then the modified Gross Reproduction Rate is called the Net Reproduction Rate or Net Replacement Rate (NRR). The NRR is interpreted as the number of daughters who will be born to a hypothetical cohort of women, considering the mortality of women from the time of their birth. This measures the replacement of a cohort of mothers by their daughters if the population is closed for migration.

Indices of short-term changes in fertility may be utilized to study the impact of government policies, such as family planning programs. Measures of short-term changes in fertility include open and closed birth intervals, Parity Progression Ratios, Pregnancy Rate, straddling interval, birth order statistics, and so on. In the study of fertility, two factors are important: how frequently women have children, and how many women of a given birth order ever proceed to the next parity. For example, the closed birth interval measures the first dimension of fertility, while the Parity Progression Ratio gives an idea of the second. The open birth interval, i.e., the duration between the last live birth to the survey date, has been frequently used to measure fertility. One can use a probability model to account for more than one type of pregnancy termination.

Pearl (1939) suggested the Pregnancy Rate per 100 years of exposure for contraceptors, as a more efficient method for assessing the effectiveness of a particular contraceptive. He compared the total reproductive performance of women who had never practiced birth control in any form at any time during their married lives with that of women who had practiced it during part or all of their married lives. Note that this takes into consideration the period of exposure to conception.

Stix and Notestein (1940) suggested that this method could be further improved by computing pregnancy rates separately for periods of married life during which contraception was practiced and for periods during which it was not. They computed pregnancy rates, which could also be described as contraceptive failure rates, for each method of family planning used by the couples under investigation.

Birth order statistics and other measures of fertility based on numerator analysis are useful diagnostic tools for determining trends in fertility. The analysis of birth order statistics is based on the assumption that changes occurring in birth order distribution over a period are mainly due to changes in the pattern of reproduction, rather than due to changes in the composition of the population. Thus, for studying the impact of family planning programs, the proportion of first-order births may be treated as an index of fertility changes.

1.3.2. Mortality Indices

As in the case of fertility measurement, the simplest measure of mortality is the Crude Death Rate. This is defined as the ratio of the total registered deaths for a particular year of a particular population to the total midyear population for that year. The Crude Death Rate is affected by age composition. In other words, the population in the denominator differs in its death risk. For instance, infants and those over 50 are more prone to death than other age groups. To account for these variations, Age-Specific Death Rates are calculated by taking the ratio of deaths that would occur in a particular age group in a particular year of a given population to the midyear population of that age group for that year. One can also calculate sex-specific and cause-of-death-specific mortality rates. Finally, there are various techniques for calculating standardized rates which control for differences in population age composition (see Section 1.4).

One of the most important indicators of mortality in any given population is the Infant Mortality Rate (IMR). This is defined as:

IMR =

$$\frac{\text{Deaths to children under 1 year of age during a given year of a population}}{\text{Number of births during the same year for the same population}}$$

The infant deaths that occur in a given year are not necessarily from the births that occurred in the same year. The infant deaths that occur during a year may represent deaths from two cohorts of births. Therefore, the denominator, births that occur in a single calendar year, is not necessarily the population at risk for the deaths that occur in the same year. Hence, infant mortality rate is sometimes referred to as infant mortality ratio.

In the discussion of rates and ratios, we have suggested that the Infant Mortality Rate is, strictly speaking, not really a rate; the numerator is not properly related to the births at risk in the denominator. Hence, the computation of the Correct Infant Mortality Rate requires an adjustment factor.

Consider the calculation of the rate for the year, T. The numerator is the number of infant deaths that occur in year T. The denominator is the births that are at risk. It is possible that some of the infant deaths that occur in year T might have come from births that occurred in the previous year, $T - 1$. Similarly, infant deaths that occur in year $T + 1$ might have come from births that occur in year T. In order to relate infant deaths that occur in year T and $T + 1$ to the corresponding births of year T, an adjustment is necessary such that the infant deaths of two years in the numerator belong to the births that occur in a single year. Another way of adjusting the computation of the Infant Mortality Rate is to relate infant deaths that occur in a given year to the births in the appropriate year and cohort. A detailed discussion of this issue, including actual computations, may be found in any introductory text on demographic methods text (see Barclay, 1958; Shryock and Siegel, 1976; Smith, 1991).

1.3.3. Migration Indices

The measures of migration are not as straightforward as either fertility or mortality. Part of the problem in developing migration measures is the lack of data. In the absence of direct data on migration, indirect measures of migration are used. For instance, if one knows the population counts at two points of time, say two successive census counts P_t and P_{t+n}, and B and D are the total births and deaths during the interval "n," then the net migration (Net M) is obtained as:

$$\text{Net } M = (P_{t+n} - P_t) - (B - D)$$

The second indirect method is based on survival probability. If S is the Survival Ratio estimated from the census, or from a life table, then the net migration among survivors of persons aged x at the first census in a given area can be obtained as:

$$\text{Net } M(x) = P_{x+n,t+n} - SP_{x,t}$$

where $P_{x,t}$ is the population aged x years in that area at the first census, $P_{x+n,t+n}$ is the population aged $x + n$ years in the same area at the second census taken n years later.

1.4. STANDARDIZATION APPROACH

Changes in population size are the result of the structure of the population at a particular time and of the cohort processes at that time. A task of the demographer is to measure the respective impact of these two components on population change. The process of separation in the study of population change, i.e., the separation of the impact due to population structure from the impact due to the cohort processes, is called standardization.

To compare levels (e.g., fertility, mortality) of different populations, a population composition is chosen arbitrarily as the standard such that population composition of study populations are controlled. Similarly, by choosing category-specific levels of an arbitrary population as a standard, the effects of population composition can be understood. The measures computed using the standard approach are called adjusted measures. The adjusted measures contain interaction terms indicating the association between category-specific rates and population composition. "These terms are erroneous, to the extent that they result from an arbitrary choice of standard rates or standard structure (indirect and direct standardization respectively). The use of different standards yields different interaction terms and thus different values of the resulting rate or index" (Burch and Madan, 1986, p. 152). Burch and Madan further argue that the seriousness of the error contained in the interaction terms depends on the relationship between the arbitrarily chosen standard with the populations under study. Though Burch and Madan do not provide firm guidelines in the choice of the standard structure or category-specific rates, they do suggest a simple method of estimating a convenient summary measure of error associated with the arbitrary choice of standard rates or structure. Their approach is based on treating rates and population composition as vectors and utilizing the concept of the Euclidean norm. In this section we will not provide a further discussion on the Burch and Madan approach nor, for that matter, a detailed discussion on any standardization approaches.

1.4.1. Direct Standardization

In the case of direct standardization, different age-specific rates are applied to a standard population. If one is interested in summarizing a set of age-specific rates independent of the age composition of the population, then direct standardization is appropriate. Essentially this is performed to eliminate the effect of differences in population age composition. In this method, a "standard age composition" is selected and age-adjusted rates are computed for each subgroup of the population. This procedure is based on the weighted average of the age-specific rates in a given area, with the age distribution of the standard population as weights. The computational formula is:

$$M_1 = \frac{\sum m_a P_a}{P} \times 1000 \quad \text{or} \quad \sum m_a \frac{P_a}{P} \times 1000$$

where $m_a = d_a/P_a$ = age-specific rate (e.g., death rate) in the given area. P_a represents the standard population at each age, and P or $\sum P_a$ represents the total standard population (see Shryock and Siegel, 1976, for a detailed discussion).

Wunsch and Termote (1978) argue that a sound approach to summarizing data standardized for population structure is to apply principal component analysis to the set of specific rates (e.g., age or duration). For example, if there are n areas for which one has computed a sequence of specific rates $f_{i(j)}$ at a specified period of time, j indicating the time at a particular area, then the various specific rates at each duration can be considered as a set of scores for each area from which principal components can be derived, such as $F = a_0 f_0 + a_1 f_1 + \cdots + a_w f_w$. An advantage of this method is that it avoids an arbitrary choice of a standard population structure. The use of different standard structures yields different values of the resulting rate.

1.4.2. Indirect Standardization

Indirect standardization is used if the data are not available for computing specific rates (e.g., age or duration), but the population structure as well as the total number of events (say, births or deaths) during a particular calendar year are known. With this information, a crude rate can be calculated. However, this rate is not able to distinguish between the respective influences of specific rates and population structure on population change. For this purpose, one can use the method of indirect standardization. Since population structures are known, one has to arbitrarily choose specific (e.g., age or duration) rates as the standard schedule. The practice in selecting standard rates has been to use rates from one of the populations being compared, or rates from a similar population. The use of maximum rates was popularized by Coale (1969) in connection with his fertility indices. An advantage of employing maximum rates is that values of the resulting index will be less than 1.0, so that they are more easily interpreted relative to that convenient reference point (Burch *et al.,* 1987). In case a suitable maximum set is difficult to obtain, and if the available standard set results in indices exceeding 1.0, then one may assess the effects of using different standards by means of a sensitivity analysis (Burch *et al.,* 1987). The formula for adjusting the crude death rate by an indirect method is given by Shryock and Siegel (1976, p. 242) as follows:

$$m_2 = \frac{d}{\sum M_a P_a} M$$

where M_a and M represent age-specific death rates and the crude death rate for the standard population, d represents the total number of deaths, and P_a

represents the study population at each age. The formula is meant for adjusting the crude death rate of the standard population by a factor representing the ratio of the recorded number of deaths to the number expected on the basis of the age-specific death rates of the "standard" population and the population by age of the study population.

1.5. COMPONENT AND DECOMPOSITION ANALYSIS

In the case of the two standardization approaches discussed above, to eliminate the influence of population composition in the study of population change, population composition was held constant (Direct Standardization). Similarly, to eliminate the influence of age- or duration-specific rates, the specific rates were held constant (Indirect Standardization). Wunsch and Termote (1978) discuss a technique known as "double standardization." This technique can be considered as the product of the ratio of specific rates indirectly standardized (φ_i being used as standard) by the ratio of structures directly standardized (φ_i again being used as standard):

$$\frac{\sum_i L_i\varphi_i/\sum_i L_i\varphi_i}{\sum_i P_if_i/\sum_i P_i\varphi_i} \times \frac{\sum_i L_i\varphi_i}{\sum_i P_i\varphi_i} = \frac{E'}{E}$$

where P_i and L_i are the population structures for populations A and B; f_i and φ_i are the specific rates for the corresponding populations. The sole influence of differential specific rates will be $\sum_i P_if_i$ and $\sum_i P_i\varphi_i$; the sole influence of differential population structures is expressed by the comparison between $\sum_i \times P_i\varphi_i$ and $\sum_i L_i\varphi_i$ where $\sum_i P_if_i = E$ and $\sum_i L_i\varphi_i = E'$, i.e., the number of events observed in populations A and B. The ratio E'/E is the relative difference between the total number of events observed.

Wunsch and Termote (1978) further argue that instead of applying double standardization to the relative differences between the total number of events observed, one can also resort to double standardization of the absolute differences between the number of events. One can derive the following expression:

$$E' - E = \sum_i L_i\varphi_i - \sum_i P_if_i$$

$$= \sum_i \varphi_i(L_i - P_i) + \sum_i P_i(\varphi_i - fi)$$

The first part of the right-hand side of the above expression represents the component due to differential population structures and the second component due to differential specific rates. This method can be extended to the method of Kitagawa (1955), which measures the components of a difference between two crude "rates." In her classic article on "Components of a Difference between Two Rates," Kitagawa (1955) developed a method which is superior to the standardization approach because the latter cannot explicitly explain which factors account for the differences between standardized rates, in comparison with corresponding differences between their unstandardized rates. Kitagawa's method is meant to explain the difference between the total rates of two groups in terms of differences in their specific rates and differences in their composition. Hence, this technique is broader in scope than that of standardized rates, because standardization is meant to summarize and compare differences in two (or more) sets of specific rates.

Having made a conceptual distinction between the two methods, a components analysis will be conducted by considering standardized rates in a components framework. Using the notations mentioned above, the relative difference between crude "rates" is given by Wunsch and Termote (1978) as follows:

$$\frac{E'/L}{E/P} = \frac{\sum_i (P_i/P)\phi_i \sum_i (L_i/L)f_i}{\sum_i (P_i/P)f_i \sum_i (P_i/P)\phi_i}$$

This indicates that it is possible to decompose population change during a given period of time, into two components: the differences between specific rates, and the differences between population structures. An extensive discussion and further development of this theme can be read directly from Kitagawa's article.

To study the decline of fertility in various European populations, Coale (1969) decomposed the Index of Overall Fertility into three components: marital fertility, nonmarital fertility, and proportion married. Roy and Nair (1983) have extended Coale's method of comparison of fertility levels of different populations by including interaction terms reflecting the degree of interrelations between patterns of married women and marital fertility. This type of methodology is quite useful because crude rates summarize behavior across both sexes, all adult ages, and all marital status categories, and thus fail to reveal different sources of variation. It is useful to decompose aggregate rates into separate components, reflecting the impact of different relevant characteristics. As an illustration, let us consider the index of overall headship (I_H) standardized for age and sex by Burch (1980), given by the following formula:

$$I_H = \frac{H_h}{\sum_i H_i^W \times W_i + \sum_i H_i^m \times M_i}$$

In order to understand the notations used in the formula given by Burch as well as subsequent mathematical decomposition formulas (the proof of the identities is omitted since it is straightforward) presented in this section, let us consider the following definitions.

H_h = Actual number of households in a population

H_{md} = Actual number of households formed by married persons

H_{umd} = Actual number of households formed by unmarried persons

W_i = Women in the age group i

M_i = Men in the age group i

W_i^{md} = Married women in the age group i

M_i^{md} = Married men in the age group i

H_{md}^W = Actual number of households formed by married women

H_{umd}^W = Actual number of households formed by unmarried women

H_{md}^m = Actual number of households formed by married men

H_{umd}^m = Actual number of households formed by unmarried men

H_i^W = Assumed maximum headship rate for women in the ith age group

H_i^m = Assumed maximum headship rate for men in the ith age group

In the following text, we sometimes refer to H_i^W and H_i^m as standard headship rates for females and males, respectively. The decomposition of I_H by marital status is given as:

$$I_H = I_{md} \times J_{md} + (1 - I_{md}) \times J_{umd} \qquad (1.1)$$

where

$$I_{md} = \frac{\Sigma_i\, H_i^W \times W_i^{md} + \Sigma_i\, H_i^m \times M_i^{md}}{\Sigma_i\, H_i^W \times W_i + \Sigma_i\, H_i^m \times M_i}$$

= index of the proportion married among the population that indicates the extent to which marriage is contributing to the achievement of the highest potential of household formation in the study population;

$$J_{md} = \frac{H_{md}}{\Sigma_i\, H_i^W \times W_i^{md} + \Sigma_i\, H_i^m \times M_i^{md}}$$

= index of how closely the married population approaches the number of households this population would produce if it were subject to the standard age-specific headship rates;

$$J_{umd} = \frac{H_{umd}}{\Sigma_i H_i^W \times W_i^{umd} + \Sigma_i H_i^m \times M_i^{umd}}$$

= index of how closely the unmarried population approaches the number of households this population would produce if it were subject to the standard age-specific headship rates.

The equation above would be reduced to the following:

$$I_H = I_{md} \times J_{md} \tag{1.2}$$

If, in the populations, unmarried persons form a negligible proportion of households, Eq. (1.2) then is only a measure of overall headship that can be factored into an index of proportion married and an index of household formation by married persons.

The three measures of household headship (I_{md}, J_{md}, and J_{umd}) embody a form of indirect standardization for age and sex within the household formation interval, since the age distribution of a given population is the same in both the numerator and the denominator. As we hypothesize that there is a variation in the household headship index by sex, we think that it is important to develop a similar formula like the one presented in Eq. (1.1), which provides a measure of overall headship that can be factored into an index of proportion females or proportion males and an index of household formation by the female and male populations.

Therefore:

$$I_H = I_W \times I^W + (1 - I_W)I^M \tag{1.3}$$

where

$$I_W = \frac{\Sigma_i H_i^W \times W^i}{\Sigma_i H_i^W \times W_i + \Sigma_i H_i^m} \times M_i$$

= index of the proportion female among the overall population measuring the extent to which the female sex is contributing to the achievement of the highest household formation potential in the study population;

$$I^W = \frac{H^W}{\Sigma_i H_i^m \times W_i}$$

= index of how closely the female population approaches the number of households females would produce if subject to the standard age-specific headship rates;

$$I^M = \frac{H^m}{\Sigma_i \, H_i^m \times W_i}$$

= index of how closely the male population approaches the number of households males would produce if subject to the standard age-specific headship rates.

In societies where marriage itself is a major determinant of the household headship index, the age-specific household headship rate will be unusually high around the average age at marriage. On the other hand, in societies where widowhood and divorce rates contribute substantially to the household headship index, the age-specific household headship rates will be high around the average ages at divorce and widowhood. In these situations, the index of proportion married (I_{md}) is strongly affected by the proportion married around average age at marriage; also the index of proportion unmarried ($1 - I_{\text{md}}$) is strongly affected by the proportion divorced and widowed around average ages at divorce and widowhood. In these circumstances one should use the alternative formula for I_{md} given below:

$$I_{\text{md}} = \frac{\Sigma_i \, W_i \times H_i^W \times \dfrac{W_i^{\text{md}}}{W_i} + \Sigma_i \, M_i \times H_i^m \times \dfrac{M_i^{\text{md}}}{M_i}}{\Sigma_i \, H_i^W \times W_i + \Sigma_i \, H_i^m \times M_i}$$

= the weighted average of the proportion married in each age interval, where the weights ($W_i H_i^W$) and ($M_i H_i^m$) are the number of households that would occur in each age interval if the standard schedule of household headship rates prevailed.

Now, the number of households by age interval depends on the age distribution of the persons between the two limits of household formation, as well as on the standard schedule of household headship rates. This means that in societies where marriage is the major determinant of household formation, more weight must be assigned to the proportion married around average age at marriage, than in societies where marriage is not the major determinant of household formation. In the case of comparing two populations where both have the same proportions married in each age interval, and still maintain differential variation in household headship rates due to marriage (i.e., in one population marriage is more important in household formation than in the other population), one should use an index which is independent of the age distribution.

It may be mentioned here that the overall headship index can also be decomposed simultaneously by marital status and sex. In this case, the decomposed formula for I_H is:

$$I_H = I_{md} \times J_{md} + (1 - I_{md}) \times J_{umd}$$

$$= I_{md} \times (J_{md}^M + J_{md}^F) + (1 - I_{md}) \times (J_{umd}^M + J_{umd}^F)$$

$$= I_{md} \times J_{md}^M + I_{md} \times J_{md}^F + (1 - I_{md}) \times J_{umd}^M + (1 - I_{md}) \times J_{umd}^F$$

where

$$I_{md} = \frac{\sum_i H_i^W \times W_i^{md} + \sum_i H_i^m \times M_i^{md}}{\sum_i H_i^W \times W_i + \sum_i H_i^m \times M_i}$$

$$J_{md}^M = \frac{H_{md}^M}{\sum_i H_i^W \times W_i^{md} + \sum_i H_i^m \times M_i^{md}}$$

$$J_{md}^F = \frac{H_{md}^F}{\sum_i H_i^W \times W_i^{md} + \sum_i H_i^m \times M_i^{md}}$$

$$J_{umd}^M = \frac{H_{umd}^M}{\sum_i H_i^W \times W_i^{umd} + \sum_i H_i^m \times M_i^{umd}}$$

$$J_{umd}^F = \frac{H_{umd}^F}{\sum_i H_i^W \times W_i^{umd} + \sum_i H_i^m \times M_i^{umd}}$$

1.5.1. Why We Should Decompose I_H

The decomposition of I_H by marital status and sex is based on two general hypotheses. The first pertains to developing societies. In transitional societies, such as South Asia, the extended family system is dissolving gradually as a result of industrialization and modernization. An evolving norm among younger couples is to form nuclear households, subsequent to the event of marriage. Consequently, the extended kinship system is eroding due to the massive increases in internal migration. This latter phenomenon is a response to the growing economic pressures on married couples. Thus, a rise in nucleation of households is evident.

In order that we may observe the effect of such changes on household structure and formation, it is essential that the overall index of household headship, I_H, be decomposed into married and unmarried components. Comparisons can therefore be made *between and/or within areas of different points in time.*

In the developed world this decomposition can be made to reflect changes in family formation/dissolution processes. A host of economic and social factors are responsible for a recent increase in household headship rates among the sexes. A change in status from unmarried to married, married to divorced, divorced to remarried, married to widowed are a few examples of contributing forces to a rise in household complexity and headship rates. Moreover, the recent trend toward increasing individualism, and the independence of teenagers and women also account for a significant contribution to the household formation process.

A special case in point can be mentioned in connection with the application of the proposed decomposition method in places such as America. In this region, family and household patterns are characterized by varying cohabitation arrangements.

In addition to the applications above, the decomposition is also a refinement of the Household Headship Index. Now the index has a better interpretation especially in terms of marital status and sex. Moreover, the decomposition formula will be able to answer the questions posed by Burch (1980) about the reasons why Eastern societies, as well as Western ones, maintained household complexity in spite of the fact that the two types of societies are based on different socioeconomic and cultural conditions.

1.6. MATHEMATICAL MODELS

Mathematical modeling may not always be an easy task, but the mathematical analysis of demographic relationships derived from empirical observation has been a very useful exercise in estimating fertility and mortality levels. For instance, the United Nation's Manual IV, Methods of Estimating Basic Demographic Measures from Incomplete Data, illustrates the application of mathematical models to age distribution analysis for the purpose of supplementing incomplete data and correcting inaccurate data. Similarly, other indirect estimation procedures based on logical relationships for pragmatic purposes have been quite useful for facilitating an understanding of demographic processes in countries with incomplete data. In this context, a short note on mathematical models is included in the discussion of basic demographic analysis.

Mathematical models have been developed based mainly on an empirical regularity in age patterns of demographic phenomena. Recently, Coale and Demeny (1983) reconstructed the model life tables of stable relative age distribution by modeling age patterns of mortality. The practice of curve fitting existed in the study of mortality long before Coale and Demeny's model life tables (e.g., Graunt, 1662). Coale's (1972) seminal work, *The Growth and Structure of Human Populations,* illustrates the relationship between fertility and mortality schedules and age distribution. Coale's contribution to mathematical models based on an empirical regularity in age patterns is not restricted to the works cited above. Upon discovering an empirical regularity in marriage distributions, Coale (1971b) developed a mathematical model of an age pattern for marriage. Based on the idea of the age pattern of nuptiality and limited variability in the age structure of marital fertility, Coale and Trussell (1974) developed model fertility schedules. The development of model schedules of fertility is explained by Coale (1977) as follows: "The model of human fertility schedules is the product of two constituent sets of model schedules, one set of schedules approximating the proportion cohabiting, and the other set approximating the rate of childbearing of cohabiters. Our model fertility schedules are based on the assumption that control always causes a proportionate reduction of fertility below the natural fertility schedule in a fixed pattern by age" (p. 147). In order to understand the detailed underlying ideas and procedures, we suggest that readers refer to the excellent review paper by Coale (1977).

Identification and mathematical modeling of patterns in mortality, nuptiality, and fertility by Coale and his associates have been very important, and have been useful developments in recent demographic research. These models, which were based purely on age (especially those of fertility), were criticized by some researchers (e.g., Page, 1977). Page argues that physiological factors are not related only to age but also to marriage duration. Fecundity may vary with marriage duration, irrespective of age. Furthermore, under conditions of changing fertility, the various marriage and birth cohorts may react differently. Page also explains how differentials in fertility behavior by age at marriage may affect both age as well as marriage duration. For example, if those who marry at younger ages have higher fertility, then the younger women in every marriage duration group will be likely to exhibit higher fertility rates, relative to the older women in their duration group, than is accounted for simply by their age. Similarly, in a given age, the women who have been married longest are those who married youngest, hence they will show higher fertility rates relative to those who married more recently than is accounted for simply by their marriage duration. This is the reason why Page developed a model to account for the relative contribution of both age and marriage duration.

Similar to the ones discussed above, the use of mathematical functions to describe patterns of fertility behavior has been common in recent years. Duchene and Gillet-de Stefano (1974) have provided an excellent review of many functions employed including polynomials, beta distributions, Hadwiger functions, Wicksell or gamma distributions, and log-normal distributions. Miller (1946) developed the Gompertz function as a description of the mortality curve, but subsequently this function was considered and demonstrated to be a useful description of fertility distributions (Murphy and Nagnur, 1972).

1.7. SUMMARY

In this chapter, we attempted to introduce readers to the basic methods of population data analysis including rates and ratios, standardization approaches, decomposition procedures, and mathematical modeling. The discussion of the concepts of rates and ratios includes their limitations and a discussion of derived measures based on these concepts in demographic processes such as fertility, mortality, and migration. The discussion of standardization approaches addresses the problems of arbitrary choice of standard specific rates.

The most important contribution of this chapter is the decomposition procedure. Though decomposition of aggregate rates is nothing new, an application of the procedure to decompose indirectly standardized aggregate rates in household demography is interesting. This application is useful in our understanding of changes in household structure and formation and the aggregate indices derived based on Coale's (1969) methodology have better interpretation than prior to the decomposition.

CHAPTER 2

Life Table Approaches to Demographic Analysis

2.1. INTRODUCTION

Initially, the life table was developed to analyze the mortality process. Currently, its application is not restricted to mortality alone but to all measurable processes involving attrition or accession to aggregate size. The life table approach is being used in fertility, labor force, nuptiality, evaluation of contraceptive effectiveness, breast feeding, and so forth. As a general rule, life tables can be used when durations of exposure are central to whether the events being studied have occurred (Smith, 1980). It is important to remember that life table analysis is particularly useful if the events under study are nonrenewable. For instance, this approach is useful in the study of birth order statistics or parity-specific fertility behavior rather than age-specific fertility rates based on number of children born. Events such as births and marriages are renewable but order-specific births and marriages are not.

A wide area of application of the life table method is the analysis of survey data. One of the special features of survey data is that usually such data are censored. Different kinds of censoring are possible and will affect the results differently. For example, in fertility surveys, where the sample is often women in their reproductive years, consider the event of having first birth. In this case, censoring refers to the situation where some of the younger cohorts of women have not had sufficient time to have their first birth by the time of the survey. Thus, the censoring effect refers to the curtailment of exposure by the survey date. To circumvent this problem, population analysts found life table techniques useful for handling the censoring effect.

We mention at the outset that the discussion of different life table approaches in this chapter is quite limited both as to theory as well as to application, the reason being that the first book in the Plenum series on demographic methods and population analysis by Schoen (1988) provides a thorough exposition of the topics that we intend to discuss in this chapter. Schoen not only provides a mathematical basis for these approaches but also includes computer programs for ready use. In addition to this, Smith (1991) also covers life table methods and their application extensively. Hence, we will restrict the repetition and replication to a minimum.

2.2. LIFE TABLE MEASURES

The life table describes the experience of a hypothetical cohort based on age- or duration-specific rates observed in a single year or a short period. The current age- or duration-specific rates are converted into the probability of surviving or dying (in case of mortality) and are then applied to a hypothetical cohort to study a particular experience. If life table measures refer to a single year of age or duration, such life tables are known as complete life tables. On the other hand, if information is given only for broader age or duration intervals, they are known as abridged life tables. Though the life table measures usually refer to hypothetical cohort experience and are different from real cohort measures, the life table technique can be used to describe the experience of an actual cohort or the collection of experiences of various cohorts during a fixed period of time. Such a table is known as the generation or cohort life table. Before we discuss some of the important measures of a life table, we should mention that we will not explain all of the basic functions of a life table or provide computational procedures for the technique. These aspects of the life table are very well known and described in any of the introductory textbooks on demography techniques. For a thorough discussion on life table functions and their applications, the reader is directed to the most recent publications: Smith (1991), Schoen (1988), and Namboodiri and Suchindran (1987).

2.2.1. The Mean

One of the most important measures of a life table is the mean. In computation of a mean by life table analysis, the analyst often faces two types of situations: (1) the event under consideration is a sure event (e.g., death, weaning), and (2) the event of interest is not a sure event (e.g., birth, marriage, divorce). In the second situation, not everybody experiences the event regardless of the duration of waiting time and in such cases the computation of a mean becomes impossible and meaningless. In situations like this, it is better not to compute the mean but to look for other summary measures such as quartiles, spreads, trimeans, and so forth. In the first situation, one can compute a life table mean by using at least two different but related formulas depending upon the problem under consideration. Let l_x be the proportion surviving (did not experience the event), then the conditional mean for those who experienced the event before time Z is given by the shaded area divided by the height $(1 - l_z)$ in Figure 2.1. This value may be expressed as

$$\text{Mean} = \bar{X} = \frac{0.5(l_0 + l_z) + \sum_{x=1}^{z-1} (1 - Z \times l_z)}{1 - l_z} \tag{2.1}$$

The above formula for life table means has been suggested by Sheps and Menken (1973) and used by others (Balakrishnan *et al.*, 1975). However, one can find another type of expression used in the literature for the life table mean, which is related but slightly different from the above equation. For example, Srinivasan (1980) uses the formula given below for computing birth interval means from the life table analysis of Fijian Fertility Survey data:

$$\text{Mean} = \bar{X} = 0.5(l_0 + l_z) + \sum_{x=1}^{z-1} l_x = e_0 \tag{2.2}$$

In fact, Eq. (2.2) geometrically represents the area under the survival curve up to duration Z divided by 1 as shown in Figure 2.2.

The mean obtained using the formula given in Eq. (2.2) implicitly assumes that those who experience the event beyond Z have the exact duration Z and

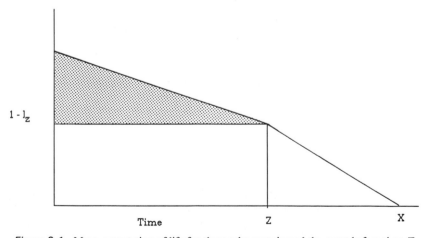

Figure 2.1. Mean expectation of life for those who experienced the event before time Z.

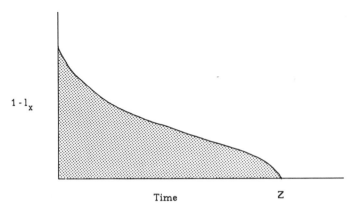

Figure 2.2. The area under survival curve up to duration.

thus make the event a sure event. Because of this assumption, the mean obtained by using formula (2.1) is always less than the mean obtained from formula (2.2), unless $l_z = 0$ or all members of the cohort experience the event by the given duration Z. The rough guide for deciding which formula to use depends on the event of interest and the nature of the event as observed from past research or experience.

2.2.2. Quartiles, Median, and Trimeans

Quartiles [i.e., $Q(1)$, $Q(2)$, and $Q(3)$] are quite informative indicators, particularly when the event of interest is not a sure event but is known to have prevalence in the study population. The survival program in the Statistical Package for the Social Sciences (SPSS) provides the median as part of the life table output. Several other measures of location and dispersion can be calculated from the quartiles such as spread $S = Q(3) - Q(1)$. Another more sensitive measure of location, given by Tukey (1977), is called the trimean. The trimean (T) can be calculated as $T = [Q(1) + 2Q(2) + Q(3)]/4$. The very nature of the trimean contains some information about the distribution, and so it is a good measure of tempo. Unlike the mean, quartiles, spread, and the trimean can be calculated for all events and are meaningful. As an example, we are reproducing a table with all of the above measures from Rao and Balakrishnan (1988a) in Table 2.1.

Table 2.1 shows quartiles and the trimean, by the year of first marriage and first birth interval length. The data are taken from the Canadian Fertility Survey and are for women who have been continuously married, married before the age of 25, have had no premarital birth, and were married between

Table 2.1. Life Table Quartiles and Trimean for the Pace of Second Birth Timing[a]

Variable	N	Quartiles (in months)			Trimean $(Q_1 + 2Q_2 + Q_3)/4$
		Q_1	Q_2	Q_3	
First birth interval (in months)					
0–7	241	19.11	30.84	46.61	31.85
8–26	686	20.60	30.32	46.06	31.83
27+	776	24.49	35.08	53.80	37.11
Marriage cohort					
1960–64	359	17.36	27.01	45.57	29.24
1965–69	419	23.15	33.54	51.71	35.49
1970–74	507	24.57	33.92	50.81	35.81
1975–79	422	23.49	33.65	46.16	34.24
Total	1707	22.04	32.46	49.09	34.01

[a] Source: Rao and Balakrishnan (1988a).

1960 and 1979. The figures were calculated from various single life tables derived from the SPSS survival program and after necessary interpolations.

2.2.3. Conditional Probabilities (q_x)

The q_x column in the life table is a pivotal column. It answers such questions as: what are the probabilities of a marriage contracted today terminating in divorce at various times say 5, 10, 15 years in the future? This question is best answered by the q_x column of a divorce table. The probabilities calculated from life table analyses are conditional and they should be interpreted as such. Hence, it is important to realize that the life table is not a method of projection or prediction but allows us to answer questions conditionally. Moreover, life table measures discussed above are synthetic measures based on the experience of all of the persons under various durations of observation, and hence in changing times is, at best, a crude indicator of the overall picture.

2.3. LOGIT MODELS

Even today, there are some countries that have no accurate or usable records of births and deaths but may have periodic censuses taken at regular intervals. In order to estimate fertility and mortality measures from available census data, model life tables have been very useful. The rationale for this estimation procedure is based on the idea that the growth and age structure of a population are determined by the fertility, mortality, and migration factors. On the other hand, model life tables are based on the idea that the mortality risks experienced by different age–sex-defined segments of a population are interrelated (United Nations, 1967). Based on this idea, different authors and organizations have constructed varying sets of life tables giving the proportions surviving from birth to each age under mortality conditions ranging from the highest to the lowest death rates observed in human populations, and a life table appropriate to a given population could then be chosen from this set of model tables (United Nations, 1967).

The United Nations took the lead in developing the model life tables (United Nations, 1955). There have been further developments since then because the United Nations's model life tables are based on only one parameter and do not provide much flexibility. In order to provide more flexibility, Coale and Demeny (1983) developed four families of tables though each family was based on single parameters. Each family of the Coale and Demeny model life tables is based on a different mortality experience. Among the four sets of model life tables, three of the sets summarize the mortality age patterns of Europe, and the fourth family is based on age patterns of mortality in 21 other countries (Australia, Canada, Israel, Japan, New Zealand, South Africa, Taiwan, the United States, and 13 in western Europe). The main limitation of the Coale and Demeny tables is that they are based mainly on European experience and unable to account for the diversity of mortality experience of non-European populations. Brass (1975) argues that the Coale and Demeny tables do not represent the mortality experience of at least Turkey, Russia, Bulgaria, Guyana, Mauritius, and Malaya, each of which exhibits a different age pattern of mortality than that of the four families in the Coale and Demeny table. It is in this context that Brass (1975) suggests that the logit system provides a more flexible alternative to existing model life tables. A thorough description of the logit system and its use is presented in Brass (1971) and Carrier and Hobcraft (1971). Nevertheless, we will provide a brief explanation of the logit system here as well for ready reference.

The logit system does not produce a set of tables. Rather it is based on a relationship for generating such tables. This relationship uses a proportion, P, between 0 and 1. Let us say that the proportion P varies with the x variable. The shape of $P(x)$ may often be described as a function similar to a logistic, and an appropriate transformation for normalizing the underlying distribution is the logit,

$$Y(X) = \text{logit} P(x) = \tfrac{1}{2} \log_e P(X)/\{1 - P(X)\} \tag{2.3}$$

Any function thus transformed can be expressed as a linear function of another function, $\phi(x)$,

$$Y(x) = \alpha + \beta \times \text{logit}\phi(x) \qquad (2.4)$$

If two or more schedules can be linearly related to the same $\phi(x)$ function, this common function may be regarded as a standard schedule that reflects the effect of variable x. As we can see, an observed schedule, $Y(x)$, is linked to the standard schedule, $\phi(x)$, by means of two parameters. The parameter α mainly describes the central tendency and β the dispersion. Since the system is based on a standard schedule and two parameters, it provides sufficient flexibility to cover a wide range of distributions. The two parameters will help to alter both the shape and the level of a standard schedule. For instance, if we fix β as 1 and α is allowed to vary, then one can produce a series of tables from the original life table. The resultant tables retain the shape of the distribution of the original table. On the other hand, if we allow only β to vary, a set of tables that intersect at a single central point will be produced. In other words, changing the values of β produces mortality variations of greater or lesser intensity at the beginning or at the end of the table.

Selecting the appropriate standard schedule depends upon the purpose of the application. In the case of mortality, one can use the model life tables of the United Nations or the West model of the Coale and Demeny system as a general standard schedule. This standard represents, basically, the European experience. Since mortality experience in Africa differs from that in Europe, a different standard should be used for Africa, one which would reflect the age pattern of African mortality. If one is interested in preparing regional estimates for a nation, the mortality table of the nation as a whole can be used as the standard. It was indicated earlier that the logit system has some advantages over the United Nations or Coale–Demeny systems. Other useful functions of the logit system as outlined by Brass (1975) are that it can be used for projecting mortality if the past and present mortality schedules are known. Based on past and present mortality schedules, trends in the values of the parameters α and β can be estimated by fitting each mortality schedule. Unlike the United Nations or Coale–Demeny systems, the logit system is very useful for computer applications as it is based on a mathematical function. Moreover, to compute life tables, other methods may require use of the computer, but the logit method does not since using it does not involve lengthy calculations. For instance, Brass (1975) illustrates how to construct a life table using an estimate of childhood mortality (say l_2) and survival probabilities from age 25. If l_2 is known, a first β value of l_{25} is obtained from the single parameter logit system (i.e., assuming $\beta = 1$). Values of $l_{32.5}$, $l_{35.7}$, and so on can then be estimated from the l_{25} and l_n/l_{25} ratios, and the logits of these values are taken from the equation:

$$Y(x) = \alpha + \beta Y_s(x)$$

$$Y(2) = \alpha + \beta Y_s(2)$$

a series of estimates of β, one for each value of x, can be estimated as

$$\hat{\beta} = \frac{Y(x) - Y(2)}{Y_s(x) - Y_s(2)}$$

Based on an average value of β from the above series, a new value of l_{25} is calculated, and then the second approximation of β is obtained. Brass suggests that one can continue this procedure to refine the estimate further but the second estimate is good enough for most purposes.

2.4. MULTIPLE-DECREMENT LIFE TABLES

The commonly used life table technique accounts for only one attrition factor. For example, the basic life table for studying mortality has "death" as the only source of decrement in the number of persons. But if one wants to take into account different causes of death in constructing a life table, the multiple-decrement life table technique is necessary. This is a simple extension of the basic life table to allow attrition, due to any number of specified causes, from the life table cohort. The multiple-decrement life table helps to answer such questions as: what is the probability that a man aged 25 y will die of a motorcycle accident before he reaches the age of 40? What is the probability that a newborn in Bangladesh will die of diarrhea before reaching its first birthday? To what will the average number of years of life in North America be extended if deaths due to cardiovascular diseases are completely eliminated? Similar to the basic life table method, the multiple-decrement life table method is also applicable to other measurable processes involving more than one attrition factor. For example, let us consider the study of nuptiality where never-married persons form the radix of the life table. This cohort of persons is exposed to both death and marriage. Unlike the situation in the basic life table, here we need to compute the attrition probabilities to take into account both *death* and *marriage*. The actual computational procedure of constructing multiple-decrement life tables is discussed in many textbooks. A thorough discussion of both computational procedures and the mathematical basis of the procedures is found in recent publications on life table techniques (Namboodiri and Suchindran, 1987; Schoen, 1988; Smith, 1991). However, in order to provide some idea of the different steps involved in the construction of multiple-decrement life tables dealing with different causes of death, the following is reproduced from Namboodiri and Suchindran (1987, p. 93):

1. Compute age-specific and age-and-cause-specific death rates and cause-of-death ratios.

2. Construct an ordinary life table using the age-specific death rates (for all causes combined).
3. Distribute by cause the total number of deaths in each age group in the life table population obtained in step 2.
4. Compute the probabilities of eventual death by each specified cause.
5. Compute the probabilities of death by cause in broad age groups, as needed.
6. Compute and plot estimated life tables by cause elimination.
7. Construct associated decrement life tables by cause elimination.

These steps are described in detail by Namboodiri and Suchindran with an illustrative example. The example is an extensive analysis of causes of death using a multiple-decrement life table technique for different populations spanning the years 1861–1964. Included are 12 different causes of death for about 180 populations in the construction of cause-eliminated life tables. In their analysis, the authors noted that in most of the developed countries cardiovascular diseases are the leading cause of death. If these diseases were to be completely eliminated, more than 60% of the cohort would survive to age 85. That is to say, the expectation of life would be increased by 17 years. On the other hand, the elimination of deaths due to cancers would increase the expectation of life by only a little more than 2 years. Similarly, the contribution by other causes of death to expectation of life due to their elimination can be found in Preston *et al.* (1972). For further discussion, computational procedures and mathematical bases, readers may refer to Preston *et al.*

2.5. MULTIPLE-INCREMENT–DECREMENT LIFE TABLES

The basic life table and multiple-decrement life table techniques are limited in scope. They are based on probabilities of attrition to form absorbing states. For example, basic life table application in mortality can be helpful in the study of movement of members of a cohort from a transient state, such as being alive, to an absorbing state, such as being dead. The straightforward extension of this technique is the multiple-decrement life table with two or more absorbing states. The multiple-decrement life table is applicable in constructing net nuptiality tables. Such tables account not only for movement to first marriage from the never-married state, but also for attrition due to mortality from the never-married state. Although this is a step forward from the basic life table where only gross nuptiality tables can be constructed, the study of nuptiality is still not comprehensive. In order to be realistic, the nuptiality process involves multiple transient states, where members of a cohort move from one state to another independently and not necessarily to absorbing states. Instead of answering the simple question such as what is the probability that never-married persons aged 20 will get married before reaching age 50?, the more comprehensive question is: what proportion of the cohort will remain unmarried, will be married once, twice, thrice, etc., before reaching age 50? In other words, it is more desirable to know the expected length of time spent in the divorced state and the widowed state by a randomly chosen unmarried person, aged 20, during the age interval 25 to 50, given that the person was first married at age 25. To answer questions of this type, the Multistate-Increment–Decrement Life Table Technique was developed. This is also known as the Multistate Life Table Technique. The multistate life table may also involve absorbing states. If a randomly chosen person is in an absorbing state, then the probability of moving to another state will be zero. Thus, the multistate life table keeps track of individuals in various states. Moreover, except for absorbing states, this technique would allow the researcher to follow people who enter or reenter transient states as they age.

In recent years, the Multistate Life Table or Increment–Decrement Life Table Technique has been very popular in the investigation of the patterns of different marital status categories, in constructing labor force status life tables, and in the study of migration and population distribution patterns. The detailed application of the multistate life table technique to the above-mentioned topics is discussed in Namboodiri and Suchindran (1987) and Schoen (1988). However, to provide some sense of the technique, we discuss briefly the application of the technique to the study of nuptiality. The discussion is heavily based on Schoen (1988).

In the case of nuptiality, we will consider five states: (1) never married (s); (2) married (m); (3) divorced (v); (4) widowed (w); and (5) dead. The first state can only be left (it cannot be returned to) and the last state is an absorbing state. The other three are transient states. The movement of members of a given cohort through a multistate system, over time, is presented in Figure 2.3, which is similar to that in Willekens *et al.* (1982).

The probability structure of the multistate life table is a continuous-time nonhomogeneous Markov process with finite state (Namboodiri and Suchindran, 1987). According to a Markov process, the probability of transition between two states, i and j, depends only on the state occupied (i). However, it actually also depends on age. It may be mentioned here that the age schedule of mortality is state-specific and the model can deal with differences in mortality by marital status.

Figure 2.3 makes it possible to study patterns of first marriage and re-marriage and separate the effects of divorce and widowhood. The calculations of these functions can be done using the computer program. In fact, Schoen (1988) provides the computer program in Appendix D. Schoen also provides

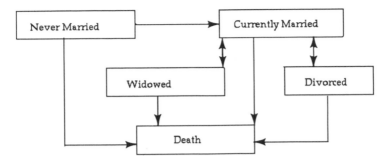

Figure 2.3. The marital-status system.

a summary table of useful indicators and that table has been reproduced here in Table 2.2. Most of the notations used in Table 2.2 are straightforward extensions of notations used in basic life table analysis. For example, $d_{ij}(y, n)$ represents the number of persons who were in state i at exact age y and who first left state i by transferring to state j in the (y, n) age interval; $l_{ij}(y + t)$ represents the group of persons who are in state i at exact age y and in state j at exact age $y + t$; and $L_{ij}(y, n)$ refers to the number of person-years lived in state j between the ages of y and $y + n$ by persons who were in state i at exact age y. Similarly, the notations and calculations can be extended to more than two-state models. Willekens *et al.* (1982) argue that the extension of a basic life table to multi-state analysis is not only simpler but also does not require restrictive assumptions if the matrix approach initiated by Rogers (1973b) is used. In the table, the matrix approach has been summarized with an application to the nuptiality process.

We must mention here that we cannot do justice to the techniques with a discussion of either multiple-decrement life tables or multistate life tables in one section of a chapter. Willekens (1985) correctly argues that multistate demography is in the process of becoming a subdiscipline by itself. The volume edited by Land and Rogers (1982) on *Multidimensional Mathematical Demography,* which is an outcome of the conference supported by the National Science Foundation, can be taken as support for Willekens's argument. Other recent works by Namboodiri and Suchindran (1987) and Schoen (1988) provide particularly good discussion on the application of the multistate life table technique not only to the study of nuptiality, but also to the study of labor force status and migration. Schoen (1988) provides the computer program for interested researchers. Since Schoen's and Smith's books are also published as part of the Plenum series on demographic methods, the discussion of the life table approaches will not be repeated in detail here.

Table 2.2. Summary Measures Available in Marital Status
Life Tables with Five States[a,b]

1. Probability a person aged 0 will ever marry	$\Sigma\ d_{sm/l(0)}$
2. Mean age at first marriage	$\Sigma\ (Y + 1/2n)d_{sm}/\Sigma\ d_{sm}$
3. Probability a marriage will end in:	
Divorce	$\Sigma\ d_{mv}/\Sigma\ (d_{sm} + d_{wm} + d_{vm})$
Widowhood	$\Sigma\ d_{mw}/\Sigma\ (d_{sm} + d_{wm} + d_{vm})$
Death	$\Sigma\ d_{m\delta}/\Sigma\ (d_{sm} + d_{wm} + d_{vm})$
4. Number of marriages per person marrying	$\Sigma\ (d_{sm} + d_{wm} + d_{vm})/\Sigma\ d_{sm}$
5. Probability of remarriage from:	
Divorce	$\Sigma\ d_{vm}/\Sigma\ d_{mv}$
Widowhood	$\Sigma\ d_{wm}/\Sigma\ d_{mw}$
6. Average duration of a:	
Marriage	$T_m(0)/\Sigma\ (d_{sm} + d_{wm} + d_{vm})$
Widowhood	$T_w(0)/\Sigma\ d_{mw}$
Divorce	$T_v(0)/\Sigma\ d_{mv}$
7. Probability of dying in state i	$\Sigma\ d_{i\delta/l(0)}$
8. Proportion of life spent in state i	$T_i(0)/T(0)$
9. Mean age at transfer from state i to state j	$\Sigma\ (Y + 1/2n)d_{ij}/\Sigma\ d_{ij}$
10. Mean age of persons in state i	$\Sigma\ (Y + 1/2n)L_i/T_i(0)$

[a] All sums run over index Y, in steps of n years, from 0 to ∞. The age interval identifiers (Yn, n) have been omitted to simplify the notation. The five-state model has four active states, never married (s), presently married (m), widowed (w), and divorced (v), and one "dead" state (δ).
[b] Source: Schoen (1988, p. 95).

2.6. STABLE AND QUASI-STABLE POPULATION MODELS

The relevance of stable population models in the chapter which deals with life table analysis is justified by the fact that life table population, also known as stationary population, is one of the family of stable population models. A life table population is a stationary population because it has zero rate of growth. The basic life table population is closed to migration and the number of births are equivalent to the number of deaths. Moreover, the age distribution of a life table population is identical to the survival function, since the rate of growth is zero. If the rate of growth is nonzero but the population still maintains a constant age distribution, then that will be a stable population. Hence, a life table population is a special case of a stable population.

A stable population is characterized by the history of a constant schedule of fertility and mortality resulting in an unchanging proportional age distribution. In other words, the population changes at a constant rate of increase (or decrease). The age distribution is determined by the mortality schedule and the annual rate of increase. The mathematical bases of the stable population theory and the algebraic expressions of births, age distribution, mean age of the population, and so forth can be found in Coale's (1972) masterpiece, *The Growth and Structure of Human Populations.* In this section, we briefly mention the potential use of stable population concepts for the estimation of demographic variables.

The model life tables are the description of typical age patterns of mortality at different mortality levels. If we incorporate rates of increase corresponding to the different levels of fertility, then we will have model stable populations. This is what Coale and Demeny (1983) have done. They have presented a set of possible stable populations for each model life table. In order to use these stable populations to estimate various demographic parameters of a particular population, one should verify whether the actual population might be considered stable (meaning that fertility and mortality have not fluctuated in the past, and that the population is closed to migration). Then one should match the actual population to one of the model stable populations. Parameters of the model stable population can then be attributed to the actual population. The actual application and detailed procedure of selecting a model stable population on the basis of recorded age distribution are described in Manual IV of the United Nations (1967). The stable population can also be used to visualize different age distributions based on schedules of fertility and mortality ranging from very high to very low levels. Coale (1972) compares the stable population to the speedometer of a car. A speedometer is a useful device for checking the speed of a running car. Although cars do not travel at constant speed, a speedometer is a useful device and so is the stable population if properly used. It is a hypothetical population but it would become actualized if specified schedules of fertility and mortality were to persist. Coale (1972) shows the usefulness of the stable population to illustrate the limits of the birth rate, the death rate, and the rate of natural increase.

So far we have discussed the stable population which is closed for migration and is generated by a fixed schedule of fertility and mortality. Rogers (1974, 1975) successfully extended the stable population characteristic equation to include migration also. This has come to be known as the multistate stable population. The multistate stable population generalizes the multistate life table. Schoen (1988) defines a multistate stable population "as a population with a fixed age and state composition that emerges from a long history of constant age- and state-specific rates of birth, death, and interstate movement. Alternatively, the stable population age–state composition can be viewed as the unique age–state structure that is constantly replicated by those rates" (p. 107). Schoen (1988) shows how multistate stable populations can be specified and calculated. He also discusses several features of multistate stable populations and identifies some new applications of the models in the area of nuptiality, labor force participation, pension system modeling, and parity progression studies, in addition to interregional and international migration. We suggest the interested readers refer to Schoen (1988).

The stable population models are only applicable to populations with a long history of constant fertility and mortality schedules. The Western countries have been experiencing widespread use of birth control methods and have been affected by international migration. Even many of the developing countries have also been experiencing a decline in fertility in the recent past and hence do not maintain constant proportional age distributions. However, there are a few countries in the world where there is no widespread use of birth control methods and which are unaffected significantly by international migration. These populations may be characterized by more or less constant fertility but a sustained decline in mortality. Coale (1972) has shown that fluctuations in fertility cause more irregularities in the age distribution compared to mortality changes. Indeed, it has been noticed by many demographers that populations with different mortality schedules but experiencing approximately constant fertility show only estimated alternations in age distribution (e.g., Coale and Demeny, 1983). Strictly speaking, these populations are different from stable populations and estimates derived for these populations based on the stable population models can be in error. Hence, the estimated parameters ought to be corrected for the distorting effects of declining mortality. The populations which have yet to experience any significant decline in fertility, but in which there is a strong and sustained decline in mortality, seem to resemble a so-called quasi-stable population. For these populations in order to estimate demographic parameters, the quasi-stable population concept is used. This concept and its application procedures are discussed in detail in Manual IV (United Nations, 1967). We will not go into details of the procedures, but we will mention briefly the philosophy underlying the technique.

It is stated in Manual IV that "the principal effect of declining mortality on age composition closely resembles the influence of steadily rising fertility. Over a specified interval of falling mortality, it is possible to find a proportionate change in fertility—say a 7-percent increase—that is equivalent to the recorded decline in mortality so far as the effect on age composition is concerned. It is possible by an extension of this idea, to determine what sequence of annually rising expectation of life in the "West" model life tables (given in annex I) would be equivalent to an annual increase in fertility of one per cent" (p. 26). Based on this idea, the adjustments are applied to preliminary estimates derived on the contrary-to-fact assumption of stability. Later, Coale (1971a) outlined a method of constructing an age distribution of the quasi-stable population consistent with the adjusted estimates of vital rates. Coale illustrates the procedure by using India, 1961, as an example. The method of estimating vital rates and age distribution described by Coale (1971a) is circular in nature. If one knows the age distribution, vital rates can be estimated. Of the estimated vital rates, Manual IV recommends that those estimated vital rates associated with C(35) (the female population proportion up to age 35) be used as the best estimates in cases where populations are subject to age misreporting.

Using this circular method, Bhat (1977) has found discrepancies between the recorded and adjusted age distribution as well as in the birth rate when it is reestimated from the adjusted age distribution. Coale also noticed these discrepancies but he attributes them to the imprecision of the technique. But Bhat traces the source of error to the procedures themselves. To be more specific, Bhat describes how Coale (1971a) made an error in calculating expectation of life at birth for females using estimated birth and death rates. According to Bhat, the estimated birth rate was wrongly assumed to be the birth rate at the end of the intercensal period. Because of this error, the expectation of life that is estimated by Coale is an underestimate. Consequently, the death rate is an overestimate because it is estimated as the birth rate minus the growth rate. Bhat suggested the way to estimate the correct birth rate and death rate at the end of the intercensal period. Once the birth rate is known, the intrinsic birth rate is estimated. Using estimates of gross reproduction rate and intrinsic birth rate, the stable age distribution is determined. We realize that this explanation of Bhat's procedure is cryptic and may not be enough to understand the computational procedure. However, our intention is to expose the reader briefly to the new developments in the application of quasi-stable population theory. For practical use of the method, we recommend that the interested user read Bhat's paper.

Before one uses the quasi-stable population theory, we must mention some of the concerns expressed by Brass (1975). Brass questions the basic premises on which quasi-stable population theory is built. Quasi-stable population theory is based on the idea that the age structure will not be greatly altered as long as fertility stays constant even if mortality is changing over time. To be more specific, even if the age structure is altered, it is similar to that of a stable population. Brass argues that the close relationship that is assumed between fertility and age structure may not be valid with actual populations. In Brass's words:

> Mortality in the first years of life can be very variable, and its level is not necessarily closely associated with adult mortality. Therefore, it is hard to distinguish whether the difference in age structure between two populations results from their having different fertility or different mortality at the beginning of life. Populations that have identical or similar age structures can nevertheless have very different fertility

rates compensated for by different childhood mortality rates. The original assumption that mortality changes have little effect on the age structure is not true; this assumption can lead to very crude results. If infant mortality is estimated at a time when mortality is changing, substantial errors can be made. [pp. 126–127].

Brass supports his argument by demonstrating how changes in the relationship between childhood and adult mortality will affect significantly the age structure using the logit system. Having made those remarks, Brass considers that the theory has some merits. He shows that the relationship between the proportion of persons approximately 2 years old and the proportion of persons between this age and 45 is very robust. Thus, one can avoid the problematic portions of the age distribution, such as the beginning of life and the end. Based on this idea of using the stable portion of the age structure, he has developed measurements. The method is very simple and uses the logit system. Moreover, this method provides tests for internal consistency as well.

2.7. RELATIONAL MODELS

Mathematical modeling of age patterns of demographic phenomena such as the model life tables of Coale and Demeny (1983) provides stable relative age distributions for the full range of mortality and fertility levels likely to be relevant either in fitting the tables to observed data, or in analyzing the hypothetical consequences of fertility and mortality schedules. In order to use these regional life tables, one must solve for the parameters that best transform the model life tables into the observed sets of mortality and fertility rates and other measures. Brass (1974) argues that these models are not very useful for prediction.

> They are based on cross-sectional arrays rather than time paths, that is the original construction did not distinguish variations in pattern with level in different populations at the same time from those for the same population at different times. A corollary is the inadequate study of the most satisfactory measure for gauging the scale of change in mortality level (or alternatively the specification of the scale of change for a familiar measure such as expectation of life which tends to increase more slowly as mortality falls). In addition, it is difficult, although not impossible, to extrapolate to life tables representing a lower level of mortality than has yet been experienced in any population. [p. 547]

Continuing on with his critique, Brass suggests relational models which retain the local features of the initial base. For example, in early life, death rates alter with age relative to a given overall level of mortality. Brass demonstrated a two-parameter transformation of the logit and of the survivorship function to reproduce many observed life tables. An important feature of the logit mortality relational model is that it describes variations among populations, or over time, without specifying the form of the pattern of mortality by age.

Interesting developments have taken place in the recent past in connection with stable population relations. Preston and Coale (1982) have generalized stable population relations to nonstable populations. Preston and Bennett (1983) have developed an important methodology of estimating not only mortality conditions but also the expected duration of stay in any state that is entered at duration zero. This method does not require assumptions of stability or use of a model life table system. "All that is required are two cross-sectional observations of the population arrayed by duration in the state. Duration-specific growth rates $(_n r_x)$ and mean populations $(_n N_x)$ are then sufficient to produce a life table of survivors and decrements from that state. In this fashion cross-sections can be converted into occurrence-exposure rates and into longitudinal information for hypothetical cohorts" (Preston and Bennett, 1983, p. 104).

Recently, Ewbank *et al.* (1983) extended Brass's relational system of model life tables based on four parameters. Inclusion of four parameters overcomes the limitation of a logit model at the extreme ages. In other words, a four-parameter model is quite flexible and matches a wide range of empirical age patterns of mortality. Moreover, this model can be reduced to three or two parameters when the data are either incomplete or not accurate for the estimation of four parameters. In sum, a four-parameter model not only provides meaningful parameters to summarize the important features of the data but also reveals a consistent pattern of mortality which may not always be possible to represent the pattern either by a single Coale and Demeny family or by a Brass logit system.

Coale (1971b) developed a relational model of nuptiality. An improvement of this model by Coale and McNeil (1972) is interesting because of its unusual use of demographic concepts. In a similar vein, Coale and Trussell (1974) developed a two-parameter model of fertility: one represents the level of natural fertility and the other represents the extent of antenatal practices. In the case of fertility studies, Brass (1974) also shows how Gompertz's model of fertility can be modified to relational form. In recent years, more relational models have been developed in demography but they are based on a larger number of parameters (Zaba, 1979; Le Bras, 1979; Hogan and McNeil, 1979).

Hobcraft *et al.* (1982) discuss the importance of relational models in age–period–cohort analysis. "For example, the parameters that transform the standard to produce an observed matrix of age–period rates can be assumed to be linear functions of corresponding parameters in periods and cohorts. In this fashion, the identification problem is readily solved" (p. 14). However, they also warn about the possibility that cohort effects may be ignored even though they are present, in cases where the distribution of cohort effects is similar to that in a particular population being compared with the standard.

2.8. SUMMARY

The discussion of life table approaches to demographic processes has been cryptic. The purpose of the chapter is not to provide a comprehensive look at these approaches, but rather to indicate the more recent developments in this area of enquiry. The life table technique is more than 200 years old and any introductory text on demographic techniques will explain the basics of life table analysis. This chapter is intended to indicate the advances made in the extension of life table techniques, the most recent of which are multistate life tables. Development of multistate life tables is based on the assumption of the Markovian condition, meaning that a transition from one state to another is affected solely by the present state from which the transition is made irrespective of the past history of transitions through which the present state is reached. Unlike the basic life table technique, multistate analysis would include multiple renewable events. In other words, multistate models are able to capture a social behavior ingrained in transitions among relevant states.

In this chapter, we have also discussed the concept of the logit system in the construction of the life table. The logit system is a useful analytical technique in the development of model life tables. It is based on a simple relationship involving two parameters: α and β. The former parameter refers to the level and the latter to the shape. Most importantly, it is quite simple to use and does not involve complicated calculations.

Since the life table population is a special case of a stable population, it is appropriate to include a brief discussion on stable and quasi-stable population concepts. In this context, we have brought to the attention of readers the recent developments in quasi-stable population theory.

CHAPTER 3

Age, Period, and Cohort Effects in Demography

3.1. INTRODUCTION

Demographic events such as birth, death, marriage, and migration are all influenced by age, period, and cohort in one way or another. For example, identification of patterns in mortality, nuptiality, and fertility by Coale and his associates is based on age (Coale and Demeny, 1983; Coale, 1971b; Coale and Trussell, 1974). Hence, age is an extremely important variable in most social and behavioral science research. Although the models based on age have been very important and useful in the development of modern demographic research, these models are still inadequate. Ignoring period and cohort effects in the interpretation of demographic processes results in error. In the study of fertility, Page (1977) developed a model which takes into account both age and duration. This model not only fits the data better than the one based solely on age, but also penetrates deeper into the structure of underlying fertility schedules and hence it is more revealing. Page argues as follows: "Age cannot bear the same relation to fertility experience in all populations, because the age at which women begin childbearing can vary widely. For populations in which childbearing occurs predominantly within marriage, duration of marriage is a more direct specification than age for detecting patterns of control" (pp. 86–87). She stresses the fact that duration alone is not sufficient as age also determines childbearing.

Ryder (1965) argues that age is interpreted in statistical analyses of social change as a point in the cohort life cycle. Omission of the cohort effect ignores an important source of variation and impedes the progress of temporal analysis.

Age-cum-cohort should be used not only as a cross-classification to explain the internal variations of other groups, but also as a group defining variable in its own right, in terms of which distributions by other variables may be compared through time. In this way, research results may be compared in cumulated fashion, linking the outputs of the various studies using the same cohort identifications, just as has been done with other quasi-group categorizations. Each such study can enhance the significance of others for the same cohort. Comparison of such composite cohort biographies would yield the most direct and efficient measurement of the consequences of social change (Ryder, 1965, p. 847).

The above discussion may be put into theoretical perspective. The analysis of demographic processes or social change should distinguish between the three levels of analysis: cross-sectional, longitudinal, and time-lag. Palmore (1978) argues that cross-sectional differences (period effects) between age groups are not only the result of age processes but also the result of cohort differences. Similarly, differences over time for the same group (longitudinal, i.e., age effects) are not only the result of aging processes and of social or environmental change. It would be useful to reproduce the summary table along with Figure 1 from Palmore (1978).

Figure 3.1 and Table 3.1 are self-explanatory. They clear up the confusion regarding conceptualization of the three effects. Palmore (1978) carefully distinguishes levels of analysis, defines essential terms, observable differences, inferred effects, and the theoretical causes of the effects.

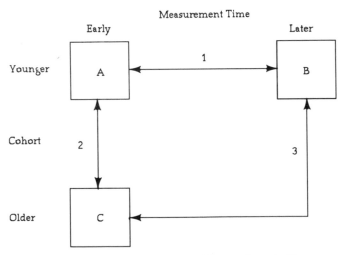

Figure 3.1. Observable differences: (1) Longitudinal difference ($B - A$), (2) cross-sectional difference ($C - A$), (3) time-lag difference ($B - C$). From Palmore (1978, p. 284).

Table 3.1. Levels of Analysis[a]

I. Differences
    A. Longitudinal: Time 2 measurement on a cohort minus
                          Time 1 measurement on same cohort
    B. Cross-sectional: Time 1 measurement on older cohort minus
                          Time 1 measurement on younger cohort
    C. Time-lag: Time 2 measurement on younger cohort
                          minus Time 1 measurement on older cohort
II. Effects
    A. Combinations of effects
        1. Age + Period = Longitudinal difference
        2. Age + cohort = Cross-sectional difference
        3. Period − Cohort = Time-lag difference
    B. Separation of effects
        1. No significant differences = No effects
        2. Two significant differences = One pure effect
        3. Three significant differences = Two unequal effects, or three effects
III. Causes
    A. Age effects = biological, psychological, and/or social role changes
    B. Period effects = changes in environment, measurement, and/or practice
    C. Cohort effects = genetic shifts, and/or interaction of historical situation with age of
       cohort

[a] Source: Palmore (1978, p. 294).

3.2. AGE ANALYSIS

The components of population change, fertility, mortality, and migration, are all directly affected by age factors. The influence of age on these demographic processes, as mentioned by Palmore (1978), can be through biological, psychological, social, and cultural mechanisms. Davis and Blake (1956) in their classic article on social structure and fertility have discussed how the age of entry into sexual union directly affects fertility. Age of entry into sexual union, in turn, is affected by sociocultural factors, especially in societies where marriage is a prerequisite for childbearing. In these societies, illegitimate fertility or the proportion of conceptions outside wedlock is negligible. In fact, Malthus suggested late marriage as one of the "preventive" checks on fertility. Age restricts the reproductive period in women, usually to between ages 15 and 50. Moreover, fecundity varies in the reproductive period favoring the younger end of the span. Thus, the fertility level of a society depends upon the age distribution of its female population, the sociocultural factors that affect age at marriage, and the proportion of persons married.

Similarly, age has a direct bearing on mortality. Model life tables derived by Coale and Demeny (1983) are based on this evidence. In all societies death rates are higher among the youngest and oldest age groups. Like fertility, mortality is also affected by sociocultural factors as is evident when one studies differential mortality by age. "Such forms of mortality as infanticide, parricide, and suicide are socially significant and age related" (Goldscheider, 1971, p. 227).

Most migration studies use age as a conditioning variable. The rationale for this lies in the fact that the influence of age on migration peaks at age 29 (Stone, 1978). Hence, age selectivity operates on migration. Goldscheider (1971) argues that age not only acts as a biological determinant of migration, but also throughout the life cycle in such age-related processes as marriage and family formation. In Goldscheider's words: "Given different political, social, economic, cultural, and demographic contexts, age remains as a critical differentiation of migration. . . . The different ways in which age is related to family formation and career and social mobility determine the specifics of the relationship of age and mobility" (p. 311).

Age models have been used quite extensively in demographic analysis. For instance, the theory of Stable Population or Model Life Tables based on period mortality data are based on age variations. Age patterns of marriages developed by Coale (1971b), age patterns of fertility in the absence of deliberate control developed by Henry (1961), and age patterns of migration by Rogers *et al.* (1978) are all examples of age models in demographic analysis.

3.3. PERIOD ANALYSIS

In order to understand the conceptual distinction between cohort and period analysis, let us consider some demographic behavior. The outcome of that behavior depends upon the past experience of the cohort, on the one hand, and the distinctive environmental stimuli characterizing the period, on the other. A judgment of the relative importance of these two components would favor one or other of the approaches.

To understand better, it is useful to discuss the concept of "synthetic" or "hypothetical" cohort. If the purpose is to develop a period analog to that of a measure for a cohort, arrangements of the data for a period in such a way that they resemble in form the history of a cohort are required. The arrangements are called *synthetic cohort constructions* (Ryder, 1982). The construct of synthetic cohort is useful, because sometimes it is impossible to wait until members of the real cohort complete their experience (in reference to the study process) to get the required information. For instance, if one needs a summary of the mortality of a short period, the life tables are the only answer. Life tables do not provide the life history of an actual cohort. Rather, a life history is synthesized from the mortality rates by age during a year or short period, and thus represents synthetic cohort measures as a summary of the mortality experience of many cohorts. Thus, synthetic cohort measures are based on life table techniques and period measures. It should be mentioned that usage of the three measures (cohort measures, synthetic cohort measures, and period measures) depends upon the research questions and the data availability. In the study of divorce, period measures relate the number of divorces in a given year to the stock of marriages in that year. Real cohort measures get the proportion ever divorced in real cohorts. Synthetic cohort measures aim at estimating the eventual incidence of divorce among the cohorts currently marrying. The proportions ever divorced are based on age- or duration-specific divorce rates experienced by real cohorts throughout their life up to a given point in time. In contrast, the corresponding proportions in synthetic cohorts are observed at a given point in time or period.

In order to understand the limitation of cohort measures, let us consider a group of women who belong to a particular birth cohort which contains women marrying at different ages. As the incidence of divorce differs by age at marriage because of varying periods of exposure to divorce, for purposes of comparison or for studying trends, the measure is not entirely satisfactory (Basavarajappa and Nagnur, 1988). Thus, compositional effects are very important in real cohort comparisons, as in those of conventional period measures. On the other hand, the usefulness of synthetic cohorts is to answer questions such as: if a hypothetical cohort of marriages contracted by either males or females, all at the same moment in time at birthday "x," were to be exposed to a fixed schedule of age-specific divorce rates (period measures), what proportion of these marriages would terminate in divorce prior to birthday "y," some specified number of years later? Hence, the construction of a synthetic cohort using the life table technique is an analysis to show the implications of certain conditions. It shows the lifetime implications of divorce rates observed at a given time. The limitations of the synthetic cohort approach revolve around the validity of assuming that age-specific divorce rates will remain constant into the future. If divorce rates are rising as they now are, the synthetic cohort approach underestimates future divorce rates, but if divorce rates are falling as they did between 1982 and 1984 in Canada, this approach overestimates future divorce rates. The limitation of the real cohort approach is that it confounds period and age at marriage effects, and because of this, its interpretation may be misleading.

Note that the comparison between the cohort approach and the synthetic cohort approach is not to suggest that they are alternative ways of providing an answer to the same question. In fact, each approach answers a different question. The real cohort approach answers the question: what proportion of the population has ever been divorced? Thus, it focuses on past and present experience. The synthetic cohort approach answers the question: what proportions will eventually be divorced under certain assumptions? Thus, it focuses on future experience. We think that both questions are valid, and as demographers, we will have to provide answers to both questions. Apart from the analytical distinction made between the cohort and synthetic approaches, they depend upon different types of data requirements. The cohort measures are derived from the retrospective sample surveys, whereas the synthetic cohort measures are derived by the application of life table techniques.

As stated earlier, period analysis deals with the study of different cohorts at the same point in time, to understand population change using annual vital statistics and census data. Population change depends upon the population composition at a particular time and of the cohort processes at that time. Period analysis is useful to discriminate between these two factors to identify their respective impact on population change. Period measures are most commonly used to indicate the current levels of demographic processes such as fertility, mortality, and migration. These are the conventional rates, namely birth and death rates. As discussed in Chapter 1, the precision of rates depends on how closely one tries to relate demographic events to the denominator. Apart from this limitation, period measures are affected by the peculiarity of the period that is considered for study. For example, period measures of fertility computed during the Great Depression in the 1930s yielded quite surprising conclusions on the future population in developed countries; these measures were, however, drastically influenced by temporary postponement of births during that period (Wunsch and Termote, 1978). Ryder (1956) argues that even if the period of time is not peculiar, period measures of intensity, that summarizes the behavior of many cohorts, normally do not adequately reflect the true cohort intensity, as the period measures are also dependent on the tempo of events in the cohorts considered. Similarly, period tempo measures also do not normally correspond to true cohort measures, as these are also influenced by cohort intensities. Ryder names this bias as "distributional distortion." Detailed discussion of this topic can also be seen in Wunsch and Termote (1978).

3.4. COHORT ANALYSIS

Cohort refers to a group of persons experiencing a particular event (e.g., birth or marriage) during the same period of time. If the event experienced is birth, then the corresponding cohort will be called a birth cohort. Members of this cohort not only were born together but they age together as well. Ryder

(1965) explains in detail the cohort as a concept in the study of social change. At a conceptual level he argues that the cohort resembles the ethnic group: "membership is determined at birth, and often has considerable capacity to explain variance, but need not imply that the category is an organized group" (p. 847).

Ryder (1968) defines cohort analysis as the quantitative description of dated occurrences, from the time a cohort is exposed to the risk of such occurrences. The most important application of cohort analysis is in the study of temporal variations in the population behavior of particular interest. More specifically, it is useful to analyze time series data to study aggregate change in the population. This is not the same as longitudinal analysis. Longitudinal analysis deals with change in, and the behavior of, individuals over time.

The usefulness of cohort analysis especially in population studies is recognized by many demographers. For instance, Frost (1939) made an important contribution to the study of tuberculosis mortality by using the cohort approach. When period analysis was used to explain the rise in the modal age of tuberculosis mortality, an examination of cohort mortality by age indicated that the age pattern from cohort to cohort was relatively fixed, and that the rise in the modal age for successive periods was a reflection of the steady decline in the level of tuberculosis mortality from cohort to cohort (Frost, 1939). Similar advantages of cohort analysis can also be seen in other demographic processes such as nuptiality and fertility. For instance, calculation of the Parity Progression Ratios using the cohort approach, for specific birth and marriage cohorts, has an advantage over the period approach which has no reference to either age or marriage cohorts, since it distinguishes the variations in the "marriage mix," i.e. the variations from cohort to cohort in the relative proportions of females marrying at specified ages (Wunsch and Termote, 1978). Moreover, cohort analysis is useful in identifying distributional distortions of births due to the cohort tempo of births, i.e., the timing of births that differ from one birth cohort to another. Whelpton (1946) demonstrated this point when computing birth-order-specific fertility measures for cohorts of white American women. He was of the opinion that the Age-Parity-Specific Birth Rates are better measures of fertility, simply because the computed birth performance prior to a given age of women in a hypothetical cohort will differ in most cases from the actual birth performances prior to the same age of women in the actual population. Both cohorts, the hypothetical and the actual, will yield the same values for fertility measures if there was no change in the timing of the births among the two cohorts. This is important because fertility at a given age is affected by fertility at younger ages. For example, if higher order births are being observed, it is quite possible that women in question started their reproduction at an early age. The Age-Parity-Specific Birth Rates for a given year provide weight to fertility in prior years of each age cohort in the actual population, and hence they measure fertility more accurately than would an Age-Specific Period Rate (Whelpton, 1946). In Ryder's words:

> If the tempo (distribution) remains fixed from cohort to cohort, but the quantum (total) varies, the period quantum will be a weighted average of quantum for the cohorts represented in that particular period, where the weights are the (fixed) temporal distribution and add up to unity. The period tempo, however, will tend to be shifted upwards (in age) by a downward trend in cohort quantum, and downward (in age) by an upward trend in cohort quantum, relative to the (fixed) cohort tempo. Variation in cohort quantum creates distortion in period tempo. As a first approximation, the difference between the means of the cohort and period age distributions of fertility is equal to the product of the relative change in cohort quantum, and the variance of the cohort age distribution of fertility. If the quantum remains fixed from cohort to cohort but the tempo varies, the period quantum will ordinarily differ from that value because in such circumstances, it will be a weighted average in which the sum of the weights departs from unity. [Ryder, 1982, p. 23]

Cohort effects are difficult to incorporate into models of demographic processes. Moreover, it is found that the explanatory gain per cohort parameter is much less than the gain per period parameter (Pullum, 1980). This may be because cohort effects are partly captured by an age variable and the difficulty involved in separating out their sole effects is not worth the cost (Hobcraft *et al.*, 1982). However, the importance of the cohort concept as a theoretical tool in the study of demographic process in particular and social change in general has been emphasized by Ryder (1965) in his paper:

> The case for the cohort as a temporal unit in the analysis of social change rests on a set of primitive notions: persons of age a in time t are those who were age $a - 1$ in time $t - 1$; transformations of the social world modify people of different ages in different ways; the effects of these transformations are persistent. In this way a cohort meaning is implanted in the age–time specification. Two broad orientations for theory and research flow from this position: first, the study of intracohort development throughout the life cycle; second, the study of comparative cohort careers, i.e., inter-cohort temporal differentiation in the various parameters that may be used to characterize these aggregate histories. [p. 861]

Social scientists and demographers today are placing particular emphasis on cohort effect identification. Examples would include the study of fertility or migration if one is interested in how many children are born on average to a woman during her reproductive period, or in how many changes of residence one has made during one's life. Studies of this type require consideration of cohort analysis to relate demographic events to the span of life (Ryder, 1986). Cohort analysis also can be used to improve the quality of short-term projections of fertility, mortality, and migration. Cohort analysis involves a record of demographic events extending over a life span and covers past experience. The projection requires the extrapolation of this past behavior into the future by the use of cohort parameters.

Although we have emphasized the usefulness of cohort analysis in population data analysis above to understand demographic processes, a word of caution is in order. At least in case of fertility research, in general, cohorts have been far less distinct than Ryder originally thought. Lee's (1980) approach of a moving-target model to relate reproductive goals to period fertility rates not only shows that the reproductive behavior of rates and goals in the United States during recent decades (i.e., the postwar baby boom and recent baby bust periods) has been consistent, and any discrepant changes between fertility targets and period rates are due to intrinsic characteristics of the relation between changes in fertility rates and targets. The past theory (i.e., the fixed target model) that relates reproductive goals to period fertility has been based on seriously questionable assumptions by recent figures. Lee's moving-target model has many implications for the analysis of fertility change over time. It not only supports certain strategies for collecting and using survey data but also emphasizes the need to survey the same cohort repeatedly over time in order to understand its reproductive behavior. If a moving-target model is accepted, the most serious implication with respect to cohort analysis is that the procedures which attach significance to a cohort's actual completed fertility as a measure of its target throughout its reproductive years have to be discarded (Lee, 1980).

3.5. SEPARATING AGE, PERIOD, AND COHORT EFFECTS

Hobcraft *et al.* (1982) have reviewed thoroughly the demographic research attempting to separate age, period, and cohort effects. The age, period, cohort analysis has been used extensively in fertility and mortality studies. Based on their review, the authors conclude that the approach is suitable for a wide range of applications in mortality but is not quite suitable for the analysis of fertility. This is because the widespread practice of contraceptive methods, especially in developed countries, has made possible goal-directed behavior in human reproduction. Moreover, these goals and strategies do not remain constant. Ryder (1982) argues that a difference between fertility at one parity and fertility at the next is conditional on the attained parity being a consequence of intentional interference with the reproductive process. Due to these reasons, Hobcraft *et al.* conclude that age–period–cohort investigations of fertility will have to develop hand in hand with the theories of fertility.

3.5.1. An Application of Age, Period, Cohort Analysis to Canadian Labor Force Participation

During the period 1950–1982, the composition of the Canadian labor force has undergone dramatic changes. Although there has been an increase in the labor force participation rates over the years, the rate has declined slightly for males and increased tremendously for females. The underlying reasons for and implications of the increase in female participation in the Canadian as well as the United States labor forces have become a theme of recent sociological research (Bokemeier *et al.,* 1983; Menzies, 1981; Phillips and Phillips, 1983). Demographers have also focused on this aspect. For instance, Basavarajappa and George (1979), Parnes (1982), and Ryder (1979) have studied labor force participation trends in a North American context. Farkas (1977) performed the first age–period–cohort analysis of labor force trends of white females in the United States during 1957 to 1968. Recently, Clogg (1982) has analyzed United States labor force trends, comparing sex–color groups over the period 1969–1979.

An attempt is made here to apply the age–period–cohort method to analyze age–sex composition of the Canadian labor force from 1950 to 1982. The method helps to decompose the effects of age, period, and cohort, independently and jointly, on the labor force rates. Obviously, we expect differences in the ability of each factor to explain the trend in the participation rates.

3.5.2. The Canadian Labor Force

To define labor force, Statistics Canada's (1979a) definition is used here. The labor force participation rate as used here refers to the number in the labor force divided by the total population 15 years and over and multiplied by 100. The labor force includes employed and unemployed noninmates 15 years and older. The employed are those who, in the week prior to enumeration, (1) worked for pay, (2) helped without pay in the operation of a family business or farm, or (3) had a job or business from which they were temporarily absent due to illness, vacation, labor dispute, and so forth. The unemployed category includes persons (1) actively seeking employment, (2) those on layoff for 30 days or less who expect to return to their jobs, and (3) those with definite instructions to start a new job. The population 15 years and over, the labor force participation rates, and the size of the Canadian labor force during 1950–1982 are given in Table 3.2. The population figures were obtained from Statistics Canada publications (1973, 1979b, 1982, 1983).

The size of the labor force in Canada has steadily increased from 1950 to 1982, with over 12 million people as of 1982 although the labor force participation rate decreased slightly from a high of 64.7 in 1981 to 64.0 in 1982. In the present context, the important point to be noted is the difference between male and female participation rates in the labor force. The participation trend for males shows a slight decrease between 1950 and 1982. The corresponding figures for females show a steady increase for the same years. These trends are displayed in Figure 3.2.

Table 3.2. Canadian Population, 15+ Years, Labor Force Participation Rates, and Labor Force: 1950–1982

Year	Population 15+ years (000's)[a]			Labor force participation rates[b]			Labor force (000's)[c]		
	Total	Male	Female	Total	Male	Female	Total	Male	Female
1950	9641.5	4882.6	4758.9	53.7	84.0	23.2	5177.5	4101.4	1104.1
1951	9758.7	4320.7	4838.0	53.7	83.9	23.5	5240.4	4128.5	1136.9
1952	10006.3	5051.8	4954.5	53.5	83.4	23.7	5353.4	4213.2	1174.2
1953	10216.9	5160.3	5056.6	53.1	82.9	23.4	5425.2	4277.9	1183.2
1954	10452.3	5282.1	5170.2	52.9	82.2	23.7	5529.3	4341.9	1225.3
1955	10659.1	5386.8	5272.3	52.9	82.1	23.9	5638.7	4422.6	1260.1
1956	10855.5	5488.1	5367.4	53.5	82.2	24.9	5807.7	4511.2	1336.5
1957	11153.4	5636.3	5517.1	54.0	82.3	25.8	6022.8	4638.7	1423.4
1958	11394.8	5750.4	5644.4	53.9	81.7	26.2	6141.8	4698.1	1478.8
1959	11625.3	5862.8	5762.5	53.8	81.0	26.7	6254.4	4748.9	1538.6
1960	11840.0	5961.3	5878.7	54.2	80.7	27.9	6417.3	4810.8	1640.2
1961	12046.4	6052.8	5993.6	54.1	79.8	28.7	6517.1	4830.1	1720.2
1962	12273.3	6153.9	6119.4	53.9	79.1	29.0	6615.3	4867.7	1774.6
1963	12513.1	6261.3	6251.8	53.8	78.5	29.6	6732.0	4915.1	1850.5
1964	12791.7	6388.0	6403.7	54.1	78.1	30.5	6920.3	4989.0	1953.1
1965	13087.7	6524.9	6562.8	54.4	77.9	31.3	7119.7	5082.9	2054.2
1966	13423.2	6681.6	6741.6	56.4	79.9	33.6	7570.7	5338.6	2265.2
1967	13791.1	6861.8	6929.3	56.8	79.6	34.6	7833.3	5462.0	2397.5
1968	14143.0	7032.3	7110.7	56.8	79.0	35.2	8033.2	5555.5	2503.0
1969	14489.5	7199.1	7290.4	57.0	78.6	36.0	8259.0	5658.5	2624.5
1970	14843.3	7368.8	7474.5	56.9	78.2	36.2	8445.8	5762.4	2705.8
1971	15187.4	7532.0	7655.4	57.2	77.8	37.1	8687.2	5859.9	2840.2
1972	15514.7	7683.6	7831.3	57.6	77.9	37.8	8936.5	5985.5	2960.2
1973	15859.7	7844.8	8014.9	58.7	78.5	39.4	9309.6	6158.2	3157.9
1974	16275.1	8041.5	8233.6	59.4	79.0	40.5	9667.4	6352.8	3334.6
1975	16693.1	8239.3	8453.8	61.1	78.4	44.4	10199.5	6459.6	3753.5
1976	17096.4	8429.6	8666.9	61.1	77.6	45.2	10445.9	6541.4	3917.4
1977	17466.1	8603.1	8863.0	61.5	77.6	46.0	10741.7	6676.0	4077.0
1978	17817.1	8766.9	9050.3	62.6	77.9	47.8	11153.5	6829.4	4326.0
1979	18151.1	8923.3	9227.7	63.3	78.4	48.9	11489.6	6995.9	4512.3
1980	18518.1	9095.7	9422.3	64.0	78.3	50.3	11851.6	7121.9	4739.4
1981	18860.1	9256.3	9603.9	64.7	78.3	51.6	12202.5	7247.7	4955.6
1982	19166.3	9400.9	9765.4	64.0	76.9	51.6	12266.4	7229.3	5038.9

[a] Population 15+ years from Revised Annual Estimates of Population, 1973, 1979, 1983, Statistics Canada, Ottawa (Catalogue 91-512 and 91-518).
[b] Labor force participation rates obtained from Labor Force Survey Division, Statistics Canada, Ottawa.
[c] Labor force calculated by multiplying population 15+ years by the labor force participation rates.

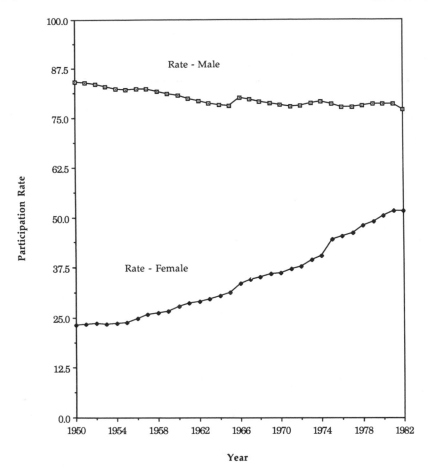

Figure 3.2. Participation in labor force: All ages, 1950–1982.

   In the context of labor force analysis, the hypotheses proposed for investigation using the age–period–cohort method are as follows. First, age effects
should be more pronounced on the labor force participation of males than
females because females enter and leave the labor force more often than males,
due to marriage and child-rearing. Second, since the participation rates for
females have steadily increased over the period 1950–1982 while the rates
have been fairly constant for males, period effects would seem to have affected
the rates for females more than for men. Finally, the cohort effects are more
difficult to hypothesize. One could expect similar cohort effects on both male
and female participation rates because there are no substantial differences in
the sizes of the male and female cohorts for the period 1950–1982 (Table 3.2,
columns 3 and 4).

3.5.3. The Data

Labor force participation rates have not been published in equal age intervals. The rates provided start from 14 or 15 (14 through 1965, 15 thereafter) years to 19 years, 20–24 years, then 25–34, 35–44, 45–54, 55–64, and 65 and older. It should be noted that application of the age–period–cohort method requires equal age intervals. In order to avoid the one-year difference in the start of the age interval, we decided to start from the 20–24 year interval. Also, two quinquennial age categories were interpolated from the 10-year intervals. The oldest age interval in the analysis was determined to be 55–59 to avoid problems with people of retirement age. Now we have eight age categories with 5-year intervals over the age range 20–59. Similarly, the period 1950–1982 was divided into 5-year intervals in order to make it consistent with the age intervals. However, the final residual interval of 1980–1982 was also included to make the analysis as recent as possible.

The eight age intervals and seven period intervals yield 14 distinct cohorts. The age, period, and cohort groups used in the analysis are given in Table 3.3. The labor force participation rates for each of the eight age groups for males and females are given in Figures 3.A.1–3.A.7.

3.5.4. Method

As a method for analyzing longitudinal data, the age–period–cohort technique has become popular in recent years (Cook and Ware, 1983). A thorough description of the technique is found in Hagenaars and Cobben (1978) and Hobcraft et al. (1982). The technique has been used for a variety

Table 3.3. Relation of Age, Period, and Cohort Groups

Age/period		1950–54 $P_1{}^a$	1955–59 P_2	1960–64 P_3	1965–69 P_4	1970–74 P_5	1975–79 P_6	1980–82 P_7
20–24	$A_8{}^b$	$C_8{}^c$	C_9	C_{10}	C_{11}	C_{12}	C_{13}	C_{14}
25–29	A_7	C_7	C_8	C_9	C_{10}	C_{11}	C_{12}	C_{13}
30–34	A_6	C_6	C_7	C_8	C_9	C_{10}	C_{11}	C_{12}
35–39	A_5	C_5	C_6	C_7	C_8	C_9	C_{10}	C_{11}
40–44	A_4	C_4	C_5	C_6	C_7	C_8	C_9	C_{10}
45–49	A_3	C_3	C_4	C_5	C_6	C_7	C_8	C_9
50–54	A_2	C_2	C_3	C_4	C_5	C_6	C_7	C_8
55–59	A_1	C_1	C_2	C_3	C_4	C_5	C_6	C_7

[a] P_1–P_7 represent the seven period groups.
[b] A_1–A_8 represent the eight age groups.
[c] C_1–C_{14} represent the 14 cohorts.

of dependent variables such as fertility (Pullum, 1980), delinquency (Maxim, 1984; Pullum, 1977), political party affiliation (Knoke and Hout, 1974), and labor force participation (Farkas, 1977; Clogg, 1982).

However, there is controversy over the use of age–period–cohort analysis (Feinberg and Mason, 1978; Glenn, 1976; Knoke and Hout, 1976; Mason *et al.*, 1973; Palmore, 1978; Rodgers, 1982; Smith *et al.*, 1982). The problem appears to be whether there are two or three distinguishable effects. We have used the method with all three effects, which is in conformity with the majority viewpoint. For instance, Maxim (1984) argues that though the three effects are not orthogonal to each other, each contributes to a substantive understanding.

We have used the "conventional linear model" approach as discussed by Hobcraft *et al.* (1982). This involves fitting "dummy" variables of each of the effects in linear, additive, regression models to a transformation of the continuous dependent variable. Since our dependent variable here is a rate, the logit transformation is employed. The logit function is: $\ln[p/(1 - p)]$, where ln is the natural logarithm and p is the rate expressed as a proportion. We have followed the procedure used by Maxim (1984) to implement the conventional linear approach. This involves performing a series of dummy variable regressions via the SPSS REGRESSION routine (Nie *et al.*, 1975), to complete the analysis. To be more specific: first, the age, period, and cohort dummy variables were run separately against the logit of the labor force participation rates for males and females to account for the overall amount of variations (R^2) removed by each of the main effects (in analysis of variance terminology). There were 7 age, 6 period, and 13 cohort dummy variables in the respective analyses. The first-order interactions of age with period, age with cohort, and period with cohort were run next. Third, although inaccurate regression coefficients were produced due to identification problems, the age–period–cohort model (second-order interaction) was run to obtain the correct R^2 for the full model. In the main effects and the first-order interaction models, A_1 (55–59 years), P_1 (1950–54), and C_1 (55–59 in 1950–54) were constrained to zero. In the second-order interaction model (i.e., age–period–cohort model), to obtain R^2 only A_1, P_1, C_1, and C_2 were set to zero to satisfy the restrictions of dummy variable regression.

The age with period model (AP) was also used to obtain the age and period regression coefficients necessary for the analysis. This model is:

$$Y_{AP} = b_0 + \sum_i a_i A_i + \sum_j p_j P_j$$

where Y_{AP} refers to the logit transformation of age–period-specific rates; A_i and P_j represent the age and period categories; and a_i and p_j are the respective regression coefficients as $i = 1$ to 8 and $j = 1$ to 7. The coefficients for the categories set to zero, a_1 and p_1, were found by subtraction since $\sum_i a_i = 0$ and $\sum_i p_i = 0$. The coefficients for the cohort categories were estimated from the residuals of the age–period model (AP):

$$(Y_{Ap} - \hat{Y}_{Ap}) = b_0 + \sum_k C_k c_k$$

where $\hat{Y}_{Ap}$ refers to the estimated Y_{Ap} values; C_k represents the cohort categories; and c_k refers to the cohort coefficients as $k = 1$ to 14. The coefficient for the first cohort, c_1, was estimated by subtraction since $\sum_k c_k = 0$.

Finally, a secondary analysis was performed to control for the effect of age. Here the age–period, age–cohort, and age–period–cohort R^2 values were examined with the impact of age removed. These calculations were based on the R^2 values obtained in the previous regressions.

3.5.5. Results

Table 3.4 shows the proportion of explained variations for each of the age, period, and cohort models. A variation as high as 82% in labor force participation for males was accounted for by age alone, whereas only 29% of the variation was explained for females. For females, period and cohort taken separately contributed strongly. Age and period together accounted for 98 and 97% for males and females, respectively. Similarly, age and cohort jointly explained the same amounts of variation for males and females, respectively.

Table 3.4. Proportion of Variation in Labor Force Participation Rates Explained by Various Age, Period, Cohort Models

Model	Parameters	Proportion of explained variation (R^2)	
		Males	Females
[A]	7	0.82050	0.29215
[P]	6	0.16186	0.67578
[C]	13	0.18941	0.83332
[AP]	13	0.98236	0.96792
[AC]	20	0.98136	0.96741
[PC]	19	0.36175	0.92492
[APC]	26	0.98993	0.97348

Table 3.5. Proportion of Residual Variation
(Controlling for Age) Explained by
Period and Cohort Effects

	Proportion of residual variation	
R^2 partition	Males	Females
$1 - A$	0.17950	0.70785
$(AP-A)/(1 - A)$	0.90173	0.95468
$(AC-A)/(1 - A)$	0.89616	0.95396
$(APC-A)/(1 - A)$	0.94390	0.96253

When the age effect is eliminated, the amount of variation explained for males was as low as 36% whereas it was 92% for females. The combined age–period–cohort models were strong predictors for both males and females.

When the effect of age was controlled, period and cohort contributed almost equally for males and females (Table 3.5). By partitioning the amount of explained variation, it is seen that period, cohort, and period and cohort together each explained 90% or more when age was controlled. Note that labor force participation is reported in an aggregate manner regarding age.

The age, period, and cohort effects by the individual categories are presented in Tables 3.6, 3.7, and 3.8. Figures 3.3, 3.4, and 3.5 correspond to these tables, showing the graphs of the regression coefficients for each category. Note that the regression coefficients presented in these tables and figures are

Table 3.6. Distribution of Age Effects
by Age and Sex

	Age effects	
Age	Males	Females
20–24	−0.78299	0.74354
25–29	−0.06154	0.23832
30–34	0.64429	−0.03258
35–39	0.71188	−0.03401
40–44	0.56935	−0.05389
45–49	0.25173	−0.08946
50–54	−0.35827	−0.24320
55–59	−0.97445	−0.52872
Constant	2.80473	−0.42328

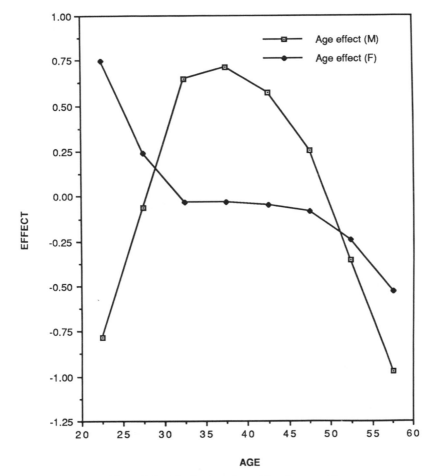

Figure 3.3. Distribution of age effects by age and sex.

unstandardized, but they are the logit transformed values rather than the original rates. As far as the age effect is concerned (Table 3.6 and Figure 3.3), the most adversely affected were the youngest and oldest males. Women, by and large, showed a high positive value and then dropped to zero at age 32, remained constant until the two oldest categories. Perhaps this is due to marriage and child-rearing. But the positive effect of age is apparent until the 30–34 year category.

Table 3.7 and Figure 3.4 show that the period effect is more profound on women reflecting the economic and social pressures exerted on the labor force participation rates from 1950 to 1982. Further, increasing influence of

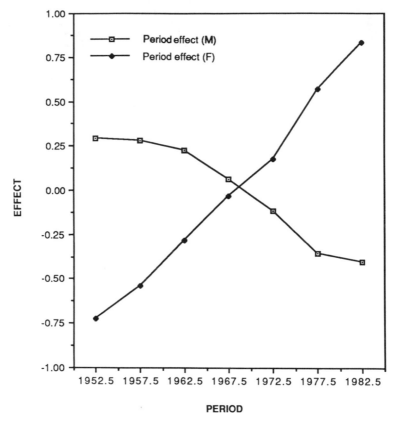

Figure 3.4. Distribution of period effects by year and sex.

the women's liberation movement may also have resulted in postponing childbearing and remaining childless to achieve economic, educational, and career goals. Grindstaff (1975) argues that temporary delay of childbearing fosters a life-style that may ultimately result in the permanent postponement of childbearing. Moreover, there has been a significant change in the value systems such that the traditional domestic role of women is changing. This also may have contributed to the unprecedented increase in female labor force participation.

The gender differential of the cohort effects is negligible (Table 3.8 and Figure 3.5). The cohort effects could be identical if they are due to changes in the age structure of the working population since the sex ratio at working ages is close to one (Table 3.2). The oldest cohort (i.e., age group 55–59 in 1950–54) had a positive effect on labor force participation for both males and

Table 3.7. Distribution of Period Effects
by Year and Sex

	Period effects	
Period	Males	Females
1950–54	0.29451	−0.72531
1955–59	0.27918	−0.54159
1960–64	0.22677	−0.28293
1965–69	0.06628	−0.02906
1970–74	−0.11270	0.17950
1975–79	−0.35405	0.56856
1980–82	−0.39999	0.83083
Constant	2.80473	−0.42328

females (Figure 3.5) and the most recent cohorts (i.e., age groups 20–24 and 25–29 in 1980–82) had negative effects on labor force participation. Perhaps the immediate explanation one may try to use is the cohort size hypothesis of Easterlin. According to this hypothesis, during the 1950s the young ones were advantaged in their participation in the labor force because of their small numbers. As mentioned above for this period, the cohort effects were significant only for the oldest cohort. Surprisingly, for all other cohorts, the effects were not significant in the 1950s. The nature of these cohort effects was explained by Smith (1981). He argues that the positive cohort effect for the period 1950–54 is due to the labor force expansion by 12%. This was possible because of a massive release of consumer wartime savings to which industries reacted by putting people to work producing goods and services. On the other hand, negative cohort effects for the postwar baby-boomers in the 1970s are due to a declining proportion in universities resulting from a rise in university costs and the economic stagnation. It is possible that the larger cohort sizes of the baby-boomers might have contributed to the high costs of university expansion, which were then passed on to students and their families. Expensive education coupled with economic stagnation resulted in crowding of the labor market by the most recent cohorts (Smith, 1981).

The age-specific labor force participation rates, based on the actual rates, are presented in Figures 3.A.1–3.A.7. The aggregate pattern (Table 3.2 and Figure 3.2) is apparent for each of the seven age groups. The 20- to 24-year-old women (Figure 3.A.1) have done well among the eight groups of women, and this is consistent with the age effects from the analysis (Table 3.6 and Figure 3.3). The 55- to 59-year-old men and the 20- to 24-year-old men (Figure 3.A.1) have been relatively more affected than the other male age groups.

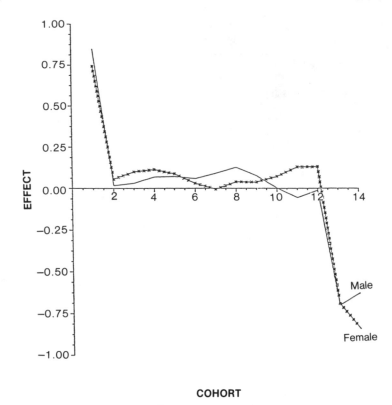

COHORT

Figure 3.5. Distribution of cohort effects by cohort and sex.

Again, the youngest age groups, especially 20–24 and 25–29, for both males and females experienced declines in their labor force participation in 1982.

3.5.6. Summary

It was clear from a cursory analysis that period had a more significant impact on women than on men with respect to their labor force participation rates. This was confirmed and elaborated by the age–period–cohort analysis. During the period under study, it was observed that the labor force participation rate for women has increased significantly in Canada. In fact, the rate in 1981 and 1982 of 51.6 is more than double the 1950 rate of 23.2. The general trend in women's participation in the labor force is an increase for all ages. The picture is not the same for men. They show more consistency in labor force participation, i.e., men enter and leave the labor force in a

Table 3.8. Distribution of Period
Effects by Cohort and Sex

Cohort	Cohort effects	
	Males	Females
1	0.84858	0.74285
2	0.01664	0.05540
3	0.03095	0.09988
4	0.06930	0.11322
5	0.07118	0.08708
6	0.05916	0.03025
7	0.09140	−0.00555
8	0.12760	0.03840
9	0.07612	0.03774
10	0.00219	0.07112
11	−0.05612	0.12875
12	−0.01074	0.13080
13	−0.69874	−0.68945
14	−0.62752	−0.84049
Cohort	−0.06034	−0.05730

linear pattern. This is in fact reflected in their age effects. For women, cohort rather than age is a better indicator of their labor force participation.

The application of the age–period–cohort technique to understand labor force participation rates for both males and females in Canada enables one to interpret labor force trends in Canada. It illustrates varying effects of age–period–cohort analysis. The application of this technique is not restricted to the study of labor force participation alone but to any demographic process where disaggregation makes sense. We also think that the method need not be restricted to the variables used here such as age, year, and sex, but may also include other discriminating variables such as occupation, education, income, and so forth. But the only difficulty is in obtaining data broken down by age, year, sex, and the other variables of interest.

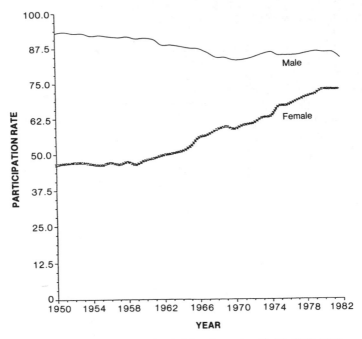

Figure 3.A.1. Participation in labor force: Age 20–24, 1950–1982.

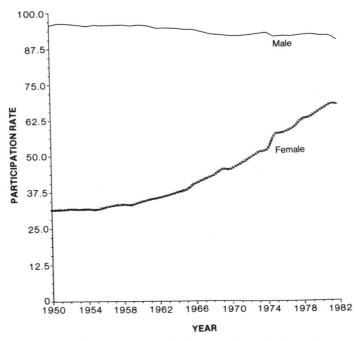

Figure 3.A.2. Participation in labor force: Age 25–29, 1950–1982.

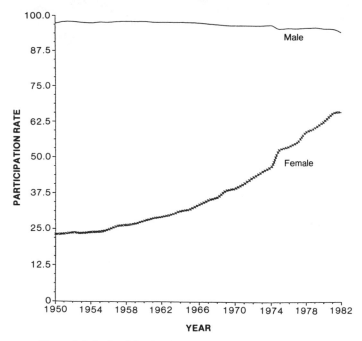

Figure 3.A.3. Participation in labor force: Age 30–34, 1950–1982.

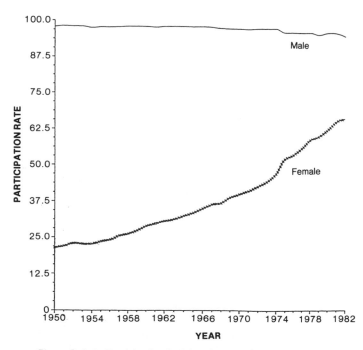

Figure 3.A.4. Participation in labor force: Age 35–39, 1950–1982.

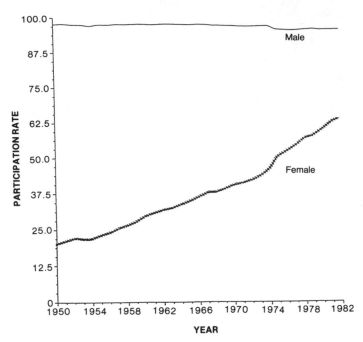

Figure 3.A.5. Participation in labor force: Age 40–44, 1950–1982.

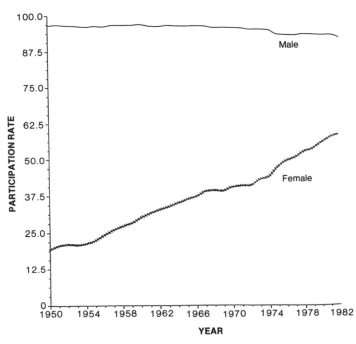

Figure 3.A.6. Participation in labor force: Age 45–49, 1950–1982.

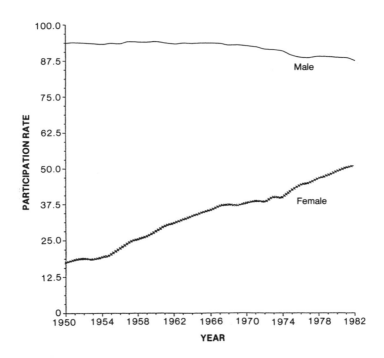

Figure 3.A.7. Participation in labor force: Age 50–54, 1950–1982.

CHAPTER 4

Causal Relationships in Population Analysis

4.1. GENERAL DESCRIPTION OF MULTIPLE REGRESSION

Demographers are concerned with the interrelationships between population and society. Hence, a major function of population studies has been not only the collection and dissemination of relevant facts regarding populations, but also the understanding of these population–society interrelationships. The relationships described above are of two types: descriptive and causal. While empirical research easily accommodates the description of relevant associations, cause-and-effect relationships are often difficult to isolate. For example, although different populations can be described in terms of recognized criteria, particular patterns and processes can only be understood in terms of a general conception of the interrelationships between variables as applied to a particular context. Research questions suggest the existence of these causal relationships, but the appropriate statistical methods are determined by the proposed answer to the research question. Multivariate statistical techniques provide the precision often required to respond to specific research needs, particularly when dealing with applied research. They have given population specialists the ability to probe more deeply than ever before into the details of causal interrelationships.

Among the large body of multivariate statistical techniques available, only four are considered in this chapter: multiple regression, path analysis, factor analysis, and LISREL (linear structural relations). The choice of these techniques is based on their popularity and the common origins of these techniques in the "general linear model" which has led in recent years to the development of a whole new branch of data analysis known as "structural equation modeling" (Bynner and Romney, 1985). Among the best known of the structural equation modeling approaches is LISREL, a procedure that encompasses all of the above statistical techniques within a single theory-testing framework, in which both substantive relations between variables (regression, path analysis), and measurement relations (factor analysis) can be investigated. In the following pages, we will discuss these statistical techniques in detail.

The multiple linear regression model is probably the most widely used multivariate technique in the social sciences for studying causal relationships between one dependent variable and several independent variables. Ideally speaking, both dependent and the set of independent variables should be measured on an interval-level scale. Independent variables are also called predictor variables as they are expected to influence the dependent variable. The dependent variable, also called the criterion variable, can be predicted from independent variables. We must mention here that one can use the regression model not necessarily for predictive purposes but also to assess the strength of relationship between a dependent variable and the independent variables. In other words, we can identify the relative importance of the in-dependent variables in accounting for variation in the dependent variable. The relative importance is represented in the form of weights to apply to the independent variables. The weights are known as partial regression coefficients and these will maximize the correlation between their combined effect and the dependent variable. The correlation coefficient is known as the multiple correlation.

The principal aim in regression analysis is to increase the value of the multiple correlation coefficient. For this reason, one should select independent variables such that they correlate minimally with each other but significantly with the dependent variable. On the other hand, if the independent variables correlate nonsignificantly with the dependent variable but significantly with each other, then the independent variables are called suppressor variables. The effect of these variables in prediction will be discussed a little later. But it is important to note that one should take some precautions about the vari-ables that are involved in the analysis. One of the basic assumptions in regres-sion analysis is that the variables have a multivariate normal distribution so that all relationships between them may be taken to be linear. In other words, for any fixed value of the independent variable, the distribution of the de-pendent variable is normal with a constant variance but may have different means. One of the ways of verifying this assumption is to inspect a scatterplot of the predicted values of the dependent variable against the residuals (i.e., difference between the actual values and the predicted values of the dependent variable). If the scatterplot shows curvature, then it is an indication that the relationship between the dependent variable and the independent variables is not linear. Some of the ways of handling the problem include raising the powers of some of the independent variables to greater than 1, including interaction terms in the model (i.e., by multiplying two or more independent variables together), or using nonlinear logarithmic transformation, or the reciprocal of some of the independent variables or the square root to achieve normality. The use of a particular transformation should be guided by theory; that is, one should know the form of the true model governing the relationship. Otherwise, one should choose the transformation by examining the plotted data or residuals. In one way, the examination of residuals is practical because one may not know the appropriateness of a model in advance. In the process of model building, a residual is what is left after the model is fit. If the model is appropriate for the data, the computed residuals (i.e., the difference between an observed value and the value predicted by the model) should have characteristics similar to those of the true errors. Since the true errors are assumed to be normally distributed with a mean of 0 and a constant variance of σ^2, and the residuals are the estimates of the true errors, then the residuals are expected to follow the above-mentioned characteristics of the residuals. Examination of the residuals is also useful to verify another assumption of regression analysis, homoscedasticity, meaning the standard deviations of errors of prediction are approximately equal at all predicted dependent variable levels.

It may be useful to describe the actual forms of residuals in order to search for violations of assumptions. Nowadays almost all computer programs provide scatterplots of residuals and one should develop a habit of examining them as part of initial regression analysis. Figure 4.1a, reproduced from Tabachnick and Fidell (1989), helps to check for violations of the assumptions. If all assumptions are met, the patterns of residuals should follow the shape of the scatterplot as in Figure 4.1a. It shows that the shape is nearly rectangular with a concentration of scores along the center.

To check for the violation of normality assumption, look at the shape of the scatterplot in Figure 4.1b. It displays a skewed distribution of residuals. If the assumption is met, the residuals would pile up in the center of the plot at each level of a predicted score, with a normal distribution of residual errors around the center. It is important to know that a failure of normal distribution of residuals could be other than actual nonnormality: misspecification of the model, nonconstant variance, due to a small number of residuals, and so forth. Because of this, researchers should investigate other forms of tests such as construction of a histogram of the standardized or studentized residuals. This test is included in the recent SPSS package as well as BMDP programs for regression. For example, the NEW REGRESSION histogram procedure in SPSS contains a tally of the observed number of residuals in each interval and the number expected in a normal distribution with the same mean and variance as the residuals. Then a histogram of expected values is superimposed on that of the observed. Although it is unreasonable to expect a complete

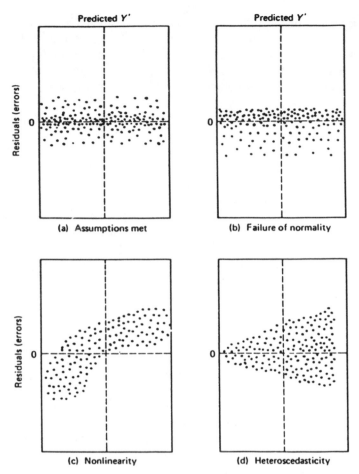

Figure 4.1. Plots of predicted values of the DV (*Y'*) against residuals, showing (a) assumptions met, (b) failure of normality, (c) nonlinearity, and (d) heteroscedasticity.

correspondence between the two frequencies, because of sampling variation, any significant deviations should be considered as evidence of failure of the normality assumption. Bock (1975) explains the effect of several deviations from normality. For a detailed discussion of this procedure and for other tests of normality assumption, refer to Norusis (1982) and Bock (1975).

If the linearity as well as homogeneity of variance assumptions are met, then there should not be any patterns in the residual plots. That is, the residuals should be randomly distributed. If there is any evidence of a pattern, researchers should be concerned about Figure 4.1c. Should the shape of the scatterplot be curved, this indicates nonlinearity. Similarly, the last scatterplot, Figure 4.1d, indicates the failure of the assumption of homoscedasticity. If the assumption was met, the residuals could have been approximately equal in width across all values of the predicted variable. Tabachnick and Fidell (1989) warn that in some cases heteroscedasticity could be a function of something inherent in the order of cases: subjects who are interviewed early in a survey might be expected to exhibit more variability of response owing to interviewer inexperience with the questionnaire. According to them, this can be checked using SPSS or BMDP programs by entering cases in order of time of interview and requesting a plot of residuals against sequence of cases. One may also check the Durbin–Watson statistic, which is an indicator of auto-correlation of errors over the sequence of cases.

4.1.1. The Regression Model

Let X_i ($i = 1, 2, \ldots, \beta$) represent the p independent variables and Y represent the dependent variable. The predictive equation to obtain an expected value of the dependent variable to be represented by the lowercase letters y, x_1, x_2, $\ldots$, x_p is as follows:

$$y = a + b_1x_1 + b_2x_2 + b_3x_3 + \cdots + b_px_p + e \qquad (4.1)$$

where y is the predicted value of Y and b_1, b_2, $\ldots$, b_p represent best-fitting regression weights, with a (intercept) as the value of y when all independent variables x_1, x_2, $\ldots$, x_p are zero, together with a residual variable e. Note that for optimal prediction of the y's, the regression coefficients, also known as slopes, should be chosen to minimize the e's. In other words, the best-fitting regression coefficients are those that produce a prediction equation such that squared differences between Y and y are the minimum ones. The estimation procedure that satisfies the above condition is known as a least-squares solution.

As mentioned above, the intercept (a) represents the predicted value of y when the predictor variables have value zero. On the other hand, the regression slope b_1 represents the change in y that would be predicted for one unit change in x_1 controlling for other independent variables, x_2, x_3, $\ldots$, x_p. Similarly, the regression slope b_2 represents the change in y that would be predicted for a unit change in x_2 controlling for other independent variables. The nature of the predictive equation (4.1) indicates that causal variables are additive and the overall effect of these independent variables is the sum of the effects of the changes in each independent variable individually.

In population studies the variables employed in a regression analysis generally have arbitrary scales and differ significantly in units of measurement.

If we want to know the relative importance of independent variables, the magnitude of the regression coefficients cannot be used. In order to make them comparable, we have to standardize regression coefficients by multiplying the coefficient by the ratio of the standard deviation of the independent variable to the standard deviation of the dependent variable. The standardized coefficient is free from the original unit of measurement and is usually known as the *beta* coefficient. The standardized coefficients are only meaningful in the comparison of the influence of independent variables on the dependent variable and should not be used in any absolute sense to reflect the importance of the independent variables.

Another way of calculating the relative importance of independent variables is by partitioning the sum of squares of the dependent variables in order to account for the proportion of the variation in the dependent variable explained by the individual independent variables. If one wants to assess the contribution of a particular variable to the model, consider the goodness of fit of the model, R^2 (square of the multiple correlation coefficient) which lies in the range 0 to 1; $R^2 = 0$ means there is no linear relationship between the dependent and independent variables, and $R^2 = 1$ indicates the perfect linear relationship. In order to compute the relative importance of the ith variable, consider the increase in R^2 when the ith variable is entered into the model that already includes the other independent variables. That is:

$$R^2_{change} = R^2_{(i)} - R^2$$

where $R^2_{(i)}$ is the square of the multiple correlation coefficient when the ith variable is added to the list of the independent variables in the model; and R^2 is the corresponding multiple correlation of the model containing all of the independent variables except the ith variable. Now the R^2_{change} provides the unique contribution of the ith variable to explain the variation in the dependent variable that is not explainable by the other independent variables. The computational procedure of the R^2 itself in an analytical fashion is as follows:

$$R^2 = 1 - \frac{\text{Residual sum of squares}}{\text{Total sum of squares}} \qquad (4.2)$$

The R^2 is interpreted as the proportion of variation in the dependent variable explained by the best linear combination of the independent variables. Since there is no reference to any particular variable in the R^2 calculated above and the model includes all the independent variables, it is used as an optimistic estimate of how well the model fits the data. One can test the significance of R^2 in order to indicate the importance of the independent variables in predicting the dependent variable. Larzelere and Mulaik (1977) suggested the following F test, which keeps Type I error below the level of significance (α):

$$F = \frac{R^2/P}{(1 - R^2)/(N - P - 1)} \tag{4.3}$$

where P is the total number of independent variables and N is the total number of observations. The calculated F is compared with the tabled F, with P and $(N - P - 1)$ degrees of freedom at α required level of significance. Using similar statistics as those in Eq. (4.3), the test of significance can be performed for the individual regression components. Some computer programs use Student's t-test statistic for the test of significance for regression coefficients.

4.1.2. Some Precautions—Problem of Outliers

In any multivariate analysis, cases with extreme values will have deleterious effects on the regression solutions. Hence, before undertaking regression analysis, one should check for the outliers. Although it is not easy to detect outliers in multivariate situations, the computer programs can be used to obtain the *Mahalanobis distance* statistic. This is a chi-square (χ^2) statistic, which measures the distance of cases from the average values of the independent variables. To check the acceptable distance for each case from the centroid of all cases, one has to calculate a critical value by referring to the chi-square table at the desired level of significance. Another method of detecting the outliers is to inspect the residuals for each case. The suspected cases with larger residuals can be deleted from the analysis, and then we compare the residuals obtained to the earlier one where all cases were included.

Sophisticated data analysts may consider using outlier diagnostics statistics to handle the problem of outliers. Diagnostics are certain quantities computed from the data with the purpose of pinpointing influential points, after which these outliers can be removed or corrected, followed by a least-squares analysis on the remaining cases (Rousseeuw and Leroy, 1987, p. 8). Many of these are based on the residuals resulting from the least-squares method. Some other diagnostics are based on the principle of deleting one case at a time, then regression coefficients are computed at each step to evaluate the impact of the deleted case. One may also delete more than one case at a time in order to evaluate their impact on regression coefficients. The statistical methods of estimating the effect of deleted cases on regression coefficients are discussed in Rousseeuw and Leroy (1987). They also discuss recent developments such as the hat matrix approach, "elemental sets," and the high breakdown diagnostics. The hat matrix approach and "elemental sets" are not as good as the high breakdown diagnostics for dealing with a large number of outliers.

Once the outliers are detected, the next problem is how to deal with them. Tabachnick and Fidell (1989) have suggested several strategies. Before anything can be done with the outlier cases, it is necessary to check the accuracy of the data. Examine the outliers for the cases to make sure that they are entered in the data processing device correctly. If genuine outliers are found, transform the data for the entire distribution of a variable such that extreme scores are moved nearer the central tendency of the distribution. An easy solution is to delete cases with extreme values from the analysis. The danger of this solution is that the sample size will be affected. If generalization is the objective of this study, rationale should be provided as to how exclusion of such cases would not affect the generalization. For instance, one could argue that the outlying case may be considered not to be a member of the population. Another alternative is to change the scores of a variable which has extreme values; sometimes, measurement of variables is arbitrary. One could also assign a new score to the offending variable based on the next extreme score in the distribution.

The most commonly used method of estimation in regression analysis is the least-squares method. This method is extremely sensitive to outliers in the data as it attempts to fit the regression line by minimizing the squared deviations. Toward the end of the first paragraph of this section, we stated that one of the methods of detecting outliers in the case of multivariate situations is to inspect the residuals. But in the case of residuals derived from the least-squares method, the outliers remain invisible even though a careful analysis of the residuals (Rousseeuw and Leroy, 1987). As an alternative to the above-suggested procedures which use the least-squares method, Rousseeuw and Leroy suggest a "robust regression" approach, an attempt to devise estimators that are not so strongly affected by outliers. There are many robust methods available. Rousseeuw and Leroy compare different robust methods and measure their effectiveness by counting the number of outliers that they can deal with.

4.1.3. Multicollinearity

The problem of multicollinearity arises whenever two or more of the independent variables are highly related. This high degree of relationship will affect the estimates of regression coefficients because the estimation of the coefficients involves a correlation matrix of the independent variables. If independent variables are perfectly correlated or any independent variable is a perfect linear combination of other independent variables, then the correlation matrix will have zero determinant making it impossible to calculate the regression coefficients. This would rarely occur in the regression analysis. However, situations in which the determinant is nearly zero result in multicollinearity, and the multivariate solution becomes unstable. Thus, before one performs multiple regression, it is important to inspect the correlation matrix. One way to detect multicollinearity is to compute a determinant of a correlation matrix or else examine the coefficients. The large coefficients or a determinant close to zero can be considered as indicators of multicollinearity. Another method of detecting multicollinearity is to inspect tolerance levels. Whenever a low tolerance level, say 0.01 (1 minus the squared multiple correlation of a variable), is noticed, one ought to be seriously concerned about the calculations.

If multicollinearity is found, one of the simple ways of handling it would be to delete the offending variable/variables from the analysis. The information may not be lost by deleting the offending variable since it is a combination of other variables. In case offending variable/variables are too theoretically important to be deleted, one could construct a composite index of these variables or subject the variables to principal components analysis and then use the score on components as the variables (Tabachnick and Fidell, 1989). Tabachnick and Fidell also suggest use of stepwise, or hierarchical entry of variables into the analysis so that only one or a few of the variables that are multicollinear are used.

If the above-mentioned procedures do not eliminate the problem of multicollinearity, the use of ridge regression may be considered. Ridge regression is based on some arbitrary assumptions and tries to stabilize estimates of regression coefficients by inflating the variance that is analyzed. Some researchers are skeptical about the technique and we recommend that the researcher considering use of this technique should first refer to Rozeboom (1979).

4.1.4. Other Issues

One of the problems often encountered by an analyst is the case-to-variable ratio. That is, how many cases per variable must one have for meaningful results? This is a practical problem not easily answered. It is realized that the lower the case-to-variable ratio, the more it is necessary that the residuals be normally distributed. Some argue that ideally one should have 20 times more cases than variables, and 40 times more cases than variables in the case of stepwise regression procedures (Tabachnick and Fidell, 1989). In any case, it is not advisable to have less than 4 to 5 times more cases than independent variables. Tabachnick and Fidell argue that especially at low case-to-variable ratios, one must check for skewness in dependent variable and measurement errors. If these are present, more cases are needed. More cases are also needed to demonstrate a small effect because as the number of cases becomes large, almost any multiple correlation will differ significantly from zero.

Sometimes it may become important to check for interaction effects in addition to the main effects of the independent variables. Inclusion of interaction terms in the regression equation may be directed by theoretical considerations. In other situations, an examination of the analysis may indicate that the magnitude of the effect of one variable on another may differ depending on the particular value possessed by some third variable. In those situations, it is necessary to include interaction terms in regression analysis. For a detailed discussion on interaction terms and their effects in the regression model, we refer the reader to Hayduk and Wonnacott (1980) who provide an excellent discussion.

As mentioned at the beginning of this chapter, multiple regression is probably the most widely used multivariate technique in the social sciences. In the last three to four decades, it has revolutionized multivariate analysis in the social sciences. Thus, almost all multivariate statistics books, either applied or theoretical, include a discussion of multiple regression. It is redundant to include here the mathematical formulas or a detailed discussion on all aspects of regression analysis. Rather, we strongly recommend that the interested researcher refer to Tabachnick and Fidell (1989).

4.2. INTRODUCTION TO PATH ANALYSIS

Although path analysis was developed by Wright in 1934, the application of this technique, especially in demography, was popularized by Duncan (1966); hence, the discussion of path analysis in this section is heavily based on Duncan's work. Path analysis helped to develop linear causal modeling, but causal models are not themselves of great importance to social scientists. The role of path analysis in causal model developments is in the interpretation and the decomposition of a dependent variable rather than discovering causes (Duncan, 1966). More importantly, it helps in making explicit the logic of conventional regression calculations. As discussed in an earlier section, an application of regression analysis to a data set is based on some assumptions. In this context, path analysis "makes the assumptions explicit and tends to force the discussion to be at least internally consistent, so that mutually incompatible assumptions are not introduced surreptitiously into different parts of an argument extending over scores of pages. With the causal scheme made explicit, moreover, it is in a form that enables criticism to be sharply focused and hence potentially relevant not only to the interpretation at hand but also perhaps, to the conduct of future inquiry" (Duncan, 1966, p. 7). Another useful function of path analysis, unlike regression which provides only the direct effect of the independent variables on the dependent variable, is to identify the indirect effects and spurious effects of the independent variables.

Path analysis deals with observed variables and unobserved latent variables. The observed variables are interrelated, and it can be assumed that there are several "ultimate" variables that completely determine them. The ultimate variables could be observed or unobserved (latent) variables. Let us consider Figure 4.2 to understand better the type of variables that we are discussing.

According to Figure 4.2, X_1 and X_2 are observed ultimate variables, and X_u and X_v are unobserved (latent) variables. According to the model, variables X_1 and X_2 determine the observed variables X_3 and X_4. It may be noted that X_4 is not only directly affected by X_1 and X_2 variables but also indirectly through the intermediate variable, X_3. Variables X_u and X_v are not only independent of each other but also do not have any relationship with X_1 and X_2.

As indicated earlier, path analysis specifies linear equations. The equations which are equivalent to the system represented in Figure 4.2 can be written as follows:

$$X_3 = p_{31} + p_{32}X_2 + p_{3u}X_u + p_{3m}R_m \qquad (4.4)$$

where X_3 is the dependent variable written as a function of its predictors X_1, X_2, and X_u with the associated coefficients p's known as path coefficients. Note that path coefficients have two subscripts: the first identifies the dependent variable, the second the variable whose direct effect on the dependent variable is measured by the coefficient. R_m is a residual variable. Similarly, we can write X_4 as a function of X_1, X_2, X_3, X_v and R_n as per Figure 4.2.

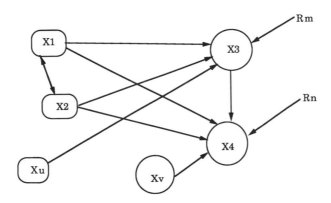

Figure 4.2. Causal model of path analysis.

$$X_4 = p_{41}X_1 + p_{42}X_2 + p_{43}X_3 + p_{4v}X_v + p_{4n}R_n \tag{4.5}$$

Since the value of X_3 is given in Eq. (4.4), if we replace the value of X_3 in Eq. (4.5) the resultant equation will be as follows:

$$\begin{aligned} X_4 &= p_{41}X_1 + p_{42}X_2 + p_{43}(p_{31}X_1 + p_{32}X_2 + p_{3u}X_u + p_{3m}R_m) \\ &\quad + p_{4v}X_v + p_{4n}R_n \\ &= p_{41}X_1 + p_{42}X_2 + p_{43}p_{31}X_1 + p_{43}p_{32}X_2 + p_{43}p_{3u}X_u \\ &\qquad + p_{43}p_{3m}R_m + p_{4v}X_v + p_{4n}R_n \end{aligned} \tag{4.6}$$

Now Eq. (4.6) indicates that the dependent variable X_4 is a function of only ultimate variables and residual variables. Let us standardize all the variables, including residual variables, by subtracting their respective means and dividing the difference by their corresponding standard deviations, i.e.,

$$X_i = (X_i - \bar{X})/\sigma_{xi}$$

Now the expectation of standardized variables, X_i and X_j where $i \neq j$, will be equal to the correlation coefficient, i.e., $r_{ij} = (\sum X_{ij})/N$. It may be mentioned that unlike in the case of path coefficients, the order of subscripts is immaterial for correlation coefficients.

The next problem is to identify the path coefficients p in the equations if the correlation coefficients between variables are known. Let us consider the correlation coefficient between two variables. According to the principle that follows from Eqs. (4.4) and (4.5), the correlation coefficient can be written in terms of the path coefficients from common antecedent variables. For instance,

$$r_{34} = \sum \frac{X_3 X_4}{N}$$

This equation can be expanded by substituting the value of X_4 from Eq. (4.5) (Note: the variables in the equation are not standardized but the form of the equation remains the same even for the standardized variables, i.e.

$$r_{34} = \frac{1}{N} \sum X_3(P_{41}X_1 + P_{42}X_2 + P_{43}X_3 + P_{4v}X_v + P_{4n}R_n) \tag{4.7}$$

$$r_{34} = P_{41}r_{13} + P_{42}r_{23} + P_{43}$$

after making use of the fact that $\sum X_3 X_4/N = 1$ and the assumption that r_{3v} and r_{3n} are equal to zero. The correlation coefficients on the right-hand side of Eq. (4.7) can be further expanded by the same above procedure, i.e.,

$$r_{13} = \frac{1}{N} \sum X_1 X_3 = \frac{1}{N} \sum X_1(P_{31}X_1 + P_{32}X_2 + P_{3u}X_u + P_{3m}R_m)$$
$$= P_{31} + P_{32}r_{12} \tag{4.8}$$

and

$$r_{23} = \frac{1}{N} \sum X_2 X_3 = \frac{1}{N} \sum X_2(P_{31}X_1 + P_{32}X_2 + P_{3u}X_u + P_{3m}R_m)$$
$$= P_{31}r_{12} + P_{32} \tag{4.9}$$

The expression r_{12} in Eqs. (4.8) and (4.9) cannot be further expanded as long as we retain the path diagram given in Figure 4.2. Based on the procedure followed in Eqs. (4.7), (4.8), and (4.9), the general equation can be written and Duncan (1966) labels this general form as the basic theorem of path analysis:

$$r_{ij} = \sum_q P_{iq}r_{jq} \tag{4.10}$$

where i and j represent two variables in the system and the index q runs over all variables from which paths lead directly to X_i. This general form can be expanded by successive applications of (4.10) itself to the r_j. By repeated use of the general formula given in (4.10), one may easily master the art of reading path diagrams and develop his/her own verbal algorithm rather than using the theorem. The systematic rule provided by Duncan (1966) to read directly from the path diagram instead of using the general form given in Eq. (4.10) is as follows:

Read back from variable i, then forward to variable j, forming the product of all paths along the traverse; then sum these products for all possible traverses. The same variable cannot be intersected more than once in a single traverse. In no case can one trace back having once started forward. The bidirectional correlation is used in tracing either forward or back, but if more than one bidirectional correlation appears in the diagram, only one can be used in a single traverse. The resulting expression may consist of a single direct path plus the sum of several compound paths representing all the indirect connections allowed by the diagram in Figure 4.2.

Duncan also provides a special case of the basic theorem to include residual paths as well. But in the case of path analysis, we make an assumption that residuals are uncorrelated, and each of the dependent variables is directly related to all of the variables preceeding it in the assumed causal sequence (Duncan, 1966). One immediately notices that path analysis is nothing but regression analysis where series of regressions are performed for each of the dependent variables directed by the path diagram. For example, Figure 4.2 indicates that X_3 and X_4 are dependent variables but X_3 is also one of the independent variables affecting X_4. And path coefficients are nothing but standardized regression coefficients.

4.2.1. Numerical Illustration

We now turn to an illustration of the path analysis technique. For this purpose, consider the path diagram displayed in Figure 4.3. The relationship among the variables is provided by the zero-order correlation matrix. The task at hand is to decompose the zero-order correlation using path analysis into different components. The possible components of a zero-order correlation are as follows:

Zero-order correlation = Direct causal effect + Indirect causal effect

+ Antecedent spurious causal effect + Error term

Before decomposing the zero-order correlations using the technique, we would like to make it clear that the causal model provided in Figure 4.2 is based on some artificial data created for illustration. Using the artificial data, a zero-order correlation matrix was computed and series of regressions performed to obtain the coefficients given in the model. Since the model is a

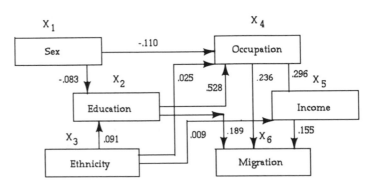

Figure 4.3. Causal diagram of migration.

hypothetical one, we will not provide a formulation of the model but the figure itself indicates the causal mechanism. The model assumes sex and ethnicity as exogenous variables and education, occupation, and income as endogenous variables. The dependent variable is migration. In other words, sex and ethnicity affect mobility behavior indirectly through socioeconomic variables.

Given this causal ordering, the numbers and associated signs are the standardized regression coefficients (betas). They indicate the type of relationship that exists among the variables. The negative coefficients of sex with education and occupation imply that females are less educated and occupy lower status occupations. Similarly, the positive relationships among education, occupation, and income imply that the higher the education, the better the occupation and the higher the income. All of these variables influence migration positively. Given this background, now let us apply the basic theorem of path analysis to Figure 4.3 in order to decompose the zero-order correlation coefficients into components such as direct causal effect, indirect causal effect, antecedent spurious causal effect, and error term. The basic theorem of path analysis given in (4.10) is as follows:

$$r_{jk} = \sum_i P_{ji} r_{ik}$$

where j = dependent variable, k = ultimate independent variable, i = all variables directly causing j, and P = path coefficient (beta). Consider case (i) where education (X_2) is a dependent variable and sex is the independent variable. In view of the above equation, $j = 2$, $k = 1$, and $i = 1$. Application of the above theorem to case (i) is:

$$r_{21} = P_{21} \cdot r_{11} = P_{21} = -0.083$$

Case (ii): The dependent variable is education and the independent variable is ethnicity. According to the decomposition equation, $j = 2$, $k = 3$, $i = 3$ and substitution of these variables in the equation is as follows:

$$r_{23} = P_{23} \cdot r_{33} = 0.091$$

Note that both in case (i) and in case (ii), the path coefficient is equal to the zero-order correlation coefficient.

Case (iii): Consider occupation as the dependent variable (X_4) and sex as the ultimate independent variable and sex and ethnicity as variables directly causing occupation. In the notations of the above theorem, $j = 4$, $k = 1$, and $i = 1, 2$. The equation is:

$$r_{41} = P_{41} \cdot r_{11} + P_{42} \cdot r_{21} = P_{41} + P_{42}(P_{21}) = -0.110 + 0.528(-0.083)$$

$$= -0.110 + (-0.044)$$

$$= -0.154$$

The r_{41} is the correlation coefficient between sex and occupation. It is decomposed into the direct effect of sex on occupation (-0.110) and the indirect effect of sex on occupation through an intermediate variable, education. That is, the total effect of sex on occupation (-0.154) is less than the direct effect of sex on occupation because there is an indirect effect of sex on occupation. The fact that total effect is close to the zero-order correlation between sex and occupation implies that the error term is negligible.

Case (iv): In this case, occupation is the dependent variable but education is the ultimate independent variable and sex, ethnicity, and education are the variables directly influencing occupation, i.e., $j = 4$, $k = 2$, $i = 1, 2, 3$:

$$r_{42} = P_{41} \cdot r_{12} + P_{42} \cdot r_{22} + P_{43} \cdot r_{31}$$

$$= -0.110 \times -0.083 + 0.528 + 0.025 \times 0.091$$

$$= 0.009 + 0.528 + 0.002$$

The decomposition of correlation coefficient between education and occupation gives the spurious and antecedent effect of sex; the second term indicates the direct effect of education on occupation; and the third term is negligible.

Case (v): Consider $j = 4$, $k = 3$, and $i = 3$:

$$r_{43} = P_{43} \cdot r_{33} = P_{43} = 0.025$$

Case (vi): Consider $j = 5$, $k = 3$, and $i = 3, 4$:

$$r_{54} = P_{53} \cdot r_{33} + P_{54} \cdot r_{43}$$

$$= 0.009 + 0.296 \times 0.025$$

$$= 0.009 + 0.007 = 0.016$$

Both cases (v) and (vi) indicate that there is no strong relationship between ethnicity, education, and income.

Case (vii): $j = 5$, $k = 4$, $i = 3, 4$:

$$r_{54} = P_{53} \cdot r_{34} + P_{54} \cdot r_{44}$$

$$= P_{53} \cdot P_{43} + P_{54}$$
$$= 0.009 \times 0.025 + 0.296$$
$$= 0.0002 + 0.296 = 0.2962$$

Case (viii): Consider $j = 6$, $k = 2$, $i = 2, 4$:

$$r_{62} = P_{62} \cdot r_{22} + P_{64} \cdot r_{42}$$
$$= P_{62} + P_{64} \cdot P_{41} \cdot P_{21} + P_{64} \cdot P_{42} + P_{64} \cdot P_{43} \cdot P_{23}$$
$$r_{62} = 0.189 + 0.236 \times -0.110 \times -0.083 + 0.236$$
$$\times 0.528 + 0.236 \times 0.025 \times 0.091$$
$$= 0.189 + 0.002 + 0.125 + 0.0005 = 0.317$$

In this case, the correlation coefficient between education and migration has been decomposed: the first right-hand side of the equation shows the direct effect of education on migration; the second term shows the spurious antecedent effect of sex on education through the intermediate variables, namely education and occupation; the third term provides the indirect effect of education through occupation on migration; the last term is almost zero. It should be mentioned that though the direct effect of education on migration is only 0.189, the total effect is as much as 0.317. In other words, path analysis helps us to reach beyond apparent direct relationships between two variables.

Case (ix): Consider migration as the dependent variable, occupation as the ultimate independent variable, and education, occupation, and income as variables directly causing migration, i.e., $j = 6$, $k = 4$, $i = 2, 4, 5$:

$$r_{64} = P_{62} \cdot r_{42} + P_{64} \cdot r_{44} + P_{65} \cdot r_{54}$$
$$= P_{62}(P_{41} \cdot P_{21} + P_{42} + P_{43} \cdot P_{23}) + P_{64} + P_{65}(P_{53} \cdot P_{43} + P_{54})$$
$$= P_{62} \cdot P_{41} \cdot P_{21} + P_{62} \cdot P_{42} + P_{62} \cdot P_{43} \cdot P_{23}$$
$$+ P_{64} + P_{65} \cdot P_{53} \cdot P_{43} + P_{65} \cdot P_{54}$$
$$= 0.189 \times -0.110 \times -0.083 + 0.189 \times 0.528 + 0.189 \times 0.025$$
$$\times 0.091 + 0.236 + 0.155 \times 0.009 \times 0.025 + 0.155 \times 0.296$$
$$= 0.002 + 0.100 + 0.0004 + 0.236 + 0.00003 + 0.046 = 0.384$$

The decomposition of the zero-order correlation coefficient between migration and occupation is as follows: the first term is the spurious antecedent effect of sex and education; the second term is the spurious antecedent effect of education through occupation on migration; the third term is negligible; the fourth term is the direct effect of occupation on migration; the fifth term is almost zero; and the final term is the indirect effect of occupation through income on migration. As in case (viii), this equation also provides information on indirect effects of occupation on migration.

Case (x): Consider migration as the dependent variable, income as the ultimate independent variable, and occupation and income as the variables directly causing migration, i.e.,

$$r_{65} = P_{64} \cdot r_{45} + P_{65} \cdot r_{55}$$

$$= P_{64}(P_{53} \cdot P_{43} + P_{54}) + P_{65}$$

$$= P_{64} \cdot P_{53} \cdot P_{43} + P_{64} \cdot P_{54} + P_{65}$$

$$= 0.236 \times 0.009 \times 0.025 + 0.236 \times 0.296 + 0.155$$

$$= 0.027 + 0.070 + 0.155 = 0.252$$

In this equation also the direct effect of income on migration is substantiated by the spurious antecedent effect of occupation.

The above computations illustrate the importance of path analysis. Unlike regression analysis, it helps to understand not just the direct influence of a variable on a dependent variable but also accounts for indirect relationships.

4.3. INTRODUCTION TO FACTOR ANALYSIS

In regression and path analysis we have examined the relationships among sets of variables in which all of the variables have been defined prior to the analysis, and the direction of the relationships between independent and dependent variables has been specified. In this section, we inspect relationships involving one set of variables that has been defined prior to the analysis and another set which is generated from the first. Hence, we take a group of observed variables and look at the interrelationships among them. In other words, every variable is both independent and dependent at the same time. This would result in a new set of variables, replacing the original set and refocusing us to study the relationships between these two sets. The motivation for replacing one group of variables by another is based on at least three considerations: (1) To identify coherent subgroups of intercorrelated variables with the given data set which are relatively independent of one another. (2) To reduce the number of variables being studied in situations where measurements are multidimensional, and the number of measurements for each subject is so large that analysis becomes very difficult. In such cases, one would be interested in reducing the dimension when analyzing multiresponse data making sure that sufficient information is retained for adequate analysis. (3) To rewrite the data set in an alternative form by constructing some set of new, composite, independent hypothetical variables from the original ones.

The three tasks outlined above can be handled by two statistical techniques: principal components analysis and factor analysis. Both are related but also based on different principles. Principal components analysis uses all of the variance in the observed variables for the solution, while factor analysis uses only the variance a variable shares with other variables (Tabachnick and Fidell, 1989). In other words, the difference between the two techniques is the way in which they treat the error term. Principal components analysis treats the error terms as segments. Here, every variable is related to a series of components, one of them could be its own error term. But factor analysis puts the error term outside of its equations. Factor analysis only takes into account the common variance of a variable with the other variables in the observed set and the common variance is divided into a set of factors (Johnston, 1978).

In this section, we will be discussing in detail the technique of factor analysis because we are interested not only in data reduction but also reproducing the correlation matrix as closely as possible with the smallest number of factors. Principal components analysis is more desirable if one is interested simply in an empirical summary of the data set (Tabachnick and Fidell, 1989). Exploratory factor analysis does this by grouping together variables that are intercorrelated. On the other hand, confirmatory factor analysis is useful for testing hypotheses or a theory about the structure of underlying processes.

4.3.1. Important Concepts in Factor Analysis

Factor Loadings. The first step in factor analysis is to compute a correlation matrix from the observed set of variables for a given data set. Using a correlation matrix, a factor matrix will be obtained. A factor matrix consists of the derived factors as columns and the original variables as rows. The cell entries of the factor matrix are known as factor loadings. Factor loadings indicate the degree to which each of the observed variables correlates with each of the factors. Hence, factor loadings are nothing but correlation coefficients between the variable and the factors. The variables with high loadings on a factor will provide the meaning and interpretation of the factor.

Factor Scores. If we assume that factors are variables and these factors are measured on the same subjects upon which the original input variables are measured, then the subjects have a value on each of the derived factors similar to the subjects having a value on each of the input variables. These values are called factor scores. In other words, factor scores represent estimates of the scores that subjects would have received on each of the factors (latent variables) had they been measured directly (Tabachnick and Fidell, 1989).

Eigenvalues. Factor analysis provides the same number of factors as the number of variables. Since the primary purpose of factor analysis is for data reduction, a researcher has to make a decision to choose as few factors as possible to represent the total variation in the data. An eigenvalue is a useful statistic for deciding how many factors we should retain from the analysis. A rule of thumb is to retain those factors which have an eigenvalue greater than 1. This is because a factor associated with the eigenvalue 1 accounts for as much variance in the data set as would one variable, on average. To illustrate this, let us consider a data set with ten variables. Since the total variation in the data is 100%, each variable on average accounts for 10% of the total variation—100% divided by ten variables. A factor with an eigenvalue of say 4 would account for $4 \times 10\% = 40\%$ of the total variation in the data and on the other hand a factor with an eigenvalue of only 0.1 accounts for only 1% of the variance in the data. The rule of thumb is to retain factors to the point where an additional factor would account for less variance than a typical variable. In the ten-variable situation where each variable on average accounts for 10% of the variance, any factor which accounts for less than 10% of the variance would have an eigenvalue less than 1, and would not usually be included as a significant factor.

Rotation of Factors. The notion of rotation in factor analysis is useful in order to interpret the factors. In a technical sense it is meant to achieve simple structure by rotating the factor loading matrix. Thurstone (1947) describes the major characteristics of *simple structure* as follows:

1. Any column of the factor loading matrix should have mostly small values, as close to zero as possible.
2. Any given row of the matrix of factor loadings should have nonzero entries in only a few columns.
3. Any two columns of the matrix of factor loadings should exhibit a different pattern of high and low loadings.

There are several rotational methods to achieve simple structure. However, there are three widely used methods, namely, varimax, quartimax, and equimax rotation techniques.

The varimax rotation technique maximizes the variance of the factor loadings for each factor by making high loadings higher and low ones lower. In other words, this technique tries to maximize the variance of the square of the loading in each column of the factor matrix. On the other hand, the quartimax method tries to maximize the variance of the square of the loadings in each row of the factor matrix. Unlike varimax, which operates on the factors, quartimax operates on the variables to increase the dispersion of the loadings within variables across factors. Equimax rotation is a compromise solution of varimax and quartimax methods. It tries simultaneously to simplify the factors and the variables. On the question of which method to use for identification of the basic structuring of variables into meaningful coherent subgroups, Kim and Mueller (1979) suggest that one should not be unduly concerned about the choice of the particular method. However, it is recommended that in many applications, the varimax rotation is probably the best.

The Naming of Factors. After rotated factor solution, the practice is to name chosen significant factors for what each factor actually means. These descriptive names are based on the high-loading variables that represent a common element. The essence of naming the factors provides a novel way of viewing the subject matter, and may contribute to the development of other hypotheses that could be tested in subsequent research studies (Kachigan, 1986).

4.3.2. An Application of Factor Analysis

So far we have described the conceptual understanding of factor analysis. Now let us examine critically the results of an empirical study and if necessary reproduce the results to overcome the limitations.

Mukherjee (1965) selected a random sample of 94 individuals to rate a particular unlabeled brand of coffee according to 14 characteristics. The 14 coffee attributes are as follows:

1. Pleasant flavor–Unpleasant flavor
2. Refreshing taste–Stagnant taste
3. Mellow taste–Bitter taste
4. Expensive taste–Cheap taste
5. Comforting taste–Irritating taste
6. Alive taste–Lifeless taste
7. Tastes real–Tastes artificial
8. Deep, distinct flavor–Shallow, indistinct flavor
9. Tastes just-brewed–Tastes reheated
10. Full-bodied flavor–Watery flavor
11. Pure, clear taste–Muddy taste
12. Roasted taste–Raw taste
13. Fresh taste–Stale taste
14. Excellent–Poor quality

If we are asked to summarize these data and come up with an effective advertising message of this particular brand of coffee, we need to use a factor analysis. Before we analyze this data set with the help of factor analysis, an initial perusal of the variables reveals several distinct characteristics. The division between taste and flavor, for example, may delineate two factors. The factor analysis should determine whether these two descriptions form distinguishing groups. Although other distinctions are less obvious, since all of the variables deal with taste preference and perception, there do appear to be other connotative divisions. Variables 3 and 5 (comforting and mellow) connote a certain relaxing quality while variables 2 and 6 (sparkling and alive) seem to contain an active element. Further, variables 4, 7, and 12 (expensive taste, tastes like real coffee, and roasted taste) all point to the quality of the coffee. Roasted and real coffee would be expected to be more expensive and of better quality than, say, instant coffee. It may be because of this that a number of advertisements for instant coffee attempt to project the idea that it tastes equivalent to brewed varieties. These variables may be expected to form a factor. Variables 9 and 13 (fresh and tastes just-brewed) may be considered also as quality variables. The factor analysis will help to resolve these issues on a scientific basis.

Mukherjee (1965) conducted this experiment by providing each of 94 individuals a cup of coffee of a particular but undeclared brand. Ten blank boxes separated each set of statements that were given in a questionnaire. Individuals checked the position which came closest to describing how they felt toward the product. The ten scale categories were assigned successive integers beginning with 1 at the favorable side of the scale and the ratings thus were treated quantitatively, and ratings could vary from 1 to 9 on an attribute. The ratings on different attributes were then intercorrelated producing a 14×14 sample correlation matrix (see Table 2, p. 36, Mukherjee, 1965). Then, on the basis of this correlation matrix, Mukherjee obtained an unrotated factor loading matrix. Because of very little contribution of the fifth factor to the total variance and apparent insignificant magnitude of the largest loading of the fifth factor, Mukherjee concluded with 4 factors and accordingly he obtained a 14×14 principal factor loading matrix, which is given in the left-hand portion of Table 3 of Mukherjee (1965). Using varimax and oblique rotation methods, he obtained a rotated varimax factor loading matrix and oblique factor loading matrix, which are shown in the middle and right-hand portion of the same table. He named the four factors as follows: Factor A (comforting quality) containing the attributes numbered 1, 3, 5, and 11; Factor B (heartiness), attributes 8 and 10; Factor C (genuineness), attributes 2, 4, 6, 7, 8, 10, and 14; and Factor D (freshness), attributes 9, 12, and 13.

Our criticism about Mukherjee's conclusions is the way he made the decision about the significant factors without any statistical basis. His conclusion regarding four factors may be appropriate to his sample of 94 individuals only. This may not be relevant in the case of another sample of 94 from the same population. If this is the case, any advertising message based on four factors as suggested by Mukherjee would not necessarily be appropriate for the entire population. The implication of this argument is that the number of factors may vary from sample to sample. In order to avoid this problem, the optimum number of factors may be determined using sampling theory, which is discussed below.

In factor analysis, we may regard each observed variable as a dependent variable that can be regressed on unobserved factors. Similarly, each factor may be considered as a dependent variable that is regressed on all observed variables. In this case the "regression coefficients" are the factor loadings that identify the number and nature of the unknown factors. In the present example, let us consider the linear factor model:

$$X_{p \times 1} = \Theta_{p \times 1} + \wedge_{p \times m} f_{m \times 1} + e_{p \times 1} \tag{4.11}$$

where $X = (x_1, \ldots, x_i, \ldots, x_p)'$, x_i denotes the observed rating for the ith characteristic of the coffee, $i = 1, 2, \ldots, p$; Θ denotes the $(p \times 1)$ location vector parameter of the distribution of X; $\wedge$ is a $(p \times m)$ principal factor loading matrix; f is an $(m \times 1)$ vector of m unknown factors; and e is a $(p \times 1)$ disturbance vector, $p = 14$ in the present case.

Let us make the following distributional assumptions for the disturbance variable e and unobservable factor random variable f.

1. The disturbance $e_{p \times 1}$ follows the multivariate normal distribution with location 0 and variance and covariance matrix ψ^2; in notation,

$$e \sim N_p(\mathbf{0}, \psi^2), \qquad \text{where} \qquad \psi^2 = \text{diag}(\psi_1^2, \psi_2^2, \ldots, \psi_p^2)$$

2. Unobservable factor $f_{m \times 1}$ also follows the multivariate normal distribution, namely, $f \sim N_m(\mathbf{0}, I_m)$, $m \leq p$.
3. Also, e and f are independent.

Under the above assumption, X in Eq. (4.11) is a linear combination of normal variates; therefore, X follows the multivariate normal distribution with location parameter Θ and covariance matrix $(\wedge \wedge' + \psi^2)$. Suppose $\Sigma = (\wedge \wedge' + \psi^2)$, then we write $X \sim N_p(\Theta, \Sigma)$. It may be mentioned that $\wedge \wedge'$ is known as the communality of X and ψ^2 refers to the uniqueness of X. Note that the distribution of X is the same as the distribution we assumed for the ratings of the attributes of coffee, in the later part of the previous section.

Our primary objective is to obtain an optimal estimate of $\wedge$, the principal factor loading matrix, which determines the components in each of m factors. We also examine the optimality of the number of factors. In estimating $\wedge$ by

$\hat{\wedge}$, the equation $\Sigma = \hat{\wedge}\hat{\wedge}' + \hat{\psi}^2$ has to be satisfied, if Σ is known. But, in our case Σ is unknown. Since, under normality, the sample covariance matrix is a consistent estimator of Σ, therefore, we estimate Σ by A, the sample covariance matrix. However, because in Mukherjee's (1965) case, both the origin and the unit in the scales of measurements have been taken arbitrarily, so only the correlation matrix, say R, is of any interest (Enslein et al., 1977). In such a case, we take A to be a correlation matrix R in what follows. Hence, R is being used for Σ.

For a fixed $m \leq p$, we estimate $\wedge$ and ψ^2 such that $\hat{\wedge}\hat{\wedge}' + \hat{\psi}^2$ converges to R. We use the generalized least square (GLS) method suggested by Joreskog and Goldberger (1972) to estimate $\wedge$ and ψ^2. This method is a rapidly converging iterative method. Suppose $\wedge^*$ and ψ^{*2} are the estimates of $\wedge$ and ψ^2, respectively, at a particular stage of iteration such that $R^* = \wedge^*\wedge^{*'} + \psi^{*2}$. Then, in the GLS method, we minimize $1/2$ trace $(R^{-1}R^* - I)$ to obtain the final estimates for $\wedge$ and ψ^2. The reader should consult Joreskog and Goldberger (1972) and Enslein et al. (1977) for the detailed methodology, and procedures.

Suppose we have the final estimates of $\wedge$ and ψ^2 as $\hat{\wedge}$ and $\hat{\psi}^2$ for a fixed $m \leq p$, by the above method, such that $\hat{\wedge}\hat{\wedge}' + \hat{\psi}^2 = R^{**}$. Then, the GLS estimator of Σ is R^{**}, that is, $\hat{\Sigma} = R^{**}$.

To test the adequacy of the estimation of $\wedge$, for a fixed m by the GLS method, we test the hypothesis $H_0: \Sigma = \wedge\wedge' + \psi^2$ versus $H_1: \Sigma \neq \wedge\wedge' + \psi^2$. Under H_0, Σ is estimated by R^{**} and under H_1, Σ is estimated by R. Now, it follows from Joreskog and Goldberger (1972, pp. 251–255) that under H_0',

$$-2 \ln\lambda = n_1\{\ln|\hat{\Sigma}| - \ln|R| + \text{trace}(R\hat{\Sigma}^{-1}) - P\} \qquad (4.12)$$

for large n_1, is distributed asymptotically as χ^2, chi-square with degrees of freedom $y = \frac{1}{2}\{(p - m)^2 - (p + m)\}$. In Eq. (4.12), n_1 is known as the Bartlett corrected sample size defined as $n_1 = n - [(2P + 5)/6] - (2/3)m$, where n is the actual sample size which is 94 in Mukherjee's case. Therefore, at a particular level of significance, the adequacy of the number of factors m (fixed) as well as the adequacy of the estimation of $\wedge$ can be verified simply by comparing the theoretical and calculated χ^2 values. We keep on changing the value of m starting from 1, until the preassigned level of significance for the test is attained. Thus, we obtain optimal m and the optimal estimate of $\wedge$.

Numerical Results. Using the sample correlation matrix from Table 2 of Mukherjee (1965), we run the computer program OFCOM, IMSL subroutine, to compute $\hat{\wedge}$ and $\hat{\psi}^2$. The χ^2 values with d.f. are also computed using Eq. (4.12) for different m ($m = 1, 2, 3, 4, 5$). These values of χ^2 are presented in Table 4.1.

Table 4.1. Test for Number of Factors for Mukherjee's Data

No. of iterations	No. of factors m	χ^2	d.f.	Attained level of significance	Coefficient
6	1	125.731	77	$0.0004 < 0.05$	0.9627
13	2	93.0467	64	$0.0103 < 0.05$	0.9733
15	3	66.7731	52	$0.0816 < 0.05$	0.9833
11	4	42.2328	41	0.4175	0.9982
11	5	25.9386	31	0.7243	1.0000

We note that in Table 4.1, the values of χ^2 for $m = 1$ and 2 are significant; for $m = 3$, the value of χ^2, though not significant at the 5% level of significance, is very close to being significant. This suggests that 3 factors are adequate to demonstrate the 14 attributes of the coffee, whereas Mukherjee arrived at 4 factors without any statistical justification. Thus, it is possible to reduce the number of factors by one, which is one of the objectives in factor analysis. In Table 4.1, we also calculated the Tucker and Lewis (1973) reliability coefficient, which represents a ratio of covariation explained by the number of factors m, to total covariation. For $m = 3$, the Tucker and Lewis reliability coefficient is fairly large, which also justifies the selection of 3 factors.

Now to determine the components of 3 factors, we write the element of $\hat{\lambda}_{ij}$ of $\hat{\wedge}$ and $\hat{\psi}^2$ of ψ^2 for $j = 1, 2, 3$ and $i = 1, 2, \ldots, 14$ in Table 4.2.

To interpret what each factor means is not always possible from the

Table 4.2. Unrotated Principal Factor Loading Matrix

i	$\hat{\lambda}_{i1}$	$\hat{\lambda}_{i2}$	$\hat{\lambda}_{i3}$	$\hat{\psi}_i^2$
1	−0.7161	−0.4970	−0.1250	0.1951
2	−0.7858	−0.4572	−0.0859	0.1065
3	−0.6476	−0.6182	−0.1220	0.1650
4	−0.8153	−0.4096	0.0473	0.1192
5	−0.6972	−0.5904	−0.3094	0.0618
6	−0.8061	−0.4834	−0.0822	0.0833
7	−0.7563	−0.4976	0.1744	0.1204
8	−0.8411	−0.0689	−0.1177	0.2032
9	−0.6750	−0.3932	0.3830	0.1889
10	−0.9998	0.0121	−0.0004	0.0003
11	−0.8344	−0.3465	−0.1127	0.1178
12	0.6547	−0.3829	0.0301	0.2031
13	−0.7252	−0.4072	0.2320	0.1432
14	−0.7660	−0.4627	0.2054	0.1125

Table 4.3. Varimax Rotated Factor Loading Matrix

i	Col. 1	Col. 2	Col. 3
1	−0.3959	−0.6716	0.4093
2	−0.4455	−0.5406	0.5860
3	−0.2777	−0.7380	0.4411
4	−0.4996	−0.5371	0.5446
5	−0.3604	−0.8435	0.2983
6	−0.4511	−0.5685	0.6030
7	−0.3882	−0.5089	0.6636
8	−0.7099	−0.3894	0.2654
9	−0.3391	−0.2826	0.7497
10	−0.8696	−0.3110	0.3831
11	−0.5692	−0.5905	0.3954
12	−0.3762	−0.4761	0.4560
13	−0.3969	−0.3979	0.6555
14	−0.4091	−0.4678	0.6759

unrotated factor solution. Considering the magnitude of the loading, it is clear from Table 4.2 that the first column of the matrix $\hat{\Lambda}_{14\times3}$ contains relatively large entries; that is, regardless of which attribute is considered, the loading is fairly large. This means there is a basic factor operating which has a major effect on all attributes. The entries in the second column of $\hat{\Lambda}$ are much smaller than the corresponding entries in the first column. Further, except for variables corresponding to attributes 5, 9, and 13, loading of all other variables in column 3 of $\hat{\Lambda}$ is almost insignificant. Hence, classification of the attributes into 3 factors from the unrotated factor loading matrix is not plausible in this case. To achieve a simple structured factor loading matrix, we use the varimax rotation. We operate the computer program OFROTA, IMSL subroutine, and then obtain the rotated factor loading matrix as shown in Table 4.3. In interpreting the factors, we cluster the attributes in a group or factor in the following way. In Table 4.3, we compare the loadings of three columns by attributes. The attribute will fall in the jth factor ($j = 1, 2, 3$) if the loading is highest in the jth column for that attribute. For example, attribute 1 will fall in Factor 2, because for that attribute, loading is highest in the second column. Thus, we obtain the following three factors.

	Factor 1		Factor 2
Variable	Attribute	Variable	Attribute
8	Deep distinct flavor	1	Pleasant flavor
10	Hearty flavor	3	Mellow taste
		5	Comforting taste
		11	Pure clear taste

Factor 3

Variable	Attribute
2	Sparkling taste
4	Expensive taste
6	Alive taste
7	Tastes like real coffee
9	Tastes just-brewed
12	Roasted taste
13	Fresh taste
14	Overall performance

From the above classification, it is clear that Factor C and Factor D, proposed by Mukherjee (1965), merge together to make a new factor, Factor 3, in our case. Factor 1 and Factor 2 are the same as Factor B and Factor A of Mukherjee, respectively. We name the third factor in our case as "Realness." Thus, we may recommend these three new factors "Heartiness," "Comforting quality," and "Realness" instead of the four factors suggested by Mukherjee (1965).

Our review shows that unlike Mukherjee (1965), three factors, namely, Factor 1 (Heartiness), Factor 2 (Comforting quality), and Factor 3 (Realness), are adequate to govern the consumers' coffee preferences, instead of four. In selecting these three factors, we choose the large sample distribution of the statistic -2 ln-likelihood which is a function of the sample correlation matrix and of the estimate of the factor loading matrix. Then, on the basis of this distribution, we test the validity of the estimate of the factor loading matrix of three factors at a 5% level of significance. At this level, the estimation of the factor loading matrix with three factors is found to be satisfactory. This means that although the estimation has been on the basis of one sample (of size 94), the estimated results would remain valid for 95% of samples, each of size 94, of the community. Hence, we may conclude with three factors instead of four as concluded by Mukherjee (1965).

4.4. INTRODUCTION TO LISREL

LISREL (*linear* structural *rel*ations) was developed and popularized by Joreskog and Sorbom. In an earlier section of this chapter we discussed regression analysis, factor analysis, and path analysis as independent techniques. For instance, factor analysis is used to investigate the dimensionality of a group of variables; regression techniques examine the linear functional relationships among a set of variables; and path analysis is for structural equation modeling. Essentially, LISREL is nothing but a combination of all of these techniques. Simultaneously, one can explore both substantive and measurement relationships in analyzing data from surveys, experimental designs, and longitudinal studies. LISREL permits a researcher to make a distinction between latent theoretical concepts and observed indicators. It consists of the structural equation model and the measurement model; the former model describes the theoretical causal relationships among the latent variables through a set of general linear equations and the latter model describes the measurement of the latent variables by the observed indicators and evaluates the reliability of such indicators. Joreskog (1973) specifically compares LISREL with correlation and regression techniques and lists the limitations of these techniques as follows: (1) in case of errors of measurement in the independent variables, regression estimates could be inconsistent; (2) in case the parameters in the structural equations and the parameters in the reduced form are not in a one-to-one correspondence, one or more of the parameters of the structural equations may be either overidentified or underidentified; and (3) in testing a theoretical model, regressions are applied to each equation separately, but this would not provide an overall test of the entire causal structure. LISREL can overcome these limitations, and thus has become a widely accepted technique in structural equation modeling. Since the early 1980s, the number of researchers using LISREL has been increasing steadily in all social sciences, and in demography as well.

4.4.1. The LISREL Model

The popularity of the LISREL model for analyzing causal linkage is partly because of the LISREL computer program based upon it. For instance, the LISREL VII program permits multiple group analyses, analyses with means and intercepts, and provides the standard errors of the estimates, assigns automatic start values, choice of estimation techniques, provides modification indices, normalized residuals, and so forth. The parameters can be estimated by any one of five methods:

1. Instrumental variables
2. Two-stage least squares
3. Unweighted least squares
4. Generalized least squares
5. Maximum likelihood

The program also contains many powerful tools for assessing the goodness of fit of the model and for detecting specification errors.

The latest version of the program is LISREL VII. Along with this, Joreskog and Sorbom also developed a program called PRELIS. PRELIS is a preprocessor for LISREL. PRELIS can read raw data on continuous, censored, and ordinal variables, transform variables in various ways, and compute many different measures of association between pairs of such variables. It can also estimate the asymptotic covariance matrix, which can be used in LISREL VII to perform a more accurate and powerful analysis than with previous versions of LISREL. PRELIS can also be used for data inspection to identify problems in the raw data. Hence, PRELIS can be used as an independent data analysis program especially for computing descriptive statistics as well as an accompaniment with LISREL VII. Joreskog and Sorbom in their users manual for LISREL VII identify the following new features of LISREL VII:

1. A thorough check of the syntax in LISREL Control lines.
2. An admissibility check of the model with options to stop before iterations begin or after a specified number of iterations if a nonadmissible solution is produced.
3. Options to constrain variances to be positive and covariance and correlation matrices to be positive definite.
4. Options to have arbitrary constraints between parameters.
5. Options to specify model by means of a set of "equations" of the form: left-hand variables and right-hand variables.
6. Two new estimation methods, namely, weighted least squares and diagonally weighted least squares, are added to those already available in LISREL VI.
7. It provides useful information about the sensitivity of the model to changes in each parameter and about the power of the χ^2 test.

Having discussed the computer programs of LISREL, we will describe the LISREL model to study structural relationships. Before we discuss the model, it is useful to know some of the concepts used in describing the model. As mentioned earlier, it incorporates both latent theoretical concepts and observed indicators. These theoretical concepts and observed variables are classified as either endogenous or exogenous. Instead of repeating the most commonly used model of LISREL for illustration, we will provide a model which is useful for the study of longitudinal data. The general form of the model which is based on factor analysis is:

$$Y_t = \mu_t + \wedge_{yt}\phi_t + \Sigma_t$$

$$X = V_t + \wedge_x\theta + \delta$$

$$\Phi_1 = A_1\theta + \psi_1$$

$$\Phi_t = A_t\theta + \beta_t\Phi_{t-1} + \psi_t$$

$$(4.13)$$

where

Y_t = a vector of the value of the p dependent measures at the tth time of measurement

μ_t = the mean vector of Y

Φ_t = the common factor structure of the p dependent measures, consisting of m_t correlated common factors

Σ_t = a vector of error terms (residual factors)

$\wedge_{yt}$ = the $p \times m$ matrix of factor loadings

X = a vector of the values of the q independent measures

V = the mean vector of X

θ = the common factor structure consisting of n common factors

δ = a vector of residual factors

$\wedge_x$ = the $q \times n$ matrix of factor loadings

A_t = a matrix of regression coefficients of order $m_t \times n$

β_t = a matrix of regression coefficients of order $m_t \times m_{t-1}$

ψ_t = vectors of residuals possibly correlated at measurement time t, but not between t and $t \pm a$.

To provide an idea about the type of structure one might expect to obtain with a causal model having no independent variable, Figure 4.4 is presented.

Note that the values linking the measures and the implicit variables are directly relatable to variance–covariance matrices among the variables. The strength of the relationship of the implicit variable to its measures is also shown by factor loadings, λ's. Note also that in a true analysis these values are estimated in the case of more than one indicator (Φ_1 and Φ_2); in cases where there is only one indicator variable, values either are specified prior to analysis (sometimes as 1) or cannot enter into the analysis due to overspe-

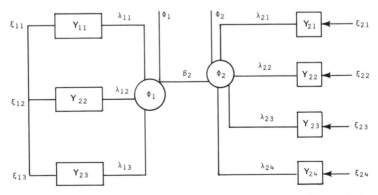

Figure 4.4. Causal linkage between implicit variables at two different times.

cification. The arrows between the Σ's represent assumed correlations between certain of the error contributions.

The important features of the LISREL model are the constraints on the data it implies. For example, in the case of an overspecified model, the constraints would ensure that the model is "identified"; that is, all the parameters can be uniquely estimated. In LISREL modeling, two such restrictions are available:

1. Any parameter can be set to zero or a specified value.
2. Two or more parameters can be constrained to be equal.

All other parameters are "free," i.e., estimated by the program (Bynner and Romney, 1985). Bynner and Romney described the LISREL program as follows: "Starting from any set of values for the parameters, the program works out the implied correlations between the variables, compares these with the observed correlations, and then changes the parameter values to reduce the discrepancy between them. The process is repeated until no further improvement between the model and the data can be achieved" (p. 45). The parameters estimated by the best fitting model to the data provide the relative importance of different explanatory variables in accounting for the variance of the dependent variables. The program also provides direct and indirect effects and total effects.

The factors (ϕ, ϕ_t) themselves can be considered implicit variables underlying the whole process. The independent measures are simply measurable manifestations of these implicit variables. The validity of the underlying implicit variables will need to be statistically demonstrated. There can be times at which there are measures taken which could be deemed manifestations of the factor structure. There is no simple independent variable–dependent variable breakdown. In fact, if the vector X is thought of as a causative precursor to the vectors, X appears to be more of a matrix or set of vectors than a single vector.

Figure 4.5 is included to show the type of structure one might expect to obtain with causal modeling given an independent variable.

4.4.2. An Application of LISREL to Fertility

The LISREL model has been used by many researchers in demography to study fertility behavior. For instance, Bagozzi and Van Loo (1978) adopted LISREL to test their general theory of fertility which incorporates the knowledge of both economic and noneconomic factors. Beckman *et al.* (1983) also used LISREL to study fertility decisions and outcomes among the young couples. To illustrate the use of LISREL here, we will discuss the recent study

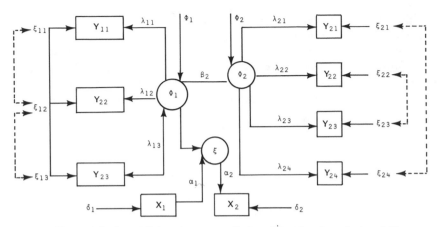

Figure 4.5. Causal linkage in overspecified model with a dependent variable.

of Jayachandran (1986) who applied LISREL to understand fertility determinants in two Canadian populations. Jayachandran's causal model is presented in Figure 4.6.

The model has three exogenous variables (husband's education, wife's education, and household income) and five endogenous variables (the total number of children the respondent is planning to have, taste for children, modern objects scale, satisfaction in life, and interaction between husband and wife). The theoretical links of these variables are discussed in detail by Jayachandran. We will only present here the definitions of symbols used by Jayachandran:

ξ_1 = husband's education (HEDUC)
$\quad X_1$ = husbands' completed years of education
ξ_2 = wife's education (WEDUC)
$\quad X_2$ = wife's completed years of education
η_1 = fertility
$\quad Y_1$ = the total number of children the respondent is planning to have (in addition to the number of surviving children)
η_2 = taste for children (TASTE)
$\quad Y_2$ = does the respondent approve or disapprove of a married couple not bearing or rearing children? (strongly disapprove = 1, ..., strongly approve = 7)
η_3 = modern objects scale (MO)
$\quad Y_3$ = possession of a dishwasher, microwave oven, automatic washer, dryer, freezer, color TV, gas barbecue, skis, etc.

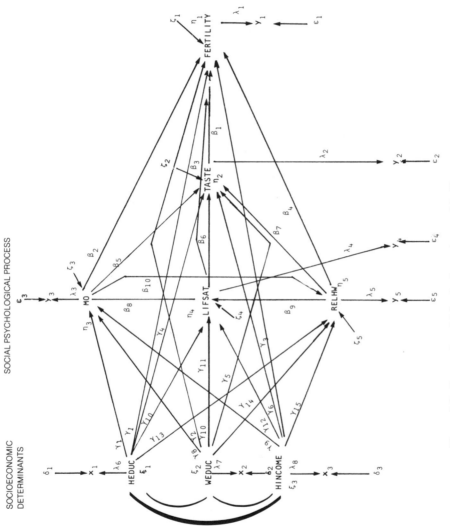

Figure 4.6. Proposed model for the determinants of fertility.

η_4 = satisfaction in life (LIFSAT)

Y_4 = respondent's satisfaction with family life, friends, neighborhood, etc. (very dissatisfied = 1, ..., very satisfied = 7)

η_5 = the social exchange processes or interaction between husband and wife (RELHW)

Y_5 = (a) spouse disagreement about housekeeping, work schedules, spending money, and visiting or writing relatives (never = 1, ..., very often = 5)

(b) husband–wife communication, discussion about work (jobs, housework), and sharing personal problems (never = 5, ..., very often = 1)

λ_s = structural coefficients relating unobserved or theoretical variables to observed variables

ϕ_s = covariance of the exogenous theoretical variables (ξ_1, ξ_2, and ξ_3)

Σ_s = structural coefficients relating exogenous, theoretical variables (ξ_s) to endogenous variables (η_s)

β_s = structural coefficients relating the endogenous theoretical variables

δ_s and ϵ_s = measurement errors in observed variables, X and Y, respectively.

ζ_s = errors of prediction

The structural relations among the variables in the model could be expressed in the form of the following structural equations. These equations are same as the ones presented by Jayachandran in his appendix. These are:

$$\eta = \beta\eta + \Gamma\xi + \zeta \tag{4.14}$$

where

η is a vector of endogenous variables
β and Γ are matrices of structural coefficients
ξ is a vector of exogenous variables
ζ is a vector of errors in the conceptual model

Let us translate this equation for the model of Figure 4.6:

$$
\begin{bmatrix} \text{FERTILITY} \\ \text{TASTE} \\ \text{MO} \\ \text{LIFSAT} \\ \text{RELHW} \end{bmatrix}
=
\begin{bmatrix}
0 & \beta_1 & \beta_2 & \beta_3 & \beta_4 \\
0 & 0 & \beta_5 & \beta_6 & 0 \\
0 & 0 & 0 & 0 & 0 \\
0 & 0 & \beta_7 & 0 & \beta_8 \\
0 & 0 & \beta_9 & 0 & 0
\end{bmatrix}
\begin{bmatrix} \text{FERTILITY} \\ \text{TASTE} \\ \text{MO} \\ \text{LIFSAT} \\ \text{RELHW} \end{bmatrix}
$$

$$+ \begin{bmatrix} \gamma_1 & \gamma_2 & \gamma_3 \\ \gamma_4 & \gamma_5 & \gamma_6 \\ \gamma_7 & \gamma_8 & \gamma_9 \\ \gamma_{10} & \gamma_{11} & \gamma_{12} \\ \gamma_{13} & \gamma_{14} & \gamma_{15} \end{bmatrix} \begin{bmatrix} \text{HEDUC} \\ \text{WEDUC} \\ \text{HINCOME} \end{bmatrix} + \begin{bmatrix} \xi_1 \\ \xi_2 \\ \xi_3 \\ \xi_4 \\ \xi_5 \end{bmatrix}$$

The measurement equations are:

$$Y = \wedge_y \eta + \varepsilon \tag{4.15}$$

$$\begin{bmatrix} Y_1 \\ Y_2 \\ Y_3 \\ Y_4 \\ Y_5 \end{bmatrix} = \begin{bmatrix} 1 & 0 & 0 & 0 & 0 \\ 0 & 1 & 0 & 0 & 0 \\ 0 & 0 & 1 & 0 & 0 \\ 0 & 0 & 0 & 1 & 0 \\ 0 & 0 & 0 & 0 & 1 \end{bmatrix} \begin{bmatrix} \text{FERTILITY} \\ \text{TASTE} \\ \text{MO} \\ \text{LIFSAT} \\ \text{RELHW} \end{bmatrix} + \begin{bmatrix} \varepsilon_1 \\ \varepsilon_2 \\ \varepsilon_3 \\ \varepsilon_4 \\ \varepsilon_5 \end{bmatrix}$$

where Y is a vector of the value of the dependent measures at the time of measurement and $\wedge_y$ is the matrix of structural coefficients.

$$X = \wedge_x \xi + \delta \tag{4.16}$$

$$\begin{bmatrix} X_1 \\ X_2 \\ X_3 \end{bmatrix} = \begin{bmatrix} 1 & 0 & 0 \\ 0 & 1 & 0 \\ 0 & 0 & 1 \end{bmatrix} \begin{bmatrix} \text{HEDUC} \\ \text{WEDUC} \\ \text{HINCOME} \end{bmatrix} + \begin{bmatrix} \delta_1 \\ \delta_2 \\ \delta_3 \end{bmatrix}$$

where X is a vector of observed exogenous indicators and $\wedge_x$ is a matrix of structural coefficients.

The structural coefficients (λ_s) are set to 1 so that the theoretical elements and the observed indicators have the same units of measurements. This would be useful for the interpretations.

The error variance for the exogenous (δ) and endogenous (ε) variables are estimated by subtracting reliability coefficients from 1 and multiplying by the variance of the respective indicators in order to get the portion of true and error variance components of the total variance of the indicators. The covariance matrix for the exogenous concepts (ϕ) and error variances for the endogenous concepts (ψ) are left free for the LISREL program to estimate.

The LISREL program finds maximum likelihood parameter estimates by minimizing the following function:

$$F = \ln|\Sigma| + \mathrm{tr}(S\Sigma^1) - \ln|S| - (p + q)$$

where Σ is the covariance matrix among all the observed indicators, that is implied by our estimated model; S is the actual observed contrivance among the indicators; and p and q are indicators of exogenous and endogenous variables, respectively.

The goodness of the fit of the model is assessed by the likelihood ratio x^2 test. The null hypothesis is tested against the most general hypothesis that the Σ is unconstrained. The probability level of x^2 is the probability of obtaining a x^2 value larger than the value actually obtained given that the model is correct. The degrees of freedom for x^2 are

$$df = 0.5K(K + 1) - t$$

where K is the number of variables analyzed and t is the total number of parameters estimated. The degrees of freedom are important to assess the fit of the model, since the x^2 measure is sensitive to sample size. The goodness of fit index (GFI), on the other hand, is independent of sample size and relatively robust against departures from normality and therefore useful to assess the fit of the model in general" (Jayachandran, 1986, pp. 81–82).

The test results of the model presented in Figure 4.6 for a Fort McMurray population indicate perfect fit between observed data and theoretical model ($x^2 = 0.01$, d.f. $= 7$, $p = 1.000$, GFI $= 1.000$, $R^2 = 0.212$). The parameters for the model were estimated only including significant paths. Table 4.4 provides indirect (IN) and total effects (TE) of exogenous and endogenous variables.

According to Table 4.4, it is clear that with the exception of life satisfaction, the endogenous variables within the social-psychological processes have a significant influence on fertility. On the other hand, the exogenous variables husband's and wife's education both have a direct effect on fertility. But the

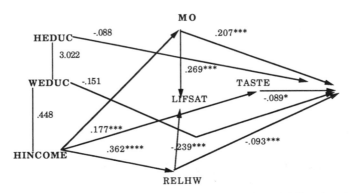

Figure 4.7. Findings for Fort McMurray and the model for Figure 4.6 (Jayachandran, 1986, p. 71).

Table 4.4. Indirect and Total Effects of Endogenous and Exogenous Variables for the Fort McMurray Model[a]

	TASTE		MO		LIFSAT		RELHW		HEDUC		WEDUC		HINCOME	
	IN	TE	IN	TE	IN	TE	IN	TE	IN	TE	IN	TE	IN	TE
FERTILITY		−0.089		0.207				−0.093		−0.088		−0.151	0.006	0.006
TASTE														0.177
MO														0.270
LIFSAT				0.269				−0.239					−0.014	−0.014
RELHW													0.362	0.362

[a] From Jayachandran (1986).

household income has an indirect effect. The level of significance of these direct and indirect effects of both exogenous and endogenous variables are presented in Figure 4.7. Table 4.5 presents the standardized coefficients and disturbance terms to understand the relative importance of the variables and amount of measurement errors. For instance, the large magnitudes of disturbance terms for life's satisfaction (1.238) and the social exchange processes between husband and wife (1.103) are indicative of the problems involved in measuring these concepts by their respective observed indicators. Jayachandran gives a thorough interpretation and discussion of the results presented here and we will not repeat here.

Table 4.5. Standardized Coefficients, Disturbance Terms, and Degree of Determinacy for the Fort McMurray Model[a]

	Fertility	Taste	MO	Lifsat	Relhw	Heduc	Weduc	Hincome
			Standardized coefficients					
Fertility		−0.095	0.250		−0.151	−0.155	−0.227	
Taste								0.149
MO								0.200
Lifsat			0.141		−0.169			
Relhw								0.199
R^2	0.193	0.029	0.047	0.048	0.045			
			Disturbance terms, variance and covariances					
PSI	1.886	2.614	3.293	11.911	5.967			
TE	0.260	0.299	0.384	1.238	1.103			
						0.819	0.591	0.211

[a] From Jayachandran (1986, p. 69).

4.5. SUMMARY

The study of demographic behavior, especially as it relates to fertility, is extremely complex. Though this area of research has dominated in demography, the complex nature of causation in fertility behavior is not fully understood. Responding to this challenge, population specialists are constantly in the process of developing a comprehensive theoretical framework by including all relevant variables. In order to operationalize the complicated causal relationships, sophisticated multivariate statistical data analysis techniques are necessary. In this chapter we have attempted to introduce some of these techniques. The principles of these techniques are useful not only for identifying relationships between sets of empirical data and testing of theoretical frameworks, but also for the theoretical modeling of the process or processes that generate the data.

The statistical techniques discussed in this chapter belong to the family of the general linear model. The main characteristics of the general linear model are that linearity is assumed in the relationship between each pair of variables. In the case of nonlinear relationships among variables, they have to be transformed or dicustomized such that the assumption of linearity is fulfilled. The general linear models are also based on the assumption of additivity. For instance, the nature of the regression model is to increase the number of independent variables to predict the dependent variable. It is here that the additivity of the model becomes evident by way of a weighted sum of independent variables to predict the dependent variable. The regression model deals only with direct relationships of the independent variables with the dependent variable. To account for indirect and specious effects, path analysis has to be used.

It often becomes necessary to reduce or summarize the large masses of unorganized numbers beyond anyone's comprehension. Factor analysis will reduce large sets of data into smaller sets that describe the original observations without sacrificing critical information. The smaller sets or factors are the manifestations of an abstract underlying dimension. Factor analysis can also be used for screening of variables for inclusion in subsequent investigations. Factor analysis application can also be found in clustering of people or objects into homogeneous groups based on interrelations among the variables.

To understand complex situations, one may require more than one research strategy. One may want to first understand the multiple correlation of each variable with all the others; if some of them are highly related to combinations of others, then one may want to choose among them or combine them; and the researcher may decide to use the latent variables in the subsequent analysis. In other words, in order to use regression analysis, path analysis, and factor analysis simultaneously, one would have to use the LISREL method.

CHAPTER 5

Logistic and Probit Models

5.1. INTRODUCTION

In demographic research, we often face situations where the dependent variable of interest is a dichotomy, such as dead or alive, divorced or still in marriage, accept or reject contraception, and so forth. In recent years, logistic regression has been used to study topics as diverse as marital formation and dissolution (Abdelrahman and Morgan, 1987; White, 1987; Trussell and Rao, 1989), contraceptive use (Studer and Thornton, 1987), premarital sexual experience (Newcomer and Udry, 1987), premarital pregnancy (Robbins *et al.,* 1985), childlessness (Rao, 1987a), and spouse abuse (Kalmuss and Seltzer, 1986). These and other studies that have employed logistic regression analysis have something in common—the dichotomous dependent variable. It is relatively easy to create dummy explanatory variables whenever we consider nominal scale variables in the regression model and employ the linear regression procedure available in many standard statistical packages. However, when the dependent variable of consideration is dichotomous, the usual assumptions underlying the linear model are rarely satisfied. The most serious problem arises because predictions may lie outside the (0,1) interval. To circumvent this problem, we have to consider alternative distributional assumptions for which all predictions must lie within the appropriate interval. One immediate solution is to transform the original model so that prediction will be in the (0,1) interval for all X. In attempting transformation, we would like to maintain the property that increases in X are associated with increases (or decreases) in the dependent variable for all values of X (i.e., monotonic transformation). Several cumulative probability functions are possible, but we will consider only two, the logistic and the normal (probit model). Like in any other model fitting, the goal of our analysis using logistic or normal distribution is to find a best-fitting and most parsimonious model that describes the relation between the dependent variable and a set of predictors.

Some statisticians tend to distinguish between a logit model and a logistic model based on the treatment of independent variables. In the logistic regression model, independent variables are assumed to be continuous and if the researcher wants to include nominal independent variables in the model, they must be dummy coded (Hanushek and Jackson, 1977). The logit model (sometimes also called the categorical logit model) is not a function of continuous independent variables. These two models also differ in the number and interpretation of parameters. For example, a logit model with K categories in each of N predictors will have $N \times K$ parameters. But in the logistic model, we will have $N \times (K - 1)$ parameters (due to dummy coding of nominal independent variables). The parameters in the logistic regression model represent the increment (or decrement) in log odds for the category coded one, as opposed to those coded zero (i.e., dummy coding) throughout (also called contrast category). The parameters in a logit model represent, again in log odds, being in a category as opposed to what would be expected if there were no relationship between that independent variable and the dependent variable (DeMaris, 1990). Also, for any given predictor in a logit model, the sum of all parameters would be equal to zero. It is important to note that if independent variables are all nominal, one can obtain the same results with either a logit or a logistic model. In this chapter, we will consider a more general case, the logistic regression model and the probit model.

The use of logistic function for transformation leads us to the logistic regression model to data sets with a binary response and one or more independent variables. One advantage of this model is that the analysis and interpretation are quite similar to the well-known procedures of multiple regression (Draper and Smith, 1981; Kleinbaum *et al.*, 1988). However, there are some differences between the two approaches—no good measure of explained variation such as R^2 (though some suggested a pseudo R^2, see Aldrich and Nelson, 1984); since the observed values are either 0 or 1, plotting residuals against predicted values is not quite informative; and computations are much more difficult and time-consuming in the logistic model.

Logistic regression provides a convenient forum for comparing several categorical data analysis procedures. For example, when all of the factors are categorical, the logistic model is equivalent to a log-linear model containing the multifactor interactions (see our discussion of logit model above). Maximum likelihood and weighted least squares are the two most commonly used estimation techniques to fit the model. It has been pointed out that when the sample sizes are adequate, the two estimation methods are equivalent and optimal. As noted in the literature, one also can use ordinary least squares (OLS) as a computationally efficient algorithm since the underlying probabilities of a positive response lie between 0.2 and 0.8 (Cox, 1970; Magidson, 1982).

The initial development of logistic regression is due to Berkson (1944, 1951, 1953). It has been recognized as an alternative to discriminant analysis, particularly when assumption of a normal distribution is not appropriate (Truett *et al.*, 1967; Halpern *et al.*, 1971). A number of authors discuss detailed procedures for estimation and comparison with hazards models (Haberman, 1978).

The odds ratio concept forms the backbone of logistic regression and it is important to have a clear idea about this ratio. The odds ratio is the ratio of two odds. Odds, in turn, are themselves ratios of the number of events to the number of nonevents. For example, if our variable of interest is marital dissolution, the odds are calculated as the number of marriage dissolutions to the number of marriages still intact. Conversion between odds and proportion can be expressed as O (odds) $= P/(1 - P)$, where P is any proportion. The logistic equation is one where the natural logarithm of the odds of the dependent variable is predicted by a linear function of the independent variables. The odds ratio is the central concept to our understanding of the logistic regression model and it has several desirable properties as a measure of association (Fienberg, 1977):

1. The odds ratio has a clear interpretation and is somewhat straightforward. If two totals are fixed, the odds ratio gives the multiplicative change required to move from one odds to the next. Like in the survival analysis, an odds ratio of greater than 1.0 suggests an increased likelihood of the event occurring (more likely to divorce), while an odds ratio of less than 1.0 indicates a decreased likelihood of the event occurring.
2. The odds ratio is invariant under the interchange of rows or columns (sign will change).
3. It is also invariant under the row and column multiplications. Shifts in sample size or marginal shifts do not affect its value.
4. It can be used in tables of variable sizes and dimensions.

5.2. THEORETICAL ISSUES IN LOGISTIC REGRESSION

This technique operates on individual or micro-level, rather than aggregated data, and is analogous to linear regression in that a continuous response variable is modeled as a linear function of a set of continuous predictors. As in OLS regression, a categorical predictor can be entered into the equation as a set of dummy variables. Logistic regression assumes that each member of the population has some underlying probability of success on a given independent variable. Therefore, in the population, each member with a given set of characteristics has a P chance of success and $1 - P$ chance of failure. If you are using individual data, each member has either a 1 or 0 chance of success.

Let P_i be the probability that the ith person in the sample is in the category of interest (success) on a dichotomous dependent variable, and $(1 - P_i)$ the probability that he or she is in the other category (failure). For the moment we will only consider dichotomous response variables, although shortly we will expand the model to include polytomous ones. Clearly, $P_i/(1 - P_i)$ equals the odds of being in the category of interest for the ith individual. Now $\log(P_i/(1 - P_i))$, the log odds of being in the category of interest, is a continuous variable that theoretically can take on any value in the range $(-\infty, +\infty)$. Also, let $X_{i1}, X_{i2}, \ldots, X_{iK}$ be a set of K continuous (and/or dummy) predictor variables measured on the ith individual in the sample. Then the logistic regression model for the log odds, given a particular vector of scores on the K predictor variables, is

$$\ln \frac{P_i}{1 - P_i} = \beta_0 + \beta_1 X_{i1} + \beta_2 X_{i2} + \cdots + \beta_K X_{iK} \tag{5.1}$$

and the corresponding multiplicative model for the odds is

$$\frac{P_i}{1 - P_i} = e^{\beta_0} e^{\beta_1 X_{i1}} e^{\beta_2 X_{i2}} \cdots e^{\beta_K X_{iK}} \tag{5.2}$$

Estimates for the betas, or regression coefficients, in Eqs. (5.1) and (5.2) are obtained by the method of maximum likelihood. As in linear regression, one employs both a global test of the model as well as individual tests for significance of the coefficient estimates. The global test is the likelihood ratio chi-squared statistic, or L^2, equal to $-2\ln(L_0/L_1)$, where L_1 is the value of the likelihood function evaluated at the maximum likelihood estimates for all of the betas, and L_0 is the maximum value of the likelihood function if all coefficients except the intercept are zero (Aldrich and Nelson, 1984). This statistic is asymptotically distributed as chi-square under the null hypothesis that all of the betas except the intercept are zero, and therefore provides a test for whether any of the predictors are needed to model the event of interest. When L^2 is significant, we conclude that at least one of the betas, $\beta_1, \beta_2, \ldots, \beta_K$, is different from zero.

Individual predictors can be tested by examining the ratios of the coefficient estimates to their standard errors, which are approximately standard normal under the null hypothesis that the coefficient is zero in the population. The interpretation of the regression coefficients is quite straightforward. For example, β_1 represents the increment to the log odds for every one unit increase in X_1, holding all other factors constant. Or, $\exp\{\beta_1\}$ represents the multiplicative factor by which the odds change for every one unit increase in X_1, controlling for the other predictors.

5.2.1. Multinomial Logistic Regression

The logistic regression model is readily adapted to the case of a dependent variable with three or more levels. In this section, we will demonstrate how the logistic regression model is adapted to this situation.

Suppose now that our dependent variable is trichotomous with categories 1, 2, and 3. Let P_1, P_2, P_3 be the probability that the ith individual in the sample is in categories 1, 2, and 3, respectively, on this variable (for simplicity, the subscript i will be omitted from our notation). Also, let $X_1, \ldots, X_K$, as before, be a vector of predictors measured on the ith individual in the sample. As in the dichotomous case, we model the log odds of being in the category of interest as a linear function of the explanatory variables. Only now, more than one equation is required, since there are two independent contrasts that can be constructed with the odds, instead of one. For example, we can consider the log odds of being in category 1 versus category 3. Expressed as a function of the predictors, this becomes

$$\ln \frac{P_1}{P_3} = \beta_0^1 + \beta_1^1 X_1 + \beta_2^1 X_2 + \cdots + \beta_K^1 X_K \tag{5.3}$$

whereas the log odds of being in category 2 versus category 3 is modeled as

$$\ln \frac{P_2}{P_3} = \beta_0^2 + \beta_1^2 X_1 + \beta_2^2 X_2 + \cdots + \beta_K^2 X_K \tag{5.4}$$

The superscripts on the betas are to indicate that we have two different sets of parameters, one for each separate log odds above. One could, of course, also consider the log odds of being in category 1 versus category 2, the third possible contrast among these three categories. The equation would be

$$\ln \frac{P_1}{P_2} = \beta_0^3 + \beta_1^3 X_1 + \beta_2^3 X_2 + \cdots + \beta_K^3 X_K \tag{5.5}$$

However, the third set of parameters in (5.5) is just a linear combination of those in (5.3) and (5.4), and therefore only the first two sets of betas need to be estimated from the data. This is easy to see, since

$$\ln \frac{P_1}{P_2} = \ln \frac{(P_1/P_3)}{(P_2/P_3)} = \ln \frac{P_1}{P_3} - \ln \frac{P_2}{P_3}$$

$$= \beta_0^1 + \beta_1^1 X_1 + \beta_2^1 X_2 + \cdots + \beta_K^1 X_K \qquad (5.6)$$
$$- (\beta_0^2 + \beta_1^2 X_1 + \beta_2^2 X_2 + \cdots + \beta_K^2 X_K)$$
$$= \beta_0^1 - \beta_0^2 + (\beta_1^1 - \beta_1^2)X_1 + (\beta_2^1 - \beta_2^2)X_2 + \cdots + (\beta_K^1 - \beta_K^2)X_K$$

and equating like coefficients in (5.5) and (5.6), we have that

$$\beta_0^3 = (\beta_0^1 - \beta_0^2), \qquad \beta_1^3 = (\beta_1^1 - \beta_1^2),$$
$$\beta_2^3 = (\beta_2^1 - \beta_2^2), \ldots, \qquad \beta_K^3 = (\beta_K^1 - \beta_K^2)$$

Thus, for a dependent variable with M levels regressed on K predictors, there are $(M - 1)(K + 1)$ parameters to be estimated from the data.

The interpretation of coefficients is exactly the same as before. For example, $\exp(\beta_1^1)$ is the multiplicative factor by which the odds of being in category 1, versus category 3, changes for every unit increase in X_1, controlling for all other predictors; while $\exp(\beta_1^2)$ is the multiplicative factor by which the odds of being in category 2, versus category 3, changes for each unit increase in X_1, controlling for all other predictors, and so forth.

The global test of the model is computed with L^2, as in the dichotomous case. However, now the test for an individual predictor, say X_1, is no longer a single degree of freedom test computed by taking the ratio of an estimate to its standard error. Instead, the total effect of X_1 is only zero if both β_1^1 and β_1^2 are simultaneously zero. The appropriate test for the total effect of X_1 is therefore a joint test for both coefficients, computed as $-2\ln(L_2/L_1)$ where L_1 is the likelihood function evaluated at the maximum likelihood estimates for the full model, and L_2 is the corresponding likelihood function for the model that excludes X_1. Under the null hypothesis that X_1 has no effect on the dependent variable, this statistic is asymptotically distributed as chi-squared with 2 degrees of freedom (Aldrich and Nelson, 1984). A significant result suggests that at least one of the coefficients, β_1^1 or β_1^2, is nonzero in the population. The next question is: which one? That is, it is possible for the joint test to be significant, but for only one of the two independent log odds to be significantly affected by X_1. To find out whether the individual betas are significant, we can, as before, take the ratios of these coefficients to their standard errors. Let us demonstrate these principles with an application in demography.

5.3. APPLICATION OF LOGISTIC REGRESSION

Several software packages contain programs that fit these models. For our NSFH (National Survey of Family and Household) data, we used PROC LOGIST in SAS (SAS Institute Inc., 1986) to compute a logistic regression with the log odds of first marriage dissolution as the response variable, and age at marriage and father's SES as continuous predictors. For this analysis, we included an additional predictor: whether or not the respondent cohabited with her first spouse prior to marriage ("yes," "no"). This was entered as a dummy variable coded 1 for "yes" and 0 for "no." The results are presented in Table 5.1.

The global test for the significance of the model is $L^2 = 303.14$ with 3 d.f., which is highly significant at $p < 0.00001$. Thus, at least one of the predictors is nonzero in the population. When the individual predictors are each tested for significance, we see that all three are significant at $p < 0.05$. Both prior cohabitation and age at marriage are highly significant at $p < 0.00001$, while father's SES is significant at $p < 0.02$. The latter finding is interesting since we were not able to find a significant linear relationship when SES was coded as ordinal. However, the additional information contained in the continuous level of measurement changes that picture. Since we have seen that the relationship appears to have a nonlinear component, the addition of a quadratic term for father's SES might prove quite significant here. However, this was not pursued for the current text.

The signs and magnitudes of the coefficient estimates are readily interpreted. We see that cohabitation before marriage increases the odds of dissolution. However, while the bivariate association was only marginally significant, at $p < 0.04$, the partial association, controlling for age at marriage and SES, is highly significant at $p < 0.00001$. Thus, the bivariate relationship is suppressed when age at marriage is not controlled. This is reasonable, since cohabitation increases the odds of dissolution while tending to delay age at marriage, and age at marriage is inversely related to the odds of dissolution. Hence, controlling for age at marriage enhances the impact of prior cohabitation. The multiplicative estimate for prior cohabitation suggests that co-

Table 5.1. Logistic Regression Results for the Regression of First Marriage Dissolved on Cohabitation before Marriage (Dummy Variable), Age at Marriage (Continuous), and Father's SES (Continuous)[a]

Effect	Additive estimate	Multiplicative estimate	p
Intercept	2.137		
Cohabited before marriage	0.436	1.547	0.00001
Age at marriage	−0.134	0.875	0.00001
Father's SES	0.004	1.004	0.012
L^2	303.140	0.00001	

[a] From DeMaris and Rao (1989).

habitors have odds of dissolving the first marriage that are 1.547 times the odds for noncohabitors, other factors held constant.

The coefficient estimate for age at marriage suggests that every additional year by which a woman delays first marriage is worth a reduction in the odds of dissolution by a factor of 0.875. This, again, underscores the beneficial effect of later age at marriage. Finally, the estimate for SES indicates that every unit increase in father's SES score increases the odds of dissolution by a factor of 1.004. While this estimate is statistically significant, it is of little substantive importance. The curvilinearity noted earlier in the relationship between SES and the odds of first marriage dissolution renders any attempt to model a linear relationship relatively ineffective.

For our final example we will use a trichotomous dependent variable from the NSFH data: first marriage dissolution, now coded as "no dissolution by separation or divorce," "dissolution within the first 7 years," and "dissolution after 7 or more years of marriage." Thus, we are further classifying the dissolution category into dissolution after a relatively shorter, versus a relatively longer, duration of marriage. Notice that this is still a qualitative dependent variable, since there is no natural ordering implied by these categories. That is, unless one were to make the value judgment that dissolution after a longer period of time is somehow indicative of greater marital stability than dissolution after a shorter period of time, it is not possible to place these categories on an ordinal continuum. Sixty-two percent of sample women had not dissolved the first marriage, while 19% had dissolved the first marriage within 7 years, and the remaining 19% had done so after 7 or more years.

Table 5.2 shows the results of regressing the log odds of first marriage dissolution as a trichotomous response variable on prior cohabitation, age at first marriage, and father's SES. The analysis was accomplished using PROC CATMOD in SAS (SAS, 1986). Here, first marriage dissolution is coded as 1 for dissolution within 7 years, 2 for dissolution after 7 or more years, and 3 for no dissolution, i.e., remaining in an intact first marriage. The response variable was purposely coded this way, since we wished to form odds by contrasting each type of dissolution with no dissolution. In PROC CATMOD, the highest level of the dependent variable is automatically made the contrast category. Thus, we will examine the effects of the three predictors on the log odds of dissolving the first marriage after a relatively short (less than 7 years) duration versus remaining married, and on the log odds of dissolving the first marriage after a relatively longer (7 or more years) duration versus remaining married.

The first part of Table 5.2 shows the joint tests of parameters that constitute the partial tests for the effect of each predictor on the dependent variable (CATMOD does not provide a global L^2 test). Evidently each independent variable is significant—prior cohabitation and age at marriage both at p

Table 5.2. Multinomial Logistic Regression Results for the Regression
of First Marriage Dissolved on Cohabitation before Marriage,
Age at Marriage, and Father's SES[a]

Joint tests for independent variables			
Variable	d.f.	Chi-square	p
Cohabited before marriage	2	99.00	0.0001
Age at marriage	2	240.74	0.0001
Father's SES	2	7.38	0.0249

Response variable: log odds of dissolution within 7 years vs. no dissolution

Effect	Additive estimate	Multiplicative estimate	p
Intercept	1.531		
Cohabited before marriage	0.890	2.435	0.0001
Age at marriage	−0.145	0.865	0.0001
Father's SES	0.005	1.005	0.0088

Response variable: log odds of dissolution after 7 or more years vs. no dissolution

Effect	Additive estimate	Multiplicative estimate	p
Intercept	1.355		
Cohabited before marriage	−0.216	0.806	0.0921
Age at marriage	−0.125	0.882	0.0001
Father's SES	0.003	1.003	0.1783

[a] From DeMaris and Rao (1989).

< 0.0001, and father's SES at $p < 0.03$. Examining the individual coefficients, however, we see that two of the predictors have significant effects only on the odds of dissolution after a relatively short marital duration compared to no dissolution, but not on the odds of dissolution after 7 years or more. For example, women who cohabited with their future husbands before marriage have odds of dissolving the first marriage within 7 years that are 2.435 times higher than those who did not cohabit, a highly significant finding at $p < 0.0001$. Yet the effect of prior cohabitation on the odds of dissolution after 7 or more years does not quite reach significance, and, if anything, is in the opposite direction ($\beta = -0.216$, $p < 0.1$).

Father's SES is positively related to the odds of dissolution both within and beyond the 7-year demarcation, but as with prior cohabitation, only dissolution after a short duration is significantly affected. Every unit increase in father's SES increases the odds of dissolution within 7 years by a factor of 1.005 ($p < 0.009$). Dissolution after 7 or more years, however, is not significantly affected by SES ($p < 0.18$). On the other hand, age at marriage is strongly predictive of dissolution after either period of time. The coefficients indicate that every additional year older the bride is at marriage, the odds of dissolution within 7 years are reduced by 0.865, and the odds of dissolution after 7 or more years are reduced by 0.882. Both coefficients are significant at $p < 0.0001$.

5.4. LIMITATIONS OF LOGISTIC REGRESSION

There are several important points that need to be carefully examined about the use of logistic regression. First, maximum likelihood estimation can be performed even when there is only a single response. It is important to note that the logistic model may not fit the data as well as some alternative model so it is important to assess the overall goodness of fit of the model as well as relative contribution due to various parameters. Many of the issues and concerns that arise in the use of multiple regression for continuous response variables are also relevant here. More specific limitations are described in the following with a practical example.

Consider the example of marriage dissolution. The problem is that the probability of experiencing an event (such as marriage dissolution) increases with duration of exposure to risk. Therefore, when one runs a logistic regression in which the dependent variable takes the value 1 if the event occurred and 0 if it did not, then one must account for the fact that two persons who have identical covariates except that one was exposed for 10 years and the other for only 1 year must somehow be treated differently. There are three correct solutions and one incorrect solution to this problem within the logistic regression framework; an alternative correct solution is to employ multivariate life table (or hazard model) analysis (Trussell and Rao, 1989).

In standard logistic regression in which the dependent variable is dichotomous, each person not experiencing an event contributes the probability $1 - F(x'b)$ of an event not having occurred and each person experiencing the event contributes the probability $F(x'b)$ of the event having occurred, where $F(\ )$ is the cumulative distribution function of the logistic distribution with density $f(\ )$ and x is a vector of the individual's covariates and b is the associated vector of regression coefficients. If one knows that an individual experienced the event at duration d, then if one chooses to employ this information, one must allow the individual to contribute $f(\ )$ not $F(\ )$ to the likelihood. This is the likelihood for a logistic regression, but it is not the likelihood employed in logistic regression packages that assume that either the event has occurred (and *when* it occurred is irrelevant) or it has not. Alternatively, one could measure duration as the elapsed time from the start of the process to the survey *regardless* of whether the event occurred. Then ordinary logistic regression could be employed with duration as a covariate. One would have to choose the latter option if information on the exact timing of events were not available, and one might choose this option even if the timing was recorded but was felt to be of poor quality (Trussell and Preston, 1982). The former option has the advantage of lower sampling variability (and hence lower standard errors of the parameter estimates), because all the information in the sample is employed (John *et al.,* 1988); the disadvantage is that computer software is not readily available.

A third option that involves logistic-type regression is more commonly chosen. One arbitrarily designates categories of duration, creates a sample in which each individual contributes one observation for each relevant duration category, and then employs ordinary logistic regression. For example, one might define each year of marriage as a separate analysis category for duration. Then a person who married 8.6 years before the survey and whose marriage was still intact at the time of the survey would contribute 8 observations (the last 0.6 year being discarded because the marriage could have dissolved in the 0.4 year remaining in the 9th duration category). If this person's marriage had instead dissolved at 4.2 years, then he would contribute 5 observations (if the dissolution had occurred at 8.4 years, it would be ignored, because persons censored in their 9th year of marriage are also ignored). Given our objective (to allow for the possibility that the risk of marital dissolution might vary with marriage duration), we have to use this method of analysis by defining two duration categories as 0–6 and 7+ years, respectively. For reasons given above, however, the last category cannot properly be open-ended, but it could be defined as, for example, 7–15 years (with marital experience beyond that point being discarded). One general problem with this approach is that interpretation of the parameter estimates will be difficult unless the duration categories are of equal length* (Trussell, in press; Arjas and Kangas, in press). For an example of this approach in the context of marriage dissolution, see Morgan and Rindfuss (1985). Another way one can avoid this problem is to estimate separate regressions for each category of duration, although the number of parameters may become quite large.

---

* Arjas and Kangas (in press) have demonstrated that in many circumstances the models will yield identical results. The conditions for equality include the following: (a) the risk per time unit (e.g., a month) is small, (b) the same time units are employed in both models, (c) the sample for the logistic regression is assembled by letting each individual contribute a separate observation for each unit of time, and (d) the same duration categories are used in both models. They have also prepared software for estimating such discrete-time models with logistic regression.

A final approach that avoids the complications of logistic-type regression is to employ hazard models, which are essentially multivariate life tables, discussed in Chapter 7. In this approach, rates, not probabilities (employed in logistic regression), are modeled. For example, the rate of marriage dissolution during the first year of marriage is defined as the number of dissolutions at duration less than 1 year since marriage divided by the number of person-years (or person-months) of exposure contributed by persons during their first year of marriage, where exposure is terminated either by a dissolution or by censoring (being interviewed with marriage intact before the first wedding anniversary). The probability of marriage dissolution can be computed only among those who married at least a year before the survey; among this group, it is computed by dividing the number of dissolutions occurring in the first year of marriage by the number of marriages. One advantage of hazard models is that all relevant respondents can contribute the full amount of information available to the analysis; in the example above, those who married during the year preceding the survey must be discarded from a logistic regression analysis based on probabilities. Other than this problem, which essentially is a reduction in the effective size of the sample, the two approaches must yield similar qualitative results, because rates and probabilities usually closely correspond.

5.5. THE PROBIT MODEL

Probit is an abbreviation of the term "probability unit," attributed to C. R. Bliss (Finney, 1971). Some researchers prefer to use a probit model to analyze dichotomous dependent variable over the logistic regression model. These two models are very similar and yield essentially identical results after adjusting for scale difference. The choice between a probit and logistic model is influenced by practical considerations such as availability of software, personal preference, and experience.

Logistic regression and probit analysis are closely related and in most cases, probit and logistic coefficients differ only by a scalar factor.* Some researchers have employed probit models in the analysis of binary dependent variable (cf. Bilsborrow *et al.,* 1987; Hanson *et al.,* 1987). For most research questions, the results may be the same whether it is a logistic model or a probit model. A comparison of probit and logit models is provided by Aldrich and Nelson (1984). However, logistic specification is more common due to its link to log-linear models and also the availability of computer software. The limitations we listed above under the logistic model are applicable to the probit model as well. The multinomial (i.e., more than two categories for the

---

* Multiplication by 1.8 yields results that are approximate for estimated models.

dependent variable) extension probit model is logically possible but imprac-
tical. In such cases, multinomial logistic regression is the only standard method
for estimating the model. In the following section, we provide an illustrative
application of the probit model.

As indicated in the introductory remarks, the probit model is based on
a normal distribution. A probit is the inverse of the cumulative standard
normal distribution function. For any given proportion, the probit transformation returns the value below which that proportion of standard normal
deviates is found. To understand this model, assume that there is a theoretical
index (such as SES) Z_i which is determined by a covariate X_i as in the linear
regression model. The index Z_i is assumed to be a continuous variable which
is random and normally distributed:

$$Z_i = \alpha + \beta X_i \tag{5.7}$$

Suppose we have data which distinguish only whether individual observations are in one category (high values of index) or a second category (low
values of index). We employ the probit model to obtain estimates for the
parameters α and β while at the same time obtaining information about the
underlying unmeasured scale index.

The probit model assumes that Z_i is a normally distributed random variable, so that the probability of Z^* being less than (or equal to) Z_i can be
computed from the cumulative normal probability function. To obtain an
estimate of the index Z_i, we apply the inverse of the cumulative normal function

$$Z_i = F^{-1}(P_i) = \alpha + \beta X_i \tag{5.8}$$

The interpretation of P_i resulting from the probit model is straightforward
and it is an estimate of the conditional probability that an individual falls
into one category (low SES), given the individual's education (X_i). This is
equal to the probability that a standard normal variable will be less than or
equal to $\alpha + \beta X_i$.

5.6. AN EXAMPLE OF THE PROBIT MODEL

The data for this example came from the Canadian Fertility Survey,
conducted in April–June 1984. A total of 5315 women of all marital statuses
were interviewed. This example analyzes the pattern of childlessness in Canada
by considering a host of socioeconomic factors. Though there is some fertility
outside marriage, most reproduction in Canada occurs within marriage. As

such, we selected ever-married women, married for at least 60 months by the survey time in 1984 for inclusion in our example. The dependent variable, childlessness or parity status, is a dichotomous variable. The parity status has a value 1 for being childless and 0 for having one or more children. Based on earlier research on childlessness in Canada and elsewhere, we selected a few socioeconomic variables as theoretically possible correlates of zero parity status. As an illustrative example here, we restrict ourselves to four independent variables: place of residence (urban = 1, else = 0), education (grade 11 or less = 1, else = 0), religiosity (weekly attending church = 1, else = 0), and age cohort (25–34 = 1, else = 0).

Several computer software packages are available to fit a probit model. We have chosen SPSS version 4.0 and the procedure probit to analyze childlessness in Canada. The probit model in SPSS is a slightly modified version of the model discussed above. The SPSS software employs the following model specification:

$$\text{PROBIT}(p) + 5 = \text{Intercept} + BX \qquad (5.9)$$

A constant 5 has been added to the probit to make the new values uniformly positive (Finney, 1971). To obtain the correct value for the intercept, subtract 5 from the model intercept reported in the SPSS output. For example, in Table 5.3, the reported intercept = 3.5977 and the correct intercept for the model is calculated as $3.5977 - 5 = -1.4023$. The resultant model equation is given by

$$\text{PROBIT}(p) = -1.4023 + 0.2143X_1 - 0.3376X_2 - 0.1968X_3 + 0.06X_4$$

The probit procedure in SPSS expects input data at the aggregate level. Like any other survey data, the Canadian Fertility Survey data employed in

Table 5.3. Probit Analysis of Childlessness in Canada
[Probit Model: $(\text{PROBIT}(p) + 5) = \text{Intercept} + BX$]

Variable	Coefficient (β)	Standard error (S.E.)	Coeff./S.E.
Urban (X_1)	0.2143	0.07177	2.9863
GR 11 or less (X_2)	−0.3376	0.07678	−4.3904
Weekly church (X_3)	−0.1968	0.07722	−2.5486
Age group 25–34 (X_4)	0.0600	0.69380	0.8650
Intercept	3.5977[a]	0.07655	46.9982

[a] Correct intercept = $3.5977 - 5 = -1.4023$.

this example are at the individual level, i.e., there is one observation per case. If we use individual data as input to the procedure, the overall chi-square goodness-of-fit statistic would be incorrect due to incorrect number of degrees of freedom (SPSS, 1990). However, the parameter estimates and their standard errors are accurate.

In the example, we have collapsed individual level data using another procedure called "aggregate." The aggregate procedure can be requested before the probit procedure. In the appendix, a complete program is provided for ready reference to fit the probit model with aggregated data.

The results of our analysis of childlessness show that place of residence, education, and religiosity are significant factors and age cohort is not statistically significant. The significance of the coefficients may be judged from the last column in Table 5.3, i.e., the ratio of coefficient to standard error (t-statistic). The overall fit of the model can be assessed by examining the significance of the chi-square goodness-of-fit statistic provided in the output. The coefficient for an explanatory variable (such as place of residence) may be interpreted as measuring the effect of this variable on the odds of being childless relative to being a mother. The sign of the coefficient indicates positive or negative effect on the odds of being childless. For example, place of residence is positive and significant. This is in the expected pattern as urban women are more likely to opt for a childless life-style than women living in farm or small communities. Similarly, women with grade 11 or lower education, and highly religious are more likely to become mothers (see the negative sign) and these two effects are statistically significant. Age cohort is the only explanatory factor that is not statistically significant; nevertheless, it is an important factor in our understanding of childlessness. The overall chi-square goodness-of-fit statistic is 9.764 (d.f. = 11, $p = 0.552$) and is not statistically significant.

Logistic regression and probit are two models in the probit procedure in SPSS. Table 5.4 presents the results obtained from logistic and probit models for the above example. The logistic model fit in the SPSS is a modified version of the model [5 added to intercept and logit divided by 2, i.e., $\ln(p/(1-p))/2 + 5 = \text{Intercept} + BX$]. As pointed out in earlier sections, both models yield identical results and the chi-square goodness-of-fit statistic is not significant for either model. One may compute a number of pseudo-R^2 type measures to assess the overall model.

For example, a pseudo-$R^2 = \chi^2/(N + \chi^2)$, where χ^2 is the chi-square statistic for the overall fit and N is the total sample size. In the childlessness example, the sample size is 16 and the pseudo-$R^2 = 9.764/(16 + 9.764) = 0.379$. This measure approaches zero as the quality of fit diminishes and reaches one as the fit improves. For a detailed discussion on advantages and problems with this measure, see Aldrich and Nelson (1984).

Table 5.4. Comparison of Probit and Logistic Regression Models

Variable	Probit model coefficient (β)	Logistic model coefficient (β)
Urban (X_1)	0.2143**	0.2198**
GR 11 or less (X_2)	−0.3376**	−0.3532**
Weekly church (X_3)	−0.1968**	−0.2059**
Age group 25–34 (X_4)	0.0600	0.0657
Intercept	3.5977	3.7750
Chi-square goodness of fit	9.764 (d.f. = 11)	8.897 (d.f. = 11)

** Statistically significant.

5.7. SUMMARY

In this chapter, we deal with models designed to handle qualitative dependent variables with two or more categories. Two different transformations are considered and the theoretical reasoning behind these models is addressed. Both logistic regression analysis and probit analysis have the same type of limitations and advantages and differ only in the nature of transformation employed. The logistic model uses the logit transformation and is more commonly employed in social science applications. The general PROBIT procedure in SPSS package has logit and probit models among its options, and the estimated coefficients obtained from these models are generally related. Comparison of logistic regression with hazard models for event history data has been discussed to provide insight into situations where one may want to use one model over the other.

5.8. APPENDIX A: SPSS PROGRAM TO FIT THE PROBIT MODEL

```
FILE HANDLE DAT/NAME='LOGIT DATA A'   /* calling data */
DATA LIST FILE=DAT/CHILD,URBAN,GR11,WEEK,AG2534 (5F3.0)
COMMENT Use aggregate procedure to convert individual level
    data

AGGREGATE OUTFILE=*
  /BREAK=URBAN GR11 WEEK AG2534
  /NUM=N(CHILD)
  /NRESP=SUM(CHILD)   /* using aggregate procedure */
COMMENT A new data file with aggregated cases will be input
    to PROBIT procedure
```

```
PROBIT NRESP OF NUM WITH URBAN,GR11,WEEK,AG2534
  /MODEL = BOTH /*requesting both logistic and probit models
   */
  /LOG=NONE
  /PRINT = NONE
FINISH
```

5.9. APPENDIX B: PROGRAM OUTPUT (PARTIAL)

```
6  0  AGGREGATE OUTFILE=*
7  0                /BREAK= URBAN GR11 WEEK AG2534
8  0                /NUM=N (CHILD)
9  0                /NRESP=SUM (CHILD)
```

A new (aggregated) active file has replaced the existing active file.

```
10  0  PROBIT NRESP OF NUM WITH URBAN, GR11, WEEK, AG2534
11  0                /MODEL = BOTH /LOG=NONE
12  0                /PRINT = NONE
```

File: AGGREGATED FILE

DATA Information

        16 unweighted cases accepted.
         0 cases rejected because of missing data.

0

MODEL Information
      BOTH Probit and Logit Models are requested.

ML converged at iteration   5. The converge criterion
 = .00000

Parameter Estimates (LOGIT model: $(LOG(p/(1-p)))/2 + 5$)
= Intercept + BX):
      Note 5 added to intercept and logit divided by 2.

	Regression Coeff.	Standard Error	Coeff./ S.E.
URBAN	.21984	.07370	2.98282
GR11	−.35322	.08133	−4.34288
WEEK	−.20590	.08000	−2.57359
AG2534	.06572	.06916	.95027

		Standard	Intercept/
0	Intercept	Error	S.E.
	3.77503	.07824	48.25196

Pearson Goodness-of-Fit Chi Square = 8.897   DF = 11
P = .631

Since Goodness-of-Fit Chi square is NOT significant, no heterogeneity factor is used in the calculation of confidence limits.

Covariance (below) and Correlation (above) Matrices of Parameter Estimates

	URBAN	GR11	WEEK	AG2534
URBAN	.00543	.07262	.09195	.04817
GR11	.00044	.00661	.01807	.12598
WEEK	.00054	.00012	.00640	.08551
AG2534	.00025	.00071	.00047	.00478

ML converged at iteration 4. The converge criterion = .00027

Parameter Estimates (PROBIT model: (PROBIT(p) + 5) = Intercept + BX):

Note 5 added to intercept.

	Regression Coeff.	Standard Error	Coeff./ S.E.
URBAN	.21433	.07177	2.98632
GR11	−.33759	.07689	−4.39042
WEEK	−.19681	.07722	−2.54863
AG2534	.06001	.06938	.86498
0			

		Standard	Intercept/
	Intercept	Error	S.E.
	3.59771	.07655	46.99819

Pearson Goodness-of-Fit Chi Square = 9.764   DF = 11
P = .552

Since Goodness-of-Fit Chi square is NOT significant, no heterogeneity factor is used in the calculation of confidence limits.

CHAPTER 6

Log-Linear Models

6.1. INTRODUCTION

Throughout the last 15 or 20 years, social scientists have seen a substantial body of literature published in their journals on the subject of analyzing categorical or qualitative data. Many of these articles begin by bemoaning the fact that most of the multivariate statistical tools that social scientists have at their disposal, i.e., the tools that they are trained to understand and use in their research, are not appropriate for the categorical kinds of data they often use. Much time is spent in research design devising scales that will measure a concept at an interval or ratio level, so that operationalized concept can be used in a regression model or factor analysis. Frequently the model assumptions would be violated less if variables were treated as qualitative. For instance, it does not make much sense to ask female victims of sexual assault *how much* guilt they feel, when we are really interested in whether or not they feel "guilty" at all, and how this state of guilt-feeling is related to other relevant variables.

We agree that social scientists can make good use of parametric techniques of multivariate analysis of qualitative data, and this chapter's limited references (and the references therein) reveal that there is no shortage of information on what these techniques are and how to use them. The problem is that a complete understanding of any one of these techniques is no simple mathematical matter, and most of us are well-acquainted with the fact that most social scientists would rather get on with their substantive research problems than spend time learning complex statistical procedures. This chapter will attempt to demonstrate how contingency tables (the manner in which most qualitative data are presented) can be analyzed in terms of a qualitative dependent variable being a function of any number of qualitative or nonqualitative independent variables. Most readers will, at this point, immediately think of the linear regression model or the log-linear model which is analogous to the regression model. Indeed, as we shall see, when we use the log-linear model to analyze a dependent variable, what we do is derive a regression model from the log-linear parameters. However, log-linear analysis employs maximum-likelihood estimation procedures to estimate the parameters. In a series of articles, Goodman, and also Fienberg (1977) and Bishop *et al.* (1975), together with a substantial body of journal literature, have extolled the virtues of log-linear analysis. Though log-linear analysis is analogous to familiar regression analysis, insofar as it is a form of linear modeling, it is certainly not a simple method of multivariate analysis to comprehend. It is even more difficult to use, given the current state of statistical software. Our task now is to introduce the reader to its basic techniques and utility. However, the reader is unfortunately left, for the time being, to the villainy of SAS and SPSS when it comes to actually using log-linear analysis.

The first thing to realize about the general form of the log-linear model is that, in looking at a multiway cross-tab (cross-table), no variable in particular is viewed as being the dependent variable. The general model expresses the logarithm of each cell frequency in the extended cross-tab as a linear combination of every possible interaction between the variables involved in the table. The advantage of viewing no one variable in particular as being dependent is that it enables the researcher to make sophisticated tests of independence between various combinations of variables. However, most readers of this chapter will be interested in the case where one variable is viewed as dependent, and in this case a model that looks exactly like the logistic regression model that is derived from the general log-linear model. In addition to the desired end of deriving statistically valid parameter estimates, log-linear analysis allows the researcher to "boil down" the information contained in a complicated multiway cross-tab, in order to see if the data can be reproduced in a more parsimonious form.

The log-linear model is an exploratory data analysis technique rather than an explanatory model. It is useful in the search for structure in systems of categorical data, and is helpful for decomposing data structures into component parts to represent the effects of one or a combination of variables. It provides both an individual variable effect, known as the "main effect," and the effect of composite variables, known as an "interaction effect." The two types of effects together describe the data. The main and interaction effects indicate not only the patterns of association between cross-classified variables but also their significance in the data set.

The log-linear model can be either a *saturated* model or an *unsaturated* model depending upon the number of independent parameters in it. If the number of independent parameters is equal to the number of cells in the contingency table, then it is known as a saturated model, otherwise it is said to be an unsaturated model. Often, unsaturated models are derived from saturated models by deleting some of the interaction effects. Willekens and Baydar (1983) discuss another type of log-linear model known as the *hybrid* log-linear model. Though hybrid models have not been popular in practical data analysis, they have been discussed in the literature by Goodman (1972), Bishop *et al.* (1975), Haberman (1974), and Gokhale and Johnson (1978). Unlike the saturated models, hybrid log-linear models require that the interaction effects be restricted to specified values or values that depend on other interaction effects rather than deleting them. For the saturated model, parameters are based on independence-related imposition, but for the hybrid model, parameters are the result of restrictions imposed on the parameters of the saturated model. Hence, these models are derived from the saturated model. Willekens and Baydar suggest interesting applications of these models to study age, period, and cohort effects in demography. In Chapter 3, we mentioned that the age–period–cohort models suffer from the problem of underidentification, and hybrid models may be useful in improving the identification problem and indicating the direction in which an optimal parameterization of age–period–cohort models may be found (Willekens and Baydar, 1983). The log-linear model is also used to study causal relationships and to quantify the effects of independent variables, separately and combined, on a dependent variable. In other words, the model expresses the observed dependent variable as a product of several terms each representing a particular type of effect of the cross-classified variables on the dependent variable. In addition to main and interaction effects, the model also provides the overall effect as the natural logarithm of the geometric mean of a dependent variable.

6.2. GENERAL FORM OF LOG-LINEAR MODELS

To illustrate the general form of a log-linear model, let us consider a simple two-dimensional contingency 2×2 table. Let the two variables be A and B each with two categories:

B/A	$i = 1$	$i = 2$	Total
$j = 1$	X_{11}	X_{21}	$X_{.1}$
$j = 2$	X_{12}	X_{22}	$X_{.2}$
Total	$X_{1.}$	$X_{2.}$	$X_{..}$

where X_{ij} denotes the observed cell frequency and $X_{.1}$, $X_{.2}$, $X_{1.}$, and $X_{2.}$ are marginal totals. Let m_{ij} represent the expected cell frequency. Then the model of independence can be written as:

$$m_{ij} = \frac{X_{i.} \times X_{.j}}{X_{..}}$$ (6.1)

By applying a natural logarithm for each item in Eq. (6.1), we can write the equation in an additive form:

$$\ln m_{ij} = -\ln X_{..} + \ln X_{i.} + \ln X_{.j}$$

This equation can also be written in different notations and this form is a simple log-linear mode:

$$\ln m_{ij} = \lambda + \lambda_i^A + \lambda_j^B$$

where λ is a constant independent of i and j and is known as the overall effect. λ_i^A is dependent only upon i and is known as the main effect of variable A. λ_j^B is dependent upon j and is known as the main effect of variable B. This equation is subject to the constraints:

$$\sum_{i=1}^{z} \lambda_i^A = 0 \qquad \text{and} \qquad \sum_{j=1}^{z} \lambda_j^B = 0$$

In some cases the model of independence does not fit the data adequately, and the above log-linear model is extended to include an interaction effect λ_{ij}^{AB} which measures the association between A and B. The new log-linear model is:

$$\ln m_j = \lambda + \lambda_i^A + \lambda_j^B + \lambda_{ij}^{AB}$$ (6.2)

with an additional constraint

$$\sum_{i=1}^{z} \lambda_{ij}^{AB} = 0$$

This model is a *saturated* model, for here the estimated log counts are equal to the observed log counts and the model fits the data perfectly. Similarly, the saturated model of a three-dimensional table is as follows:

$$\ln m_{ijk} = \lambda + \lambda_i^A + \lambda_j^B + \lambda_k^C + \lambda_{ik}^{AC} + \lambda_{jk}^{BC} + \lambda_{ij}^{AB} + \lambda_{ijk}^{ABC}$$ (6.3)

where m_{ijk} is the cell value for category i of a variable A, category j of a variable B_A and category k of a variable C:

λ is the overall effect
λ_i^A is the main effect of variable A
λ_j^B is the main effect of variable B
λ_k^C is the main effect of variable C

λ_{ik}^{AC} is the effect of the combined variable AC (first-order interaction effect), λ_{jk}^{BC} and λ_{ij}^{AB} are also first-order interaction effects, and λ_{ijk}^{ABC} is the second-order interaction effect or the second effect of the combined variables ABC. The λ's satisfy the constraints

$$\sum_i \lambda_i^A = 0, \qquad \sum_j \lambda_j^B = 0, \qquad \sum_k \lambda_k^C = 0,$$

$$\sum_i \lambda_{ij}^{AB} = \sum_j \lambda_{ij}^{BC} = 0, \cdots \sum_i \lambda_{ijk}^{ABC} = \sum_j \lambda_{ijk}^{ABC} = \sum_k \lambda_{ijk}^{ABC} = 0$$

Other types of log-linear models are hierarchical models. Hierarchical models are those in which higher-order terms may be included only if the related lower-order terms are included (Fienberg, 1977). In other words, in the case of a hierarchical model a higher-order effect cannot be present unless all lower-order effects whose indices are subsets of the higher-order effect are also included in the model. For instance, if λ^{ABC} is nonzero, then it implies that λ^{AB}, λ^{BC}, λ^{AC}, λ^A, λ^B, λ^C, λ are all present.

6.3. APPLICATION OF LOG-LINEAR MODELS

6.3.1. Description of the Data

Let us take as an example, data from Taylor and Chappell (1980) to illustrate the use of log-linear analysis. The units of analysis are students (N = 450), and they have been classified according to four variables, each of which has two categories. Table 6.1 is thus referred to as a $2 \times 2 \times 2 \times 2$ table, and it therefore has 16 cells.

Note that this four-way cross-tabulation is presented in a somewhat unusual form. The usual method is to present the cross-classified sample in the form of partial tables. That is, in this instance there would be a two-way partial table (of grades by IQ) for each of the four possible combinations of class and effort. At least that is the way most of the more common statistical software packages output multiway crosstables. The presentation in Table 6.1 is more economical, yet it contains all of the information that the other method contains. The advantage of the current method is that it encourages the reader

Table 6.1. Grade by Social Class by Effort by IQ[a]

Subscripts:	Social class i	1 = Middle	2 = Lower
	Effort j	1 = High	2 = Low
	IQ k	1 = High	2 = Low
	Grades l	1 = High	2 = Low

| | | | | Number with high and low grades | | Sample size |
ijk	Class	Effort	IQ	High	Low	
111	Middle	High	High	60	20	80
112	Middle	High	Low	40	24	64
121	Middle	Low	High	40	24	64
122	Middle	Low	Low	24	12	36
211	Lower	High	High	40	16	56
212	Lower	High	Low	6	32	38
221	Lower	Low	High	18	38	56
222	Lower	Low	Low	2	54	56

[a] $N = 450$.

to view the entire sample as a partitioned sample. Essentially, what occurs when a sample is cross-tabulated is that the sample is partitioned into as many subsamples as there are cells in the table. In this case, seeing that we are going to view grades as a dependent variable, and the other three variables as independent variables, we have partitioned the overall sample of 450 students into 8 *subsamples*. Each subsample (of size n) represents a unique combination of the categories of the independent variables, and we observe the distribution of the dependent variable, grades, over its two categories for each unique subsample. It is conventional that cells in a cross-table are subscripted with lowercase letters i, j, k, etc. In this manner, cells can be referred to by their numerical subscripts, and the presentation of general mathematical formulas is made simpler. For example, let us look at the fifth row in the table. This row presents the grade distribution for our subsample of lower class students, who were recognized as demonstrating high effort in their schoolwork, and who have been placed in the high-IQ group. The subscripts of the independent variable categories related to this group identify it as group 211 (i.e., $i = 2$, $j = 1$, $k = 1$). There are 56 students in this subgroup, 40 of whom received high grades, and 16 of whom received low grades.

Let us now turn our attention to matters related to the dependent variable, grades. Adding up the total for all those in the "high" column (i.e., $l = 1$), we arrive at the overall number who received high grades, which is 230; the count for low grades is 220. Because this is a dichotomous variable, we can view it in the same terms as a binomial probability experiment. That is, the proportion who got high grades (230/450 = 0.511) can be viewed as "success." Accordingly, this proportion can also be treated as the probability of being grouped in the high-grades category, and it is given the general label p (i.e., success). The other category is similarly treated and is given the general label q (i.e., failure). Note that, for a dichotomous variable, $p + q = 1$; thus, if all we know is one of p or q, then the other proportion is determined. We only need to work with the proportion falling into the "success" category for a dichotomous variable, because we know by inference what the proportion is for the "failure" category. If we know the sample size n and the proportion p or q, we know everything we need to know about the distribution of the dichotomous variable. From this information, we can infer whether our sample proportion is reasonably close to the population proportion. The variance of a binomial probability distribution is pq/n, and the standard error of this distribution is, of course, the square root of the variance. Thus, the standard error for grades is 0.024, and with this figure we can make inferences about the overall sampling distribution of the proportion of students receiving high grades according to the central limit theorem. Note that the standard error becomes large if the distance between p and q is small, and if the sample size n is small. The practical importance of this is that one ought to be careful when making inferences from a binomial distribution if the sample size is less than 20.

We can treat the proportion receiving high grades within each subsample in exactly the same manner. That is, we can observe how the proportion of students receiving high grades—or alternatively, the probability of receiving high grades—varies across all of the independent groups. Of course, this variation of p across the independent groups is precisely the information we are interested in analyzing through a log-linear analysis of these data. The log-linear analyses gives us an idea of where the significant relations are in these data, and how much each independent variable affects the probability of achieving high grades.

6.3.2. Log-Linear Analysis of the Data

The information in our original four-way, $2 \times 2 \times 2 \times 2$ cross-tab of grades by class by effort by IQ contains many subtables within the overall four-way table. That is, there are the univariate tables for each variable, there are all of the possible two-way tables of the four variables, all of the possible three-way tables, and of course, the four-way table that "generates" all of this lower-order information. All in all, there are 15 unique tables (including the univariate distributions) that can be derived from the four-way table. In order to summarize what is a complicated concept, log-linear analysis treats each of these tables as an "effect" upon the logarithm of the observed frequency in each cell of the overall table. That is, what is modeled is an expected logarithm of a cell frequency, not a probability or odds. Recall that each row of Table 6.1 actually represents two cells of the overall $2 \times 2 \times 2 \times 2$ table; i.e., the first row represents cells 1111 and 1112 in the *ijkl* notation or, in words, middle-class students showing high effort and high IQ who got high grades, and middle-class students showing high effort and high IQ who got low grades. The general log-linear model estimates the logarithm of each cell, or, in more general terms, ln *(ijkl)*. All the parameters that do not involve the variable subscripted by *l* will drop out, and we will wind up doubling those parameters left in the model. It will suffice to say that the resulting equation is interpreted precisely as is the logistic regression model. Indeed, both are one and the same logit model, except that one is determined by logistic regression, and the other is derived from maximum-likelihood log-linear analysis. This may not make much sense to the reader yet, but after a little more familiarity with the log-linear model, it will become clear how the logit model is derived from the log-linear model, and how log-linear analysis can thus be adapted to the analysis of a dependent variable as a function of independent variables.

Let us back up a few steps and return to the concept of the effects present in a multiway cross-tab. Each possible univariate and multivariate frequency distribution in the $2 \times 2 \times 2 \times 2$ cross-tab is viewed as an "effect" in log-linear analysis. A log-linear model that includes a parameter for each of these possible effects is a *saturated model:* the model is "saturated" with all possible effects. Such a model will reproduce the original cross-tab perfectly. In terms of goodness of fit, there will be no difference between the observed table and the expected table. The reader ought now to see that a fundamental purpose of log-linear analysis is to see which of the many possible effects can be deleted from the general model without causing the hypothesized model to generate expected values in a cross-tabulation that differs too greatly from the observed cross-tabulation. The idea is to find the most *parsimonious* method of interpreting and presenting the relationships existing in the data.

Let us consider the saturated model for the logit of getting high grades, and we shall determine what each "effect" in the model represents in real terms. In order to simplify matters, we shall introduce a shorthand method of referring to the variables involved. Accordingly, each variable will be represented by the first letter of its name: C will represent social class, E will represent effort, and I will represent IQ. The saturated logit model is:

$$\ln(\text{high grades odds}) = \ln(\text{mean odds of high grades}) + \ln(C)$$
$$+ \ln(E) + \ln(I) + \ln(CE) + \ln(CI) + \ln(EI) + \ln(CEI) \tag{6.4}$$

Each parameter on the right-hand side of the equation can be visualized as being a cross-tabulation of grades with the independent variable specified by the parameter. (The exception is the first parameter, which is an intercept. It represents the same thing as does the intercept in a regression equation.) That is, C represents a cross-tabulation of grades by social class, EI a cross-tabulation of grades by effort by IQ, and so forth. The computer program will estimate the "amount" of linear effect for each combination of the independent variables.

Each combination, represented by a parameter, is referred to as an *interaction*. C, E, and I are the "main effects" of class, effort, and IQ on the logit of high grades. CE, CI, and EI are the "first-order" interactions present within the saturated model. If any one of these first-order interactions proves to be substantial and significant, this will indicate that the main effects included within it are further elaborated by the interaction of the two independent variables. For example, we will obtain an estimate for the main effect of being in the middle class (the interaction C, $i = 1$), and the main effect of showing high effort in school (the interaction E, $j = 1$). Should the first-order interaction CE prove to be significant, then we will be provided with information that elaborates on what we know about the main effects of class and effort on the odds of getting high grades. We will be told that, in addition to considering a student's social class and effort in predicting the likelihood of the student getting high grades, we must also consider the combination of the student's social class and effort categories in order to improve our prediction. Similarly, we will have a more refined estimate of the controlled effects of social class and effort: there will be a different "factor" that adds to (or subtracts from) the mean logit of getting high grades for each of the four possible combinations of social class and effort.

The interaction CEI is called, logically, a "second-order" interaction, and its interpretation follows the same logic as that for first-order interactions. An important point to realize now is that our saturated logit model, derived from the general saturated log-linear model, is *hierarchical* in nature. That is, the presence of the interaction CEI in the model means automatically that all the lower-order interactions included with CEI must be included in the model. Although it is possible to deal with nonhierarchical log-linear models, they become quite complicated to explain to the log-linear novice. The more acquainted reader is advised to consult Knoke and Burke (1980) for more information on nonhierarchical models.

As stated above, the basic idea of log-linear modeling is not only to arrive at parametric estimates of the effects of independent variables (and their combinations) on a dependent variable, but also to summarize the data contained in a multiway cross-table in a more parsimonious form. Given the above information, we can now see that the strategy involved here is to subtract, in a stepwise fashion, the higher-order interactions from the model to see what effect this subtraction has on how well the resulting *nonsaturated* model "fits" the observed cross-table. Each parameter in the saturated model represents 1 degree of freedom. Our cross-table therefore has 8 degrees of freedom in all, and the saturated model uses all of them. The statistic that measures the goodness of fit (GOF) of a modeled cross-table (derived from the parameters of the log-linear model) is, of course, chi-square. The likelihood-ratio statistic is also calculated by most of the software packages, and it has a distribution almost identical to chi-square for the same degrees of freedom. A saturated model, and therefore a model with no degrees of freedom (no parsimony), will reproduce the observed cross-table perfectly and will have a chi-square and likelihood ratio of 0. This indicates that there is no difference between the observed cell frequencies and the expected frequencies under the model. In other words, no error at all is generated by this model. If we remove the only second-order interaction from the saturated model, we will have specified a nonsaturated model with 1 degree of freedom. How well will this model fit? What we will be looking for is nonsignificance of the GOF statistics: this will indicate that the error generated by this more parsimonious model is not an "amount of error" that can be considered to be statistically significant.

Let us get away from explanation, and show via demonstration with our example data how logit modeling with log-linear analysis is done. Table 6.2 shows the parameter estimates and GOF statistics for the saturated logit model given in Eq. (6.4). It is recommended that any log-linear analysis begin with an examination of the saturated model. The saturated model will give a good idea of which interactions are good candidates for deletion in a more parsimonious treatment of the data. We begin by observing that the last two effects show up as insignificant based on their chi-square statistics. We shall keep in mind these interactions as candidates for deletion when we estimate a non-

Table 6.2. The Saturated Log-Linear Logit Model of the Data
(Likelihood Ratio = 0.00, Significance = 1.00)

Effect	Estimate	Chi-square	Probability
Intercept	−0.253	3.38	0.0658
Class	0.956	48.37	0.0001
Effort	0.466	11.48	0.0007
IQ	0.698	25.74	0.0001
Class × effort	−0.365	7.03	0.0080
Class × IQ	−0.596	18.80	0.0001
Effort × IQ	0.097	0.50	0.4809
Class × effort × IQ	0.096	0.48	0.4869

saturated model. The antilog of the intercept is 0.776. This represents the overall odds of being grouped in the high-grades category. The main effect for being in the middle-class category ($i = 1$) is 2.6, the antilog of 0.956. Log-linear models employ an effect-coding scheme (most packages will generate the effect-coding automatically, and will read almost any kind of value, i.e., including alphabetic, for a variable), so the interpretation of the parameters is the same as with logistic regression. We observe that the additive parameter for class by effort is 0.365. The antilog of this value, and thus the multiplicative parameter for this interaction, is 0.694. This value holds for $i = j$. Thus, the factor according to which the mean odds is multiplied is the same for the combinations middle class/high effort, and lower class/low effort. The reciprocal of 0.694 = 1.44—is the value for the other two combinations of class and effort. Let us take a look at what this means. The multiplicative parameters for the main effects of middle class and high effort are 2.6 and 1.59, respectively. When we take into account the interactive effect of these two variables on the odds of getting high grades, we arrive at four different multiplying factors, instead of just two, reflecting the increased information we have at our disposal because of our knowledge of this interaction. For a middle-class student who shows high effort, the multiplying factor is $(2.6)(1.59)(0.694) = 2.87$. One can see that the effect of the interaction is to make the multiplying factor smaller than it would be were it based on the product of the main effects alone. Similarly, for a lower-class student who shows high effort, the multiplying factor on the mean odds is $(0.385)(1.59)(1.44) = 0.88$. In this instance, the effect of the interaction is to increase the multiplying factor beyond simply the product of the main effects of social class and effort. It is very confusing to interpret the parameters of higher-order interactions without reference to the main effects that are subsumed beneath them. We feel that it is better to interpret these interactions in combination with the main effects. The difference is one of knowing just the main effects of the variables involved, and of enriching that knowledge by considering the meaningful differences between the possible combinations of the two categories of the variables.

The last general point to consider in the explanation of log-linear models is the problem of model selection and model evaluation. As far as we know, the technique we are about to present was developed by Goodman (1972), but one sees the technique explained in many of the sources listed in the bibliography. For our money, the most lucid explanation once again is found in Swafford (1980). We must also mention that model testing and evaluation seems to be the single most annoying and fundamental flaw of the software packages we have worked with (i.e., SAS and SPSS). The amount of work required to generate this information can get to be very formidable in a research design with more than four variables. If you can put up with its other annoying flaws, SPSS is marginally superior in this regard. The software package of choice for this kind of analysis appears to be Leo Goodman's ECTA (Everyman's Contingency Table Analyzer), which is not available to us at this time.

If one takes the trouble to calculate how many different nonsaturated models are possible with these data, one will see that there are 18. This is a general weakness of log-linear modeling: the number of possible models can get *very* large if there are more than four or five variables! We will use a simplified notation for the specification of hierarchical log-linear logit models in this section. The notation {CEI} delineates a saturated model that includes all possible independent effects. Similarly, {CE}{CI}{EI} refers to a nonsaturated model that includes all independent effects except the single second-order effect. {CE}I refers to a model that includes the first-order interaction between class and effort, and therefore the main effects of class and effort alone, and the main effect of IQ. Only seven models out of the nineteen possible models (the additional one is the saturated model) will concern us in Table 6.3. Model 7 is an interesting and useful model. It hypothesizes that odds for subsample is equiprobable, i.e., that none of the independent parameters have any effect on the odds of getting high grades. We can see by observing the GOF statistics for this model that it provides an extremely poor fit with these data. It is in fact the worst possible fit. The utility of calculating this model is that it provides an index of the total amount of variation to be explained in the odds of getting high grades, based on partitioning the sample according to these independent variables. Thus, we can look at the figure for model 6 (another poor-fitting model) and calculate how much of the variance that model explains, relative to the equiprobability model. The figure is 133.42 − 31.59/133.42 = 0.763. This figure is analogous to R^2 in multiple regression; we can say that model 6 "accounts for" 76.3% of the variance in grades. See Goodman (1972) and Poppel and Willekens (1982) for more on this analogy to R^2.

What we need to do with Table 6.3 is appropriately compare the various models to see what happens to GOF when certain independent effects are

Table 6.3. The Evaluation of Several Models under
Goodman's Scheme of Model Evaluation

Model #	Model spec.	d.f.	Ratio	Likelihood–prob.
1	{CEI}	0	0.000	1.000
2	{CE} {CI} {EI}	1	0.500	0.479
3	{CI} {CI}	2	1.840	0.398
4	{CI} {EI}	2	8.080	0.018
5	{CE} {EI}	2	23.250	0.0001
6	CEI	4	31.590	0.0001
7	Intercept	7	133.420	0.0001

deleted. The only effect missing from model 2 that is present in model 1 is the effect of second-order interaction; namely, the parameter for {CEI}. If we subtract the GOF statistics for model 1 from those for model 2, we will be able to test the statistical contribution of the second-order interaction. The figures are: $0.50 - 0 = 0.5$ at $1 - 0 = 1$ degree of freedom. A likelihood-ratio difference of 0.5 to 1 degree of freedom indicates that second-order interaction can be deleted from our model without the introduction of significant error. Indeed, the overall GOF for model 2—0.5 at 1 degree of freedom—yields an error that is insignificant (probability = 0.479).

If we compare model 6 with model 2, we can test the hypothesis that none of the first-order interactions are significant. This test yields a likelihood-ratio difference of 31.09 at 3 degrees of freedom, and this would indicate that we do need some first-order interaction in our final model, as this difference is significant for 3 degrees of freedom. Our strategy now is to find out if we need all three first-order interactions. Model 3 tests the contribution of the {EI} interaction, model 4 the {CE} interaction, and model 5 the {CI} interaction. Each of these tests is conducted relative to model 2, the model that includes all three first-order interactions. The results of these tests indicate that we *can* drop the {EI} interaction without introducing significant error into our most parsimonious log-linear logit model.

We thus conclude that the "best" model for these data is model 3: {CE}{CI}. This model has an overall GOF of 1.84 with 2 degrees of freedom, and the error introduced by the model into the cross-tab is not significant. This model explains 98.6% of the variance in grades. The parameter estimates for this model are listed in Table 6.4. One may conclude that, controlling for other independent effects, social class has the most substantial effect on the odds of getting high grades. This model indicates that the only circumstance in which the odds are favorable for lower-class students getting high grades (i.e., odds greater than 1) is when they show both high effort and high IQ. No

Table 6.4. Parameter Estimates for the Best-Fitting
Log-Linear Logit Model, {CE} {CI}

Effect	Additive parameter	Antilog	1/Antilog
Intercept	−0.268	0.765	—
Class	0.942	2.566	0.390
Effort	0.483	1.621	0.617
IQ	0.715	2.043	0.489
Class × effort	−0.348	0.706	1.417
Class × IQ	−0.580	0.560	1.786

other combination of independent variables raises their odds above 1, even when interactions are taken into account.

6.4. COMPARISON OF THE LOG-LINEAR WITH OTHER MODELS

In this section, we will try to compare the log-linear technique with the more familiar linear regression model. Two of the techniques considered here—linear probability modeling and logistic regression—are forms of regression. We will not discuss the theoretical background of these techniques here, as they have been discussed in earlier chapters. However, we will attempt to demonstrate how contingency tables can be analyzed in terms of qualitative or nonqualitative independent variables. The purpose of this section is thus to bring together in one place the similarities and differences of these techniques, with their comparative strengths and weaknesses, so as to allow the researcher to judge independently exactly which technique best suits his or her research problem.

6.4.1. Linear Probability Modeling: Regression with Proportion as the Dependent Variable

As Neter and Wasserman (1974) point out, one can employ a dummy-coded dichotomous dependent variable in regression analysis; the value that the derived model specifies is the *probability* that the dependent value will take on the coded value "1," given the specified values of the independent variables. Alternatively, we can view each subsample of our cross-table as a single observation. In this case, we code each independent variable according to a dummy-coding or effect-coding scheme (see Kerlinger and Pedhazur, 1973, for a review of the difference between dummy- and effect-coding; here, we use effect-coding), and we use each subsample observation of p—the probability of getting high grades—as our observed dependent variable. The parameters of the resulting model will tell us everything we need to know. The intercept will tell us the overall mean probability of being grouped in the high-grades category, independently of the independent factors. The parameter for each independent factor represents the amount each factor adds to the intercept when that factor equals 1, *controlling for* each of the other independent factors. Thus, we model the probability of achieving high grades as a linear function of social class, effort, and IQ, and thus the name *linear probability modeling* (Swafford, 1980).

This approach is not without its problems. The astute reader will observe that, by simply using observed proportions as our dependent variable, we violate one of the fundamental assumptions of ordinary least-squares (OLS) regression, namely, the assumption of homoscedasticity. Clearly, the binomial-based variances of the observed proportions for each subsample are unequal for each combination of values for the independent variables. If we simply use these observed proportions in their current state, our resulting estimates of the statistical significance of the model parameters will be inaccurate. The solution to this problem is to use a weighted least-squares (WLS) method of estimating the model. This is the technique proposed by Grizzle *et al.* (1969). Their technique is widely cited throughout the literature, and it is most commonly referred to as the GSK technique (GSK being the acronym of the authors' surnames). The GSK method corrects for heteroscedasticity by weighting each observed proportion by the inverse of its binomial-based variance. Observed proportions with a small variance are thus given more weight in the fitting of the model than are proportions with a large variance.

Table 6.5 displays the results of regressing our observed proportions of students receiving high grades (from Table 6.1) against social class, effort, and IQ. We used Proc Reg in the SAS statistical package, and we weighted each observation by the inverse of its binomial-based variance in order to achieve a WLS fit. The independent variables were effect-coded; i.e., the first category of each variable was coded "1," and the other category "−1," meaning that the sum of the effects for each category for each variable equals 0. We can see that the overall mean probability of being grouped in the high-grades category, in the absence of the effects of any of the independent factors, is 0.454. Unstandardized betas are the parameter of choice, as all of the factors are measured in the same logical "units"; each beta represents the amount each independent variable "adds to" or "subtracts from" the intercept. Thus, we can see that the effect of being in the middle class—controlling for the effects of effort and IQ—is to add 0.171 to the mean probability of getting high grades. The effect of being in the "lower" category of social class is to *subtract* 0.171 from the intercept, in accordance with the proper interpretation of effect-coded independent variables. We can logically say with validity that, based on this sample and this hypothesized model, students who are in the middle class are 34.2% more likely to be grouped in the high-grades category than are students in the lower class, controlling for the effects of effort and IQ. [The computational reasoning is as follows: the probability of achieving high grades for lower-class students is $0.454 - 0.171 = 0.283$; for middle-class students it is $0.454 + 0.171 = 0.625$. $0.625 - 0.283 = 0.342$ (the difference between middle- and lower-class students). To obtain the difference as a percentage, one of course multiplies 0.342 by 100. Bear in mind that these figures are *controlling for* effort and IQ. The betas of the other independent variables are interpreted in exactly the same fashion.]

Note in Table 6.5 the very high figure for R^2: 0.91. Having manipulated

Table 6.5. A WLS Regression of Probability of Receiving
High Grades on Social Class, Effort, and IQ
(Independent Variables Effect-Coded) ($R^2 = 0.9057$)

Variable	Unstandardized beta	T	Probability $> |T|$
Intercept	0.454	8.84	0.0009
Class	0.171	3.01	0.0396
Effort	0.093	1.72	0.1607
IQ	0.135	2.47	0.0692

the multiple regression model to accommodate the information contained in a multiway cross-tab, we interpret this figure differently from the way we would if we were regressing individual-level data. R^2 in this case represents the amount of variation between *subsample proportions* that is explained by this model. As Swafford (1980) notes, an important source of individual-level variation is eliminated by grouping the data into a cross-tabulation. In fact, with linear probability modeling, it is always possible to account for 100% of the variation between subsample proportions, if we merely add into the model all the possible interactions between the independent variables.

This kind of regression, then, would appear to suffice for supplying us with a parametric technique of multivariate analysis of cross-tabulated data. It has given us a controlled and statistically valid estimate of the degree of effect of each independent variable on the probability of the dependent variable falling into one of two categories. There is, however, a logical flaw in this technique that makes it quite inappropriate for certain data. It is possible that, for certain data, this kind of regression could result in the researcher formulating a model that estimates p value greater than 1 or less than 0 for certain combinations of the independent variables in the model. Clearly, this will not do when we are speaking of probabilities: a probability must always be between 0 and 1 or it makes no sense. This constraint can be referred to as the "ceiling and floor" constraint on the linear probability model, and it arises out of viewing the relationship between p and each independent factor as being linear (i.e., *additive*). Swafford (1980) provides a good argument to the effect that, in practice, this will occur only rarely. However, Neter and Wasserman (1974) state that the output of invalid values is most likely to occur, as a result of the kind of estimation procedure involved here, when the overall value of p for the dependent variable falls *outside* the range 0.25 to 0.75. This rule of thumb makes a certain kind of intuitive sense, as more extreme distributions are quite likely to result in the estimation of an intercept that is relatively small or large. If "substantial" effects are added to or subtracted from an intercept of this kind, one is quite likely to have a model that estimates values of p that are invalid. The solution to this problem is to use *logistic* regression.

6.4.2. Logistic Regression: Transforming the Dependent Variable

It is perhaps misleading to introduce logistic regression as a form of multivariate analysis that is completely distinct from the general multiple regression model that we just discussed. The whole purpose of employing multiple regression with grouped qualitative (i.e., cross-tabulated) data in the first place was to arrive at parameter estimates of the *degree* of effect each independent variable has on the dependent variable, controlling for the effects of all of the other independent variables. We should not forget that this is the *purpose* of multivariate analysis. In fact, logistic regression is simply another way of manipulating the general multiple regression model in order to meet this purpose, and to provide a practical way of analyzing data with the power of multivariate analysis. Logistic regression, then, is useful in order to model data that do not suit the linear probability form of regression.

The difference is with the way the dependent variable is represented. In linear probability modeling, the dependent variable was represented as the simple observed proportion p. The problem with using p is that, with certain sets of data, the ceiling/floor constraint on p renders its use inappropriate for data where the overall observed p is either relatively small or large. This problem is avoided if we look at the dependent variable in another way. Instead of viewing the dependent variable as a proportion or probability, we can view the dependent variable as the *odds.*

In terms still of a dichotomous variable, the odds is the ratio of p to q. That is, $p/q =$ odds. For example, recall that the overall distribution for grades was 230 with high grades, 220 with low grades, out of an overall sample of 450. This yields a value of $p = 0.511$. The odds of getting high grades is p/q $= 0.511/0.489 = 1.045$. This is interpreted as follows: overall, students are 1.045 times more likely to get high grades than they are to get low grades. Alternatively, there are 1.045 students with high grades for every 1 student with low grades. Obviously, the odds of getting high grades of 1.045 are not very significant. This reflects the fact that the distance between p and q is not very great. Odds of 1 reflects a perfect split between p and q; it means that the chances of being in one or the other group are equal. Of course, this coincides with a situation where both p and q equal 0.5. The relation between odds and probability is made even more directly apparent when one realizes that one can derive p if one knows the odds of p; the formula is: $p = $ odds/(1

+ odds). This formula is derived through simple algebraic manipulation of the expression: odds = $p/(1 + p)$.

The advantage of using odds as a dependent variable is that odds do not face the same ceiling/floor constraints that proportions do. Odds will always be positive and greater than zero. The problem with using odds as the dependent variable in a regression, however, is that we cannot logically state that the effect of an independent factor on the odds is linear or, equivalently, additive. Factors that affect the odds are *multiplicative,* not *additive.* Intuitively, this is reflected in the very manner in which we state odds. We say that one condition is *x times* more likely to occur than is another condition. Clearly, this represents a problem if we want to use odds as a way of stating a qualitative dependent variable.

This problem is done away with by taking the *logarithm* of the odds, and using this quantity in the regression analysis. The utility of the logarithm for regression analysis is that it enables us to use the odds as a dependent variable. The logarithm of the odds is called a logit. In logistic regression, we use the logits of all our subsamples as the dependent variables. Thus, in comparison with linear probability modeling, we have merely performed two transformations: (1) we state the subsample proportions as odds instead of proportions, in order to do away with the ceiling/floor constraints on proportions; and (2) we convert the observed odds into a logarithmic scale, so that we can conceive of the effects of the independent variables as being additive. The parameter estimates of the logistic model thus state the linear effect of each independent factor on the logit. The value estimated by a logistic regression model is, accordingly, a logit, i.e., the logarithm of the estimated odds of falling into one category of the dependent variable as opposed to the other. If we take the antilog of each estimated beta for the logistic model, the number we get is the multiplicative effect for the associated independent factor. As most people do not think naturally in a logarithmic scale, it is strongly recommended that any reporting of the results of a logistic regression be converted back into the multiplicative form. This enables the reader to think in terms of odds, instead of logits (see Alba, 1987, for more on this).

As an example of what to do with the parameters of a logistic regression model, we recomputed the model for the data in Table 6.1 using observed logits instead of observed proportions. The results obtained are shown in Table 6.6. (Figures related to statistical significance are not supplied here, as they are very similar to the values for our first regression, and they are of questionable value in any case.) The first values to look at are in the column of unstandardized betas. These are the parameter estimates supplied directly by the logistic regression model, and these parameters represent the additive controlled effects of each independent variable on the logit. The intercept is −0.129; the effect of being in the middle-class category adds 0.738 to this

Table 6.6. A WLS Logistic Regression of the Odds of Receiving High Grades on Social Class, Effort, and IQ (Independent Variables Effect-Coded)

Independent variable	Unstandardized beta	Antilog	1/antilog
Intercept	−0.1288	0.879	—
Social class	0.7378	2.091	0.478
Effort	0.4288	1.535	0.652
IQ	0.5654	1.760	0.568

overall mean logit. The principle of effect-coding holds true here as it did with linear probability modeling. The effect of being in the lower-class category subtracts 0.738 from the intercept. Note here the problem of interpreting these parameters in the additive form, on the logarithmic scale. What do these figures mean to the average person? We are modeling odds here. The comparison of odds is inherently multiplicative, so the parameters ought to be converted back into their odds form—i.e., back into the multiplicative version of the model—and they ought to be reported in that manner for the sake of simplicity and clarity.

Thus, we have taken the antilog of each parameter. The intercept, as you will recall, is interpreted as the overall odds of falling into the category of high grades when the value of each independent variable is set to 0. In this case it is 0.879. The multiplicative parameters for each of the independent variables represent the amount this "mean" odds is multiplied by, and they represent the multiplicative effect of each independent variable. In considering the controlled effect of social class, we can see that the estimated odds of getting high grades for social class = 1 (i.e., middle-class students) is $(0.879)(2.091) = 1.838$. We can legitimately say that being in the middle group of social class *doubles* a student's odds of being grouped in the high-grades category. In order to obtain the parameter estimated for the other category of social class, we must take the reciprocal of the estimate for social class = 1. The constraint of effect-coding under the additive model that the sum of effects for a variable must equal 0 translates under the multiplicative model into the constraint that the product of the effects for a variable must equal 1. Thus, the odds of lower-class students getting high grades is $(0.879)(0.478) = 0.420$. We note at this point that a comparison of the odds for the two groups is somewhat troublesome, and can be quite misleading. We can compute a ratio of the estimated odds for the two groups. Because $1.838/0.420 = 4.38$, we can legitimately say that the odds of middle-class students receiving high grades is about 4.4 times greater than the odds for lower-class students. Under the logistic estimates, however, the difference in terms of probability is still only 0.352. That is, in any random sample, we would expect there to be about 2.2 times as many *students* in the middle class with high grades compared to the number of students in the lower class with high grades. For this reason the comparison of odds, insofar as they are inherently relativistic, can be quite misleading. Translation back into absolute terms can be quite instructive (see Alba, 1987, pp. 49–50).

6.4.3. Summary

Thus far, we have examined two ways of manipulating the multiple regression model in order to "force it" to accommodate qualitative dependent variables and grouped data from multiway cross-tabs. We have seen how WLS estimation avoids the problem of heteroscedasticity, and how logistic regression is a method of avoiding the ceiling/floor constraints inherent with probabilities, which can cause a problem when one is analyzing a dependent variable with either a relatively small or large value for p. The advantage of these two ways of adapting multiple regression is that most researchers are familiar with regression and its assumptions. Generally, there is a software package for regression that they know how to use, and for this reason they like to stick with regression. For instance, most packages will allow weighting of the observations of the dependent variable, and one can easily obtain a WLS fit in this fashion. The transformations required to fit a logistic model are performed with similar ease with most packages. Many inexpensive calculators will compute antilogs, so the researcher can quickly derive the odds-based values for the parameters of the logistic model. Also, it is no small advantage that nothing stops the researcher from including interval- or ratio-level independent variables in the hypothesized regression model.

However, these regression-based methods of analyzing cross-tabs are not without their problems. Foremost among these problems is the matter of tests for statistical significance. At this level of measurement, the standard tests are rendered questionable, to say the least (Swafford, 1980). A better test of overall significance for a modeled crosstab would be the chi-square GOF test, or its close parallel, the maximum-likelihood ratio. Such statistics can also be employed to test the significance of individual parameters. Also, maximum-likelihood estimation, using an iterative computer algorithm, has been claimed to be superior to least-squares estimation for data of this kind (Goodman, 1971). This is where log-linear modeling comes into the picture. As mentioned earlier, log-linear analysis not only is analogous to regression in its form of linear modeling but also employs maximum-likelihood estimation and appropriate tests of statistical significance. Significance testing of parameters is doubtful with linear probability modeling and logistic regression. As well, interaction seems to be treated better in log-linear analysis, although nothing prevents a researcher from including interactions in his/her regression models.

As is usual with most matters in social science, it is always best to recall occasionally first principles. We must remember first that the purpose of using parametric multivariate analysis for cross-tabulated data is to estimate the strength of the relationship of each controlled independent factor with the dependent variable. That is the only unique contribution that parametric multivariate analysis can make. The second principle to remember is that statistical tools are meant to serve the needs of the researcher, particular research designs, and particular samples of data. No one multivariate tool that we are aware of has been demonstrated to be superior for every kind of design and every kind of problem.

CHAPTER 7

Demographic Models

7.1. INTRODUCTION TO DEMOGRAPHIC MODELS

Demographic models incorporate entities and relations that are well defined and involve certain empirical regularities. According to Coale (1988), there are two categories of demographic models. The first is a set of relations that are tautologically appropriate to the basic subject matter of demography. The latter involves populations, collectivities which increase or decrease by the entry or the exit of members. At each moment, each member of the population has a specific age, and the events or risks that determine entry or exit vary with age. Suitable collectives for study include conventionally defined populations subject to birth, death, and migration, and also the set of currently married couples (age in this regard becomes duration of marriage), postoperative patients, and so forth.

The second category of demographic models is an expression (mathematical or merely tabular) of the frequency of events or the intensity of risks in a population as a function of age. These models express such variables as mortality rates, rates of childbearing, and rates of entry into first marriage, as functions of age, and require the specification of only a few parameters to obtain a full schedule of rates. Other classes of models are also found in the scientific literature, e.g., normative models and descriptive models. A normative model's main focus would be what, under certain precise conditions, may not be realistic. Descriptive models emphasize the replay of reality as closely as possible. The most usual and important measure of fertility, the Total Fertility Rate, is an example of a normative model, based on the concept of a synthetic cohort. The Total Fertility Rate and other normative measures tend to be misinterpreted as real, due to their heavy use by demographers. The other normative measures include life expectancy at birth, net reproduction rate, and most population projection models.

Descriptions of age structure, age patterns of mortality, fertility, and nuptiality are some of the preoccupations of descriptive models. These descriptive models are similar to those mentioned earlier under the second category, based on the empirical regularities observed in several populations. An example of this would be age patterns of mortality—very high during infancy, dropping to lower and lower levels during the adulthood years, and rising gradually as one ages, reaching a peak at old ages.

7.2. WHY WE NEED MODELS

Demography is known for its models, and demographers use modeling as a tool for several different purposes. First and foremost, demographic models are used to smooth questionable data. For example, the majority of the developing countries do not have reliable registration systems. Often, age distributions reported in censuses and surveys show heavy clustering at numbers ending in 5 or 0. The ASDRs (age-specific death rates) obtained may be irregular, perhaps due to such clustering rather than a genuinely peculiar pattern. Models can help smooth such data and thus produce better estimates.

Models are also used to describe some aspects of fertility, mortality, and other demographic processes. For example, if model life tables adequately represent the mortality situation in a country, the parameters of the model reveal several interesting features of the country in question. Often, the data are available in 5-year intervals. For example, ASDRs are recorded in 5-year intervals, and we may like to obtain single-year rates. One way is to identify a model for the 5-year rates and, using this model, generate single-year rates. Similarly, fertility models are used to generate a complete set of reliable rates from the few trustworthy points of data.

Simulation is another use of models to examine various policy implications on the overall growth and structure of the population. For example, Greenhalgh and Bongaarts (1987) examined various alternatives to achieve the same total population for China. Models are also helpful in developing research concerning possible effects of specific levels and changes of demographic determinants. More discussion of models and their uses and problems can be found in the introductory chapter of the United Nations Manual X (1983).

7.3. INTRODUCTION TO SURVIVAL ANALYSIS

The study of any sociological phenomenon can be undertaken either in terms of structure or in terms of process, depending upon the nature of the problem. In recent times there has been a greater interest among social scientists on the study of processes, especially those that are continuous. This was at least partly due to the development of new methodologies in the early 1970s such as the Proportional Hazards model (Cox, 1972) and other survival models. Since then, in the area of nuptiality and fertility, investigators have amply demonstrated the benefits of survival analysis in the study of nonrenewable events such as first marriage formation, first marriage dissolution, first birth timing, and so forth (Rodriguez and Hobcraft, 1980; Smith, 1980; Teachman, 1982; Rao, 1988c, 1989a, 1989b; Rao and Balakrishnan, 1989; Balakrishnan *et al.,* 1987). This chapter introduces some simple survival models, and brings together the material on the concepts and relations between various functions used to describe the processes. Also, simple life table techniques followed by application of the Proportional Hazards model to a demographic phenomenon are provided for clarification of the method.

The data used in survival analysis are sometimes called *event histories* (Tuma *et al.,* 1979), though other terms such as *failure time data* and *survival data* are not uncommon in the literature. We use the terms *survival times* and *failure times* interchangeably. In the analysis of mortality, for example, the failure time is the age at death and the survival time is the length of life, which of course is the same as age at death. Most cross-sectional surveys collect information retrospectively on various life course events. Like the World Fertility Survey (WFS), many fertility surveys collect retrospective data on the number, timing, and sequencing of events as they occur in time. These data can be efficiently analyzed using survival models.

There are two major problems associated with the analysis of retrospective histories collected in cross-sectional surveys, namely, censoring and selectivity. Censoring is caused by the incomplete experience of the event studied (see Chapter 2).

The problem of selectivity arises due to the fact that the sample selection criteria impose restraints on the group of women in the sample. In the example of age at first birth, the older cohorts may have had births at all ages (i.e., throughout the reproductive span) while the younger cohorts may only have had them at younger ages (only a part of the reproductive span). Also, the timing of first birth varies a great deal as young women generally give birth more recently than older women who may have first given birth as far back as 20 years prior to the survey time. Another example is the proportion of the population progressing from ith parity to $(i + 1)$th parity. In this study the sample is restricted to those women who had the ith child by survey time. Thus, we are left with a select group of women, who may not form a valid probability sample of the population for the study of $(i + 1)$th parity. Selectivity also arises due to the different relationships of various socioeconomic and demographic characteristics on the timing of first birth. For example, premarital conception or birth is associated with young age at first birth, while higher education and labor force participation tend to be associated with higher age at first birth. One strategy for overcoming this problem is to select subgroups of women with a specific set of characteristics and carry out a separate analysis for each group. However, this process will reduce the sample size quickly. The development of the Proportional Hazards model combining life table and regression analysis in a multivariate context allows one to overcome this problem to some extent. The following sections briefly outline the important functions, relations, and applications of survival models.

7.3.1. Terminology in Survival Analysis

Let T be a nonnegative random variable, denoting the failure time of an individual, and let us suppose that T is described by a continuous distribution. The failure time T need not be real age (as it would be in the case of mortality data), but generally it is the time elapsed between two specified nonrenewable events, the second event being failure. Let us consider an example—analysis of marriage dissolution—and let T denote the time elapsed between the age at first marriage and the age at first marriage dissolution. The time elapsed is also called exposure time to failure. The failure time T can be described generally by using three functions, namely, the probability density function (PDF), the survival functions (SF), and the hazard function (HF). These three functions are interrelated, and knowing any one of them allows one to derive the other two.

The PDF describes the probability that an event occurs during the time interval $(t, t + \Delta t)$ and is given by:

$$f(t) = \lim_{\Delta t \to 0} \frac{\Pr(t \le T < t + \Delta t)}{\Delta t} \tag{7.1}$$

and

$$\int_0^\infty f(t)dt = 1 \tag{7.2}$$

By definition, $f(t)$ is an absolute instantaneous rate of failure. Thus, $f(t)$ is not a probability, but for any small quantity Δt, the approximation $f(t) \Delta t = \Pr\{t \le T \le t + \Delta t\}$ is valid and one can thus interpret $f(t) \cdot \Delta t$ as the probability that failure occurs in the small interval $(t, t + \Delta t)$. The PDF is also called the frequency function or the unconditional failure rate. In the example of first marriage dissolution, $f(t)$ can be interpreted as the unconditional probability that a person will get divorced at time t after first marriage.

The second function in the survival analysis is the survival distribution function or survival function (SF) and is defined as the probability of surviving to at least time t, $t > 0$, and is given by

$$S(t) = \Pr(T \geq t) \qquad 0 < t < \infty$$

$$= \int_t^\infty f(t)dt \tag{7.3}$$

In our example of the process of marriage dissolution, $S(t)$ indicates the probability that a person experiences at least t years of stable first marriage. Note that $S(t)$ is a nonincreasing function with $S(0) = 1$ and $S(\infty) = 0$.

The third function is the hazard function (HF), also known as force of mortality in the demographic literature and popularly denoted by $\mu(x)$. In survival analyses and biomedical literature, the HF is most commonly denoted by $\lambda(x)$. We will use the latter notation in this chapter. The HF is also known as the conditional failure rate or instantaneous (relative) failure rate at time point t and is defined as

$$\lambda(t) = \lim_{\Delta t \to 0} \frac{\Pr(t \leq T < t + \Delta t \mid T \geq t)}{\Delta t} \tag{7.4}$$

or in other words $\lambda(t)\Delta(t)$ is the conditional probability that an individual experiences the event in the time interval $t \leq T < t + \Delta t$, given that no event occurs prior to time t. This interpretation is similar to that of $f(t) \cdot \Delta t$; however, $f(t) \cdot \Delta t$ is an unconditional probability whereas $\lambda(t)$ is a conditional probability. In our example of marriage dissolution, the HF represents the probability of experiencing marriage dissolution in the interval $(t, t + \Delta t)$, given that the person survived till time t. One can derive functions such as the cumulative distribution function, the cumulative hazard function, and others from the three basic functions discussed above.

7.4. RELATIONS BETWEEN FUNCTIONS

As indicated earlier, the distribution of failure time T can be described by just one of the above functions. In other words, knowing any one of them allows one to compute the other two using the mathematical relationships that exist among the functions. Suppose one estimates the survival function; the other functions can be derived by using the following relations:

$$\lambda(t) = \frac{-d \ln S(t)}{dt}$$

$$f(t) = \frac{-dS(t)}{dt} \tag{7.5}$$

Similarly, if one estimates the HF $\lambda(t)$, the other two can be derived by using the following relations:

$$S(t) = e - \int_0^t \lambda(u)du$$

$$f(t) = \lambda(t)S(t)$$

(7.6)

The above three key functions used in survival analysis uniquely describe any specific distribution of events over time, each providing a different view of the data. Plotting of the HF indicates the shape of the risk to which the population being studied is exposed as a function of time. A monotonically increasing HF represents positive aging while a monotonically decreasing function indicates negative aging. HFs are more distinct than PDF or SF and therefore are more useful in describing specific survival processes (Gehan, 1969; Gross and Clark, 1975).

7.5. DATA REQUIREMENTS

In event history analysis, researchers often come across two types of data on a time scale. One set of data are complete in all respects, i.e., uncensored. In the example of marriage dissolution, data of this type contain complete follow-up of all women till their marriage is dissolved by death or divorce. Survival analysis with such data is simple. One can adopt either nonparametric or parametric methods to estimate the SF and other relevant functions from such a sample. Using a parametric model for estimation assumes prior knowledge of the distributional form of the SF which is not often possible in demographic applications, an exception being the case of mortality. In general, however, the data available are censored. Censored data arise from the cross-sectional surveys (in demographic applications) or by termination of an experiment or even due to loss of follow-up (in clinical studies). Essentially censored data contain partial information on failure time. In such cases we know only that an individual has not experienced the event when last observed. One of the major contributions of survival analysis is its ability to deal with censored observations.

In survival literature, one can find a variety of names and types of censoring. Particularly in engineering applications, one is often interested in testing the efficiency of a particular process either by observing a prespecified elapsed time or by stopping the experiment after a prespecified fraction of failures. In literature, the first type is called Type 1 censoring and the second Type 2 censoring. But in failure time applications in the social sciences and biostatistics, one is faced with a different kind of censoring. In these applications, we almost always assume random censoring. Random censoring can occur in a variety of ways. For example, censoring may occur due to loss of follow-

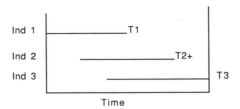

Figure 7.1. Failure and censoring intervals.

up in longitudinal studies, or due to dropout from the study in a clinical trial, and/or due to termination of study. In all of the above cases, we only know that the lifetime of those individuals is greater.

In Figure 7.1, $T1$ is the time of failure for individual 1, and $T2$ and $T3$ are the indicators of censoring times for individual 2 and 3, respectively. In our example of marriage dissolution, the first individual entered the study at time "0" (i.e., age at first marriage) and obtained divorce at time $T1$, thus providing complete information about the process. However, the other two individuals in our example were still in marriage when last observed and thus the information from them is incomplete for the study of process. (In the literature, one finds the word *withdrawn,* meaning withdrawn from the study at the time of survey.) Detailed examples on right and left censorship can be found in Smith (1991).

To apply survival models, we need the following minimum information:

1. Date of entry
2. Date of event, if any
3. Date of cutoff (generally the survey date)

The cutoff date is needed even for those experiencing the event, if data are grouped. Otherwise we would not know if events occurred in closed or open intervals, and could use only actuarial estimates for survival.

The time elapsed can be expressed in days, months, or years depending on data availability and detail required. Too elaborate and too broad time units are not recommended. Usually, where available, month is a good time unit to employ.

7.6. ESTIMATION OF FUNCTIONS

The three functions used in survival analysis, survival, hazard, and probability density function, can be estimated by adopting either parametric or nonparametric methods. In practice, SF is estimated as the proportion of individuals surviving longer than time t, assuming no censoring. In some types of data, the survival time is recorded in intervals like $(t, t + 1)$, making it impossible to study the exact failure times. In the presence of censoring and no prior information about the distributional form of SF, simple nonparametric methods are suggested. There are three such methods widely used in the literature, i.e., Actuarial method, Curtate* (anniversary) method, and Product Limit estimate or Kaplan–Meier method (Kaplan and Meier, 1958). Construction of nonparametric estimates of the SF can be seen as a first step before proceeding to parametric models for survival analysis. As indicated earlier, in a complete data set (i.e., no censored cases), the estimation of the SF and, thus, other functions is straightforward and is not discussed here. In the following section, a brief review of the actuarial, curtate, and product limit estimation methods for censored data is provided.

The actuarial method assumes that data are grouped into n number of intervals, with width b_i. Generally the width of the intervals will be equal, but one can use unequal widths without much computational difficulty. The derivation of formulas for various functions can be arrived at by considering a case in the specified interval (say, ith interval) (t_i to t_{i+1}). Let us suppose c_i censored times, and d_i failure times in this interval. The number of individuals entering at the beginning of the ith interval is equal to the number of individuals present at the beginning of the $(i - 1)$th interval minus those lost due to censoring, or experience of the event in the $(i - 1)$th interval. The actual number exposed to the risk of experiencing the event in the ith interval r_i is estimated assuming uniform distribution of failure and censored times in the unit interval, i.e., $r_i = n_i - 0.5 c_i$. The estimated conditional probability of experiencing the event in the ith interval, given that a particular individual survived at the beginning of the ith interval, is given by $q_i = d_i/r_i$ where r_i and d_i are as defined above. The conditional probability of surviving is the reciprocal of the conditional probability of failure, i.e., $p_i = 1 - q_i$. The estimation of the SF at the end of the ith interval is given by:

$$S(t_i) = \prod_{k=1}^{i} P_k \tag{7.7}$$

The HF and the PDF are usually estimated at the midpoint of the interval. The PDF is the probability of dying in the ith interval, per unit width, and is estimated at the midpoint of the small interval. Let us denote m_i as the midpoint of the ith interval and the PDF is estimated as:

---

* The term *curtate* has been introduced by Smith (1991).

$$f(t_{mi}) = \frac{S(t_i) - S(t_i + 1)}{b_i} \tag{7.8}$$

The third function, the HF, is also estimated at the midpoint of the interval and is the number of failures per unit time in the interval divided by the average number of survivors at the midpoint of the interval. The HF in the actuarial method is given by

$$\lambda(t_{mi}) = \frac{2q_i}{b_i(2 - q_i)} \tag{7.9}$$

The actuarial method is used when at least some events cannot be placed in the closed or open interval with certainty. It is the only formula available for studies in which the event is death and unscheduled losses to follow-up have occurred, since it allows the researcher to treat all deaths as belonging to closed intervals. In such a case the possibility arises that some of those dying *would have been lost later in the interval,* just as some of the living were. Hence, the censored subset includes known live withdrawals and possibly, but unidentifiable, some deaths.

Where the researcher has a choice, the actuarial method is not particularly attractive since it imputes a higher survival probability to the unobserved part of the interval than to the observed part. A constant hazard, or for general mortality an increasing hazard, is usually more appropriate. Except in the above circumstance, the curtate estimator is to be preferred.

The curtate estimator is a maximum-likelihood estimator and Fischer consistent (see Smith, 1991). The curtate estimator for a sample that includes censored and uncensored observation may be expressed as:

$$_nq_{x, \text{curtate}} = \frac{(_nD_x - _nD_{c, x})}{N(x) - N_c(x)} \tag{7.10}$$

where subscript c refers to an observation in an open (censored) interval, and

$N(x)$ = complete sample
$_nD_x$ = complete events (uncensored)
$N_c(x)$ = censored subset of $N(x)$
$_nD_{c, x}$ = events to censored subset

Detailed illustration of the curtate method to calculate survival probabilities by using expression (7.10) can be found in Smith (1991). The third method considered for estimation of survival probability in the presence of censoring is the product limit (PL) method (or Kaplan–Meier method) and the estimation procedure is discussed in the following section.

The PL estimation method developed by Kaplan and Meier (1958) to estimate the SF assumes that the exact times of failure or censoring are available for each individual at the survey time. The PL estimation uses the ordered observations instead of grouped data. It is the usual practice to treat censoring as occurring slightly after failure when a tie situation arises. Let n be the total number of individuals whose survival times are available either through censoring or through experiencing the event before the survey time. Let these n survival times be arranged in ascending order such that $t_{(1)} \leq t_{(2)} \leq t_{(3)} \cdots \leq t_{(n)}$. Then, the PL estimate of the SF is given by:

$$S(t) = \prod_{t(r) \leq t} \frac{n - r}{n - r + 1} \tag{7.11}$$

where the values of r are consecutive integers, and when there are no censored observations. The formula can easily be modified to include censored data. Let w be integers counting ordered raw data, then the function becomes:

$$S(t) = \prod_{t(r)t(w) < t} \frac{n - r - w}{n - r - w + 1} \tag{7.12}$$

The variance of the PL estimate of $S(t)$ is approximated by:

$$\text{Var}[S(t)] = [S(t)]^2 \sum_r \frac{1}{(n - r)(n - r + 1)} \tag{7.13}$$

Using the actuarial estimate for the same data constructed with very fine intervals such that no one interval contains both censored and failure time cases, the survival estimate obtained will be the same as that from the PL method. In other words, the actuarial estimate is in effect a PL estimate. The two methods differ more when one uses large intervals and/or there is heavy censoring. In such cases the basic assumption of a uniform distribution of events in arriving at the actuarial estimate does not hold. The bias is expected to be small if the total number of individuals exposed to the risk is large compared to those censored or failing in a particular interval. The PL estimate is recommended for small samples and, obviously, the curtate method is preferred when one has a substantial sample size with the exception noted above, wherein the actuarial method would be preferred. Unfortunately, the widely available computer software packages use the actuarial method (SPSS) and the PL method (BMDP, SAS) (see our comments in a later section).

7.7. COMPUTATIONAL ASPECTS

There are several software packages that generate a "simple life table" either from the actual data on time and the status variable, or from the age-specific rates. The SURVIVAL program in SPSS, BMDP1L in BMDP, and LIFETEST in SAS are three popularly employed packages for obtaining simple life table analysis. All three packages listed above assume the actuarial method for computing survival probabilities with the exception of the BMDP and SAS programs where an option allows one to specify the estimation procedure—actuarial method or Kaplan–Meier. More information on the input and output from all three packages is provided at the end of this chapter.

7.8. THE PROPORTIONAL HAZARDS MODEL

The single state survival models discussed in the above section help to identify important covariates of failure times. However, these models do not allow one to observe the covariate effects on failure time in a multivariate context. Sometimes a situation arises where a covariate seems important, but ceases to be significant when other covariates are introduced into the model. One way to deal with this situation is to select the group of women with the chosen characteristics and estimate the SF and other functions. However, this procedure, generally, greatly reduces the sample size and makes the estimates unstable. Besides, the interpretation of a large number of life tables based on small numbers becomes problematic, particularly when there are many potential covariates. The proportional hazards model introduced by Cox in 1972 was a major attempt to overcome the above problems. An excellent discussion of the model exists in the literature and so only the essential elements of the model will be outlined here (Cox, 1972; Breslow, 1974; Holford, 1976; Lagakos, 1981; Kalbfleisch and Prentice, 1980). Briefly, the proportional hazards model, a special case of the more general survival models, combines aspects of the life table and regression. Thus, the model allows the formulation of relations between a set of covariates and the SF, as in conventional multiple regression. Though the model looks parametric, it is basically nonparametric in the sense that the baseline HF is arbitrary and has an unspecified functional form. Let $\lambda(t; z)$ denote the HF at time t for an individual with the characteristics represented by the covariate vector z. The covariates can be either discrete or continuous, but some widely available computer software packages can only handle discrete covariates. The proportional hazards model, specified by hazard relationships, is given by:

$$\lambda(t; z) = \lambda_0(t) \cdot \exp(z \cdot \beta) \qquad (7.14)$$

where $\lambda_0(t)$ is an arbitrary unspecified baseline HF for continuous time t and β is a vector of parameters. The estimation of β depends only on the rank ordering of the dependent variable vector z and is invariant with respect to the monotonic transformation on the dependent variable, i.e., survival time. The HF $\lambda(t)$ is a product of an underlying age-dependent risk $\lambda_0(t)$ (baseline HF) and another factor $\exp(z \cdot \beta)$ that depends on the covariates. The baseline HF represents the HF for an individual whose covariate categories have the value zero. The HF allows us to estimate the risks of other groups in relation to the baseline group. Other specifications of the hazards relationship are possible, e.g., $\lambda(t; z) = \lambda_0(t) + z \cdot \beta$. The problem with this relationship is the possibility of predicting negative hazard rates and one therefore needs to impose extra conditions on the estimation procedure to ensure positive hazard throughout. By assuming the relation $\exp(z \cdot \beta)$, given by Cox (1972), the model becomes partially parametric and positive values of hazard are ensured. The proportional hazards model derives its name from the relationship that exists between the HFs for two individuals and the proportionality factor depends on the explanatory variables introduced into the model. In other words, the ratio of the HFs for two individuals $\lambda(z_1)/\lambda(z_2)$ is constant in time.

Another closely related function, the SF, allows us to estimate the probabilities of surviving at various ages for various characteristics of women. The SF in Cox's model with covariate vector z is derived in terms of baseline SF when $z = 0$ and is given by:

$$S(t; z) = [S_0(t)]\exp(\beta z) \qquad (7.15)$$

where $S_0(t)$ is the baseline survivorship function representing the default categories of the covariates. Using the model and the relation between the baseline SF and the SF of the model, one can compute the survivorship probabilities for various groups of women.*

The PDF in the proportional hazards model is given by:

$$f(t; z) = \lambda(t; z)S(t; z) \qquad (7.16)$$

---

* The BMDP program (BMDP2L) for the Cox model provides the estimate of the survival function evaluated at $z = z$ bar and this information can be used in the calculation of baseline survival function. Similarly, the SAS (PHGLM) program provides the estimated survival probability for the entire survival function along with $z \cdot \beta$, hazard, and minus log minus survival as optional output. These estimates are based on a final regression model as specified above and one can use them to test proportionality, and to identify the nature of survival function. Thus, the SAS program is very flexible, and the user has control over the output.

where $\lambda(t; z)$ and $S(t; z)$ are the HF and the survivorship function, respectively. In terms of the HF, one can write the PDF as follows:

$$f(t; z) = \lambda_0(t) \cdot e^{z\beta} \exp[-e^{z\beta} \int_0^t \lambda_0(u)du] \tag{7.17}$$

The vector of parameters β can be estimated by using the method of partial likelihood suggested by Cox (1975). The method involves arranging the data as required for the product limit estimation method. Let $R(t_i)$ be the set of individuals at risk to the event at time t_i. The conditional probability that an individual i experiences an event at time t_i given that the set of individuals $R(t_i)$ are at risk and that exactly one failure occurs at t_i is given by

$$\frac{\lambda(t_i; z_i)}{\sum_{i \in R(t_i)} \lambda(t_i; z_i)} = \frac{\exp(z_i\beta)}{\sum_{i \in R(t_i)} \exp(z_i\beta)} \tag{7.18}$$

for $i = 1, 2, \ldots, k$. Since $\lambda_0(t)$ is completely unspecified under the proportional hazards model, no additional information about β is obtained from a surviving individual in $(t_{(i-1)}, t_{(i)})$ $(i = 1, 2, \ldots, k)$. If one had information as to the parametric form of the baseline HF, there would be a contribution to the inferences about β from surviving individuals. The method of partial likelihood was proposed by Cox (1972, 1975) to derive estimates of β. It has been shown that the method of maximum likelihood gives essentially equivalent estimates to those given by the method of partial likelihood (Kalbfleisch and Prentice, 1980). The partial likelihood is derived by taking the product over all failure time points t_i, giving:

$$L(\beta) = \prod_{i=1}^{k} \frac{\exp(z_i\beta)}{\sum_{i \in R(t_i)} \exp(z_i\beta)} \tag{7.19}$$

The likelihood given above is not a likelihood in the usual sense, meaning that the general construction does not give a result that is proportional to the conditional or marginal probability of any observed event. However, Cox has shown informally that the method used to construct this estimate of likelihood gives maximum *partial likelihood* estimates. Thus, the asymptotic results for β hold for estimation from partial likelihood as well as from the usual likelihood function. The partial likelihood given above assumes no ties in the data between event times and censorship times. However, generalizations from such a data set are available (Kalbfleisch and Prentice, 1980). Maximizing L or its logarithm requires an iterative procedure such as the Newton–Raphson procedure. There are several other methods for the derivation of likelihoods and a detailed discussion of the merits of these methods can be found elsewhere (Kalbfleisch and Prentice, 1980). To test nested models (see Chapter 6 for a detailed discussion on these), one can use the likelihood ratio tests or other nonparametric tests, such as the Wald test. For individual β coefficients, tests may be constructed using the asymptotic covariance matrix which is estimated by the inverse of the matrix of second partial derivatives of the log likelihood. Also one can construct a conventional t statistic by dividing the coefficient by its standard error and test for significance.

7.8.1. Testing Assumptions

The proportional hazards model requires that the HFs for any two covariate sets z_1 and z_2 be related by $\lambda(t; z_1) < \lambda(t; z_2)$, $0 < t < \infty$. In some demographic applications, different levels of a covariate may produce HFs markedly different. Kay (1977) has proposed an inspection procedure for testing the proportionality assumption which is based on the log minus log SF versus time. For any two survivorship curves, these log minus log plots should be at least roughly parallel. However, this procedure requires continuous variables to be categorized. The graphical method is not entirely satisfactory because nonparallelism of graphs may be due to sampling fluctuations.

Schoenfeld (1980) developed a computationally simple test based on partial residuals of the model. These residuals are the components of the first derivative of the log likelihood function with respect to regression parameters β, computed separately at each risk set or unique failure time. A test based on the linear correlation between the residuals and rank order of the failure time seems to have reasonable power when the hazard ratio is monotonic in time.

The test statistic is a normal deviate calculated as $Z = \sqrt{n_u - 2} / \sqrt{1 - r^2}$ where r is the correlation between residual and failure time order and n_u is the total number of uncensored observations. In the case of tied failure times, the residual is taken as the total component of the first derivative derived by the number of tied failure times at the corresponding risk set and the r is weighted by the number of tied times.

Some care is required in selecting the baseline category of various covariates included in the model. McDonald (1981) suggests as a general rule category with a relatively large number of cases as baseline category to minimize standard errors of the estimates. If the researcher feels a particular category is needed for a baseline category for comparative purposes, one may ignore this general rule.

Another assumption made in the use of the proportional hazards model concerns heterogeneity. The model assumes that heterogeneity in the population under study is captured by a set of covariates included in the model.

However, it is possible that heterogeneity may not have been captured by any or all of the covariates included in the model and thus heterogeneity may remain. Trussell and Richards (1985) caution the users that failure to correct for unmeasured heterogeneity can lead to bias in the parameter estimates and the estimated hazard may decline more steeply (or rise more slowly) than the true hazard. Assuming a parametric form with prior knowledge of the hazard may help overcome this problem to some extent as shown by the authors. For example, they have arrived at identical estimates of parameters with Weibull and nonparametric hazards for child mortality without correcting for heterogeneity. Correcting for heterogeneity on the lines suggested by Heckman and Singer (1984a,b) is not entirely satisfactory, and research on this aspect is still in progress.

7.9. HAZARD MODELS WITH TIME-DEPENDENT COVARIATES

In the discussion above, we focused on time constant covariates (or fixed covariates) for the proportional hazards model. However, there may be occasions in demography where we cannot assume that the effects of the covariates are fixed throughout the period over which events (such as marriage dissolutions, first births) can occur. For example, living arrangements during the childhood years and parental education are fixed covariates whereas variables that represent current characteristics can vary across time or change prior to the event (marriage dissolution). Even if personal characteristics do not change over time, their effects on the risk of experiencing the event of interest may change depending on the age and period. For example, consider the effect of educational attainment on marriage dissolution. Two individuals with the same educational level (e.g., high school diploma) but at different ages (e.g., 24 and 44) may experience different risks of marriage dissolution. A simple analogy would be the value of a dollar, which was not the same in 1984 as in 1989, in terms of its purchasing power.

It is desirable to examine those variables representing current characteristics as time-dependent covariates, i.e., letting the effects of these covariates depend on time. When we introduce a time-dependent covariate into the model, it is no longer a proportional hazards model, but simply a hazards model. The proportionality assumption involved in the proportional hazards model is no longer required. The beta coefficient is no longer fixed, but will vary over time. The HF which includes both time-dependent and time-independent covariates (a general form) is:

$$\lambda[t; Z(t)] = \lambda_0(t) \exp\{\beta Z(t)\} \qquad (7.20)$$

where $Z(t)$ is a covariate vector consisting of both time-constant and time-dependent covariates. The time-dependent covariates take a different value at each time t. This model can be estimated using the BMDP2L program with function paragraph, or by employing specialized packages, such as RATE.

7.10. SUMMARY

This chapter began with an introduction to survival models and their application to the study of social processes. A critique of the problems associated with the analysis of retrospective data collected in surveys was provided to give an appreciation of the use of survival models. The problems of selectivity and censoring were discussed at some length. The basic terminology used in survival analysis literature was laid out before discussing various functions and their relations. Three important estimation methods, the actuarial method, the curtate (or anniversary) method, and the product limit method, were discussed.

After having discussed the three methods for survival estimation, the proportional hazards model was introduced. The relationship between the baseline hazard and the model hazard was laid out. The underlying assumptions of the proportional hazards model were discussed along with various testing procedures available in standard computer software packages. The estimation of the model is based on the partial likelihood given by Cox (1972) and Kalbfleisch and Prentice (1980). Maximization of the likelihood through a suitable iterative procedure allows one to test the significance using large sample tests, i.e., likelihood ratio tests, and other nonparametric tests.

In sum, this chapter examined the family of survival models (nonparametric) for the event history analysis. In the next chapter, we will introduce some parametric survival models and their role in demographic analysis.

7.11. APPENDIX A.1: DETAILED APPLICATION TO AGE AT FIRST MARRIAGE

In this section we illustrate the application of survival models with age at first marriage as an example. The data used in the study are from the 1984 Canadian Fertility Survey (CFS). Some of the other applications using life table and the proportional hazards model can be found in the literature (Trussell and Bloom, 1983; Rao, 1987b, 1989a, 1989b; Rao and Balakrishnan, 1989).

The first part analysis involves application of simple survival analysis to age at first marriage for selected birth cohorts. In essence, we will be constructing several life tables, one for each covariate category. We discuss the results obtained from the life table method for each covariate category. This is accomplished by comparing the cumulative probability of experiencing the event at selected ages. In the second part, we identify the covariates of age at first marriage in Canada with the help of the proportional hazards model. The covariates considered include place of residence (with two categories, urban and other), education (with three categories, less than grade 12, grade 12–13, and grade 14 plus), work status before marriage (with two categories, worked before marriage, and not worked before marriage), birth status (with three categories, premarital birth, premarital conception, and neither), and religion (with two categories, Catholic, and other). Discussion is provided on relative risks for various groups and identification of higher and lower risk groups for first marriage in Canada.

Though the CFS sample consists of women in the age range 18–49, our study will be based only on all women in the ages 20–49. We excluded the 18- and 19-year-old women due to the very short time available for them to experience first marriage, our interest in this example. Only legal marriages are considered for the purpose of our analysis. Cohabitation and other living arrangements are treated as never married. The detailed methodology of the survey has been provided elsewhere and is not our immediate concern.

7.12. APPENDIX A.2: DISCUSSION OF RESULTS

Table 7.1 displays the cumulative probability of first marriage for the birth cohort (1945–49) by various covariate categories considered. The cumulative probability of first marriage is given at ages 15, 17, 19, 20, 22, 24, 30, and 35. In general, life tables based on below 50 cases are not reliable and thus one should be cautious in interpreting the estimated probabilities. The probability of first marriage at age 17 varies from 0.01 for college or more educated women, to 0.11 for women who were not in the active labor force before marriage. More than 90% of women born during 1945–49 were married by age 35, irrespective of their characteristics. However, we find differences between urban and other place of residence, educational groups, religious categories, and by birth status, up to age 24. The BMDP and SPSS programs allow us to test for significance of these differences.

The CALCULATE subcommand in SPSS with the COMPARE option should be used for comparing covariate categories and for testing their statistical significance. Unfortunately, producing life tables (for presenting cumulative probabilities, as in Table 7.1) and the comparison of groups cannot be obtained in one run, as they are mutually exclusive options in SPSS.

Table 7.2 displays the proportional hazards coefficients in their expo-

Table 7.1. Actuarial Method Estimates of Cumulative Probability of First Marriage (1945–49 Birth Cohort, Canadian Fertility Survey, 1984)

Covariate	15	17	19	20	22	24	30	35	Sample
Place of residence									
Urban	0.00	0.03	0.11	0.20	0.45	0.67	0.89	0.93	542
Other	0.00	0.04	0.18	0.32	0.63	0.80	0.94	0.95	355
Education									
<Grade 12	0.01	0.07	0.27	0.42	0.68	0.81	0.94	0.96	303
≥Grade 12, 13	0.00	0.02	0.11	0.23	0.55	0.78	0.93	0.95	291
Grade 14+	0.00	0.01	0.03	0.08	0.32	0.59	0.86	0.91	302
Work status									
Worked before	0.00	0.01	0.03	0.08	0.32	0.59	0.86	0.91	302
No work	0.02	0.11	0.29	0.42	0.69	0.90	0.97	0.99	234
Birth status									
Premarital birth	0.00	0.04	0.17	0.24	0.48	0.61	0.93	—	54
Premarital conception	0.00	0.06	0.33	0.48	0.85	0.92	0.99	—	89
Neither	0.01	0.03	0.11	0.22	0.48	0.71	0.90	0.93	754
Religion									
Catholic	0.01	0.03	0.11	0.22	0.49	0.70	0.91	0.93	444
Other	0.00	0.04	0.16	0.28	0.56	0.74	0.92	0.95	453

nential form for age at first marriage in Canada by age cohort. A coefficient of 1.00 in Table 7.2 indicates that the variable category in question has the same impact as for the reference group on first marriage timing. This interpretation of the coefficient is valid only when we have categorical variables or continuous variables divided into categories. The program automatically sets 1.00 for the baseline group categories. The comparisons made here are with respect to the baseline group. A coefficient of value higher than one indicates higher risk for the event under study. For example, in Table 7.2, women of urban residence always have a coefficient lower than 1.00, indicating that these women are less likely to marry than their rural/small town counterparts in all birth cohorts. In particular, women residing in other places of residence in the birth cohort 1955–59 have a 33% higher chance of being married compared to urban women of the same age. These trends are consistent with the earlier finding of Grenier *et al.* (1987) using Canadian census data.

Another important and significant covariate of first marriage is education. Women with grade 14 or higher education have lower risk of first marriage compared to those with less than grade 12 education. This is true for all birth cohorts. But these differences are greatest for younger cohorts. Women belonging to the 1960–64 birth cohort with grade 14 or more education have a 45% lower chance of being married than those with grade 11 or lower edu-

Table 7.2. Estimated Relative Risks from the Proportional Hazards Model for Age at First Marriage, Canadian Fertility Survey, 1984

	Birth cohort					
Covariate	1935–39	1940–44	1945–49	1950–54	1955–59	1960–64
Place of residence						
Urban	0.757*	0.823*	0.763*	0.769*	0.672*	0.823
Other	1.000	1.000	1.000	1.000	1.000	1.000
Education						
<Grade 12	1.229	1.084*	1.211*	1.214*	0.950	1.223
≥Grade 12, 13	1.000	1.000	1.000	1.000	1.000	1.000
Grade 14+	0.693*	0.662*	0.663*	0.604*	0.591*	0.553*
Work status						
Worked before	0.617*	0.498*	0.544*	0.451*	0.463*	0.661*
No work	1.000	1.000	1.000	1.000	1.000	1.000
Birth status						
Premarital birth	0.379*	0.426*	0.421*	0.460*	0.617*	0.652*
Premarital conception	1.000	1.000	1.000	1.000	1.000	1.000
Neither	0.689*	0.583*	0.522*	0.474*	0.447*	0.129*
Religion						
Catholic	0.687*	0.765*	0.798*	0.855*	0.872*	0.887
Other	1.000	1.000	1.000	1.000	1.000	1.000
$-2 \ln L$	5241	6125	9928	11008	10739	4543
Model χ^2	85*	118*	187*	265*	256*	220*
Sample size	516	590	897	1029	1114	949

* Significant at 5% level.

cation. These trends confirm our earlier findings from single life table analysis presented in Table 7.1.

We considered religion, with two categories Catholic and other, as a covariate for age at first marriage. The study of first marriage by Grenier *et al.* (1987) with census data found that Catholics tend to have a lower mean age at marriage compared to other religious groups in 1981. Our present study with CFS data confirms their earlier finding in this regard, with a different method of analysis. Religion is found to be significant for all birth cohorts except the 1960–64 birth cohort. However, Catholics tend to have lower risks of first marriage for all birth cohorts than do other religious denominations.

The next important covariate included in the model is work status, with two categories, worked and not worked before first marriage. As expected from the earlier analysis, women having premarital work experience have a lower risk of first marriage. Work status is significant for the younger cohorts, born after 1945. This shows that young women who are actively participating in the labor force are postponing their marriages or even foregoing marriage.

Grenier *et al.* analyzing the first marriage patterns using census data conclude that the change in nuptiality patterns is not so much in increasing age at marriage, but in the proportion who eventually get married. Our earlier analysis with the Coale–McNeil model seems to confirm their view in this regard.

The results in Table 7.2 allow us to identify high- and low-risk groups of women for first marriage for various age cohorts. Women with lower education, non-Catholic, no premarital work, and residing in rural areas or small towns are more likely to marry early than women with urban residence, grade 14 or more education, Catholic, and who worked before marriage. The model χ^2 given at the bottom of Table 7.2 is the difference between the null model and the model with five covariates. It is significant for all birth cohorts, and has a maximum value of 265 for the 1950–54 birth cohort.

7.13. APPENDIX B.1: COMPUTER SOFTWARE FOR ESTIMATION: ILLUSTRATION WITH MARRIAGE DISSOLUTION (ACTUARIAL METHOD)

The Survival procedure in SPSS is a versatile program that reads raw data and produces an elaborate output: a 13-column simple life table. It has the capability to test for differences between two or more groups. Let us consider an example—marriage dissolution—and also assume we have cross-sectional data on marriage history from a survey. In this example, the time of observation starts from the date of first marriage and ends either by date of divorce or by survey time, whichever comes first.

- Step 1: First compute a time variable—MARDUR (Date of survey (or divorce) − Date of first marriage).
- Step 2: Compute a status variable—MARSTAT (=1 if divorced, =0 if still in marriage).
- Step 3: Recode the race variable—black, white, and other.

The following SPSS program generates a life table for the whole group:

```
Title 'Analysis of Marriage Dissolution by SPSS program'
Data List Fixed record=1 notable FREE/
    MARDUR, MARSTAT, RACE
Begin data
10 1 1
. . . .
. . . .
. . . .
End data
```

```
Survival Tables = MARDUR/
  Intervals = thru 60 by 6/
    status = MARSTAT (1)/
    plots = ALL
FINISH
```

Separate Life Table for Each of the Racial Groups

```
Survival Tables = MARDUR by RACE (1,3)/
  Intervals = thru 60 by 6/
    status = MARSTAT (1)/
    plots = ALL
```

Comparison of the Racial Groups in a Population

```
Survival Tables = MARDUR/
    Intervals = thru 60 by 6/
      status = MARSTAT (1)/
      plots = ALL/
  compare = MARDUR by RACE/
```

The comparison option produces mean survival score for each subgroup and a statistic D describing the probability that the subgroups come from different survival distributions.

The SPSS survival procedure can only perform a simple survival analysis; it is not possible to fit the Cox proportional hazards model with SPSS.

7.14. APPENDIX B.2: BMDP PACKAGE: BMDP1L AND BMDP2L PROGRAMS

The instructions for estimating the survival distribution by the actuarial (life table) method using BMDP1L are:

```
/problem title = 'Analysis of Marriage Dissolution -
  BMDP1L'.
/input  variables = 3.  format = free.
/variable names = MARDUR, MSTAT, RACE.
/form time = MARDUR.  status = MSTAT.  response =1.
/estimate method = life.  width= 6.  grouping = RACE.
/end
```

```
20  1  1
 -   -  -
 -   -  -
```

The instructions for fitting Cox's proportional hazards model using BMDP2L are as follows (with slight modification, one can use the same program to run a hazards model with time-dependent covariates):

```
/Problem  title  =  'Analysis  of  Marriage  Dissolution  -
   BMDP1L'.
/Input  variables = 3.  format = free.
/Variable names = MARDUR, MSTAT, RACE.
/Transform  if RACE = 1 then RACE1 = 1.
            if RACE = 2 then RACE2 = 1.
            if RACE1 = 1 then RACE2 = 0.
            if RACE2 = 1 then RACE1 = 0.
/Form time = MARDUR. status = MSTAT. response =1.
/Regress  covariate=race1, race2.
/end
20  1  1
 -   -  -
 -   -  -
 -   -  -
```

7.15. APPENDIX B.3: SAS PROCEDURE TO ESTIMATE THE SURVIVAL DISTRIBUTION

(Like the BMDP1L program, the LIFETEST procedure in SAS allows the user to specify the method to estimate the survival function—actuarial method or product limit method)

```
*THIS IS TO RUN COX'S MODEL ON SAS USING DATA FROM AN EXTERNAL
FILE - PROGRAM

TITLE 'ANALYSIS OF MARRIAGE DISSOLUTION - LIFETEST';
   DATA; INFILE DATA;
      INPUT MARDUR MSTAT RACE (3.);
  CARDS;
  20 1 1
   -   -  -
  ;

   OPTIONS LS = 67;
```

```
PROC LIFETEST WIDTH=6  METHOD= LIFE;
      TIME MARDUR*MSTAT (0);
      STRATA = RACE(1,3);
      EVENT MSTAT;
      MODEL MARDUR= RACE;
ENDSAS;
```

SAS Program for Proportional Hazards Model

A procedure can be employed in SAS to fit Cox's model: PHGLM (a user-supported SUGI program).

```
*COX'S MODEL USING DATA FROM AN EXTERNAL FILE

    CMS FILEDEF DATA DISK MAR DATA D;

  TITLE 'COX MODEL MARRIAGE DISSOLUTION NSFH DATA';
  DATA; INFILE DATA;
    INPUT MARDUR MSTAT RACE (3.);
      OPTIONS LS = 67;
  PROC SORT;
      BY DESCENDING MARDUR;
  PROC PHGLM;
      EVENT MSTAT;
      MODEL MARDUR= RACE;
ENDSAS;
```

CHAPTER 8

The Parametric Failure Time Models

8.1. INTRODUCTION

Parametric failure time distributions have been widely used in engineering but are new in demography. For example, a failure time model represents an attempt to describe mathematically the length of a first marriage, or duration at a certain parity before progressing to the next. The literature on survival models discussed in the previous chapter shows that there are many causes that affect either individually or collectively the experience of a certain event at a particular time point in the life cycle. It is not always possible to pinpoint all of these causes and mathematically account for all of them. Therefore, the choice of a particular failure time distribution to describe the process remains an art. In real time applications the choice of the hazards function $\lambda(x)$ is facilitated by considering three general types of failures recognized as having time dependence. The first one, called the initial failure, manifests itself shortly after $t = 0$ and gradually begins to decrease during the initial period. The second one is called failure by chance, and the third is wearout failure. The famous U curve of human mortality is a clear model for the above description. In general, each specific form of the hazard function leads to a specific survival distribution.

Parametric models are interesting for two major reasons. First, these models allow us to smooth out the irregularities of observed experience, and second, they can handle censoring and provide predictions. These two functions are fulfilled if we have a good to moderate fit for the observed data.

In this chapter, our focus is on parametric failure time models and their suitability for describing demographic processes. Later each of the models will be applied to a demographic problem as an illustration. Failure times cannot be negative, and this condition leaves us with the distributions of nonnegative random variation. The parametric models discussed in this chapter are the exponential, Weibull, lognormal, and loglogistic.

The exponential and Weibull models are also proportional hazards models but the parametrization for the covariates differs by a multiple of the scale parameter from the parametrization used in Cox's model (see Chapter 7). In life testing studies, the exponential family of distributions plays an important role analogous to that of the normal distribution in other areas of statistics. Though many demographic processes cannot be adequately described by the exponential distribution, an understanding of the theory behind this model is important and it facilitates the treatment of more general situations. The exponential distribution is famous for its lack of memory and is the only available distribution with this property (Feller, 1957, p. 413). In view of the general nature of the exponential family of distributions, we will start the discussion with the exponential model and move on to the Weibull, lognormal, and loglogistic in the following sections. After discussing the general properties of these four models, we will illustrate each of them with a demographic application.

8.2. THE EXPONENTIAL REGRESSION MODEL

The exponential distribution corresponds to a purely random failure pattern. Mathematically, this means that, whatever be the cause of a failure, it occurs according to the postulates of a Poisson process with some parameter λ. Consider an event such as a failure of some process. For example, consider the event of first birth. In the terminology of survival literature, the event of a woman having a first birth at time point t in her life is termed as a failure. If this failure is due to some random phenomenon such as accidental pregnancy, then the probability of its occurrence is proportional to the length of the woman's exposure, the rate of which is constant over time. If there is no other cause of failure (such as change in the probability of conception due to age), the clearly the probability of failure in a given time interval is proportional to the length of the interval. In such a case, the exponential model may be the best mathematical model to describe the birth process. The probability density function (PDF) of the exponential distribution can be obtained either from the hazard rate or by considering the waiting time between failures in a Poisson process.

The exponential model has been extensively used in applications for three main reasons: (1) Many time response data, specifically failure data, can fit quite well into an exponential model. (2) Inferences concerning the one (unknown) parameter are relatively easy. In other words, theoretical aspects of the model are not difficult. (3) Much has been written about the model and so literature pertaining to this model is readily available (Gross and Clark, 1975). In the past, the exponential model has been used as a model for waiting times in demographic applications.

We will briefly describe some of the mathematical properties of the exponential model, to assess its suitability for describing demographic processes. The exponential model is obtained by a constant hazard function λ, i.e., $\lambda(t)$ = $\lambda > 0$. As in the Cox model, larger λ indicates higher risk, and so shorter survival. The one-parameter exponential density is given by:

$$f(t/\lambda) = \lambda e^{-\lambda t} \qquad t > 0, \qquad \lambda > 0 \qquad (8.1)$$

$$f(t) = 0 \qquad t < 0 \qquad (8.2)$$

The cumulative distribution function is given by:

$$F(t) = \Pr(T \le t) = 1 - e^{-\lambda t} \qquad (8.3)$$

and the survival function is given by

$$S(t/\lambda) = \Pr(T \ge t) = e^{-\lambda t} \qquad (8.4)$$

The hazard function is defined as $\lambda(t) = f(t)/S(t) = \lambda$, a constant. This indicates that the exponential process is independent of age, or that the failure is a random event likely to occur at any time. This property is referred to as lack of memory, in the sense that those who survive to any time t have a distribution of remaining life that is also exponential, with the same parameter λ. A consequence of this property for the analysis of first birth is that it does not matter how old people are when observed, because the distribution of lifetime after the start of observation is exponential. The positive constant λ is the parameter of the exponential distribution and establishment of the value of λ completely determines the distribution. It can be shown that if the failure time t has an exponential distribution, then the mean and variance are given by $1/\lambda$ and $1/\lambda^2$, respectively. The parameter of the exponential model can be estimated by using the method of maximum likelihood. In general, there are three main reasons for using maximum-likelihood estimation (MLE): (1) conceptually it is simpler, (2) the asymptotic properties of MLE make their use desirable, and (3) MLE affords a rather general method of estimation of parameters of various survival distributions. One can also use other methods to estimate parameters of the survival models, though the MLE method is the principal method. In the following section, we briefly outline the maximum likelihood procedure in the presence of random censoring. The procedure described is a common procedure for estimating parameters in the presence of censoring and with necessary modifications, one can use this general method to estimate parameters of other models considered here.

8.2.1. Estimation of the Parameter

Our interest in the study of parametric models is to examine their suitability for describing first marriage and first birth patterns. The cross-sectional data available from the Canadian Fertility Survey, for example, contain incomplete information on those women who had not experienced the event of interest by survey time in 1984. In our case, women enter the sample independently at different points in time. Suppose there are n women in the sample. Let T_i be the maximum time for which the ith woman can be observed, $i = 1, 2, 3, \ldots, n$. Thus, if the survey is at time T and if the ith woman enters the sample at time z_i, then $T_i = T - z_i$.* The actual age at first marriage of the ith woman, say t_i, is known only if $t_i < T_i$. Thus, given a sample of n women, the complete failure time is available for those who were married by the survey time, i.e., $t_j \leq T_j$, and for others we assign survey time as the censored time. In the following estimation procedure, we assume that the sample size is fixed in advance and μ, the total number of marriages observed, is a random variable. Let $\mu = 1/\lambda$ in the probability density function given above for the exponential model. We adopt the maximum likelihood procedure to estimate μ (hence λ). The contribution of the ith woman to the likelihood of the sample is:

$$f(t_i) = \mu^{-1} \exp(-\mu^{-1}t_i) \qquad 0 \leq t \leq T \qquad (8.5)$$

$$= \exp(-\mu^{-1}T_i) \qquad t_i > T_i \qquad (8.6)$$

In the above equation, if a woman has never been married at the survey time, we can only measure the probability of her survival, which is $\exp(-\mu^{-1}T_i)$ or $S(T_i)$. The likelihood function is given by:

$$L(\mu) = \prod_{i=1}^{n} [\mu^{-1} \exp(-\mu^{-1}t_i)]^{\delta_i}[\exp(-\mu^{-1}T_i)]^{1-\delta_i} \qquad (8.7)$$

Similarly, for any survival distribution $S(t)$ with the corresponding density function $f(t)$, we can write the likelihood as:

---

* Since the hazard function λ is constant in the exponential model, we can proceed to estimate λ under the assumption that $T_i = T - z_i$.

$$L(\mu) = \prod_{i=1}^{n} [f(t_i)]^{\delta_i} [S(t_i)]^{1-\delta_i} \tag{8.8}$$

where $\delta_i = 1$ if the ith woman married in the interval $0 \le t_i \le T_i$ and $\delta_i = 0$ if the ith woman does not marry in the interval $0 \le t_i \le T_i$. One can now follow the standard procedure of taking the log of the likelihood and differentiating with respect to μ and solving by equating to zero. This gives an estimate of the parameter μ. Thus, μ is given by:

$$\mu = m^{-1} \sum_{i=1}^{n} (\delta_i t_i + (1 - \delta_i)T_i) \tag{8.9}$$

where μ is the number of marriages assumed to be greater than zero. Substantially, the m given above is the sum of the time-to-marriage of all women who marry while the study was in progress plus the sum of the study times for those never married as of the duration of observation, divided by the number of women who married by survey time. Since the maximum likelihood estimators are invariant under one-to-one transformations, we can easily write the equation for the original parameter λ of the exponential model from the equation. One can also use the delta method for estimation (see Miller, 1981). One of the important contributions of survival analysis is the estimation of survival function. Once we have the estimate of λ, the hazard function, we can easily compute the survival function $S(t)$ using the relation described earlier.

The exponential model can be extended to incorporate the fact that the lifetime of a process is influenced by a variety of covariates, thus giving a multivariate regression flavor to the model. In general, we allow the model parameter λ to depend on a set of covariates z and the resulting β's of the parameter λ are sometimes called hyperparameters. One can choose a convenient functional form to express the covariate effects. Thus, in a general case, we can write $\lambda(t; z) = \lambda c(z\beta)$ where β is a set of regression parameters, λ is a constant, and c is any specified functional form. To ensure that $z\beta$ is positive for all possible z, we consider the exponential as the functional form for c above. Thus, the PDF for the exponential regression model is given by:

$$f(t; z) = \lambda \cdot e^{z\beta} \cdot e^{-\lambda t \cdot e^{z\beta}} \tag{8.10}$$

The hazard function is given by $\lambda(t; z) = \lambda \cdot e^{z\beta}$, and the survival function for the regression model is $S(t; z) = e^{-\lambda t \cdot e^{z\beta}}$.

The exponential regression model can be written as a log-linear model if we specify the log of failure time for the hazard function. In terms of the log survival time, $y = \ln T$, the model becomes a linear function of the co-variates z. Thus, $y = \alpha - z\beta + w$ where $\alpha = -\ln\lambda$ and w has the extreme value distribution (Kalbfleisch and Prentice, 1980). Also we note that the exponential regression model is a special case of the Weibull model with scale parameter constrained to one. We follow the general method discussed earlier to estimate the parameters and hyperparameters of the model. Some graphical tests are available to check the suitability of the exponential model for a given set of data. One of them is to plot log survival time against failure time and this plot should approximate a straight line passing through the origin to have a good fit with the model.

8.3. THE WEIBULL REGRESSION MODEL

The Weibull distribution can be described as a generalization of the exponential distribution discussed above. The basic difference between the exponential model and the Weibull model is in its hazard function property. The hazard function is constant in an exponential model and it is not so in the Weibull model, thus widening the scope of application to a variety of situations. The Weibull distribution also has been extensively used in engineering and other life testing applications, but is new to demography.

Recently, the Weibull model has become very popular as a failure time distribution for the following reasons: (1) In many instances where one cannot assume constant hazard and fit with the exponential model, the Weibull model becomes an immediate choice. (2) Inferences concerning the two Weibull parameters λ and γ were difficult to make in the past, but recent advances have simplified these problems (see Gross and Clark, 1975). (3) The Weibull is one of the most frequently used parametric models in failure time data analysis. Thus, literature concerning the Weibull model is readily available, as is the needed computer software. However, the authors are not aware of any extensive discussion of the Weibull model in the demographic literature.

The theoretical explanation underlying the suitability of the Weibull model comes from its weakest link interpretation of endurance. Consider a process where a large number of subprocesses are involved, failure of any one subprocess leading to the failure of the whole system. Thus, the lifetime of the process is equal to the minimum lifetime of any of its subprocesses. If the data on lifetimes have this property, then it can be theoretically shown that the Weibull model provides a close approximation of the distribution of these data. Instead of lifetimes, let us consider waiting times until the occurrence of a certain phenomenon, and if the given phenomenon can instantaneously occur if any one of a large number of statistically independent causes comes into effect (so that the waiting time until the given phenomenon occurs is the minimum of the times which elapse until one of the causes comes into effect), the Weibull distribution again provides a close fit to the distribution of such waiting times. The timing of first marriage and first birth can be seen as an example of the waiting time instance in which case, the Weibull is expected to provide a reasonably good fit. In the following paragraphs we develop the Weibull model and define the essential functions of the regression model.

The Weibull model can be derived either from the hazard rate concept or as the asymptotic distribution of the smallest order statistic from a specified probability distribution function (see Mann *et al.*, 1974). Since our interest is in the hazard rate, we derive the model from that concept. As indicated earlier, the Weibull model is completely specified by the parameters that define the model, i.e., λ and γ. γ is sometimes called the shape parameter and λ the scale parameter. The hazard rate increases when γ increases and decreases when γ decreases and is constant when γ equals one (the exponential case). Thus, the shape parameter gives flexibility to the Weibull model in the sense that it can be adapted to a variety of situations involving increasing, decreasing, and constant hazard cases. The probability density function and the cumulative distribution function are given by:

$$f(t) = \lambda\gamma t^{\gamma-1} \exp[-\lambda t^\gamma] \qquad t \geq 0, \qquad \lambda > 0, \qquad \gamma > 0 \qquad (8.11)$$

and

$$F(t) = 1 - \exp[-\lambda t^\gamma] \qquad (8.12)$$

The survival function and the hazard function of the model are given by:

$$S(t) = \exp[-\lambda t^\gamma] \qquad (8.13)$$

$$\lambda(t) = \lambda\gamma t^{\gamma-1} \qquad (8.14)$$

respectively.

The basic model can be extended to incorporate a set of covariates and this model is termed the Weibull regression model. In the regression model, the two Weibull parameters λ and γ will depend on a set of covariates considered important (z).

The probability density function for the regression model can be written as:

$$f(t; z) = \lambda(z)\gamma(z)t^{\gamma(z)-1} \exp(-\lambda(z)t^{\gamma(z)}) \qquad (8.15)$$

where $\lambda(z)$ and $\gamma(z)$ are positive functions of covariate z and $\lambda(z) > 0$ and $\gamma(z) > 0$. The survival and hazard functions for the regression model are given by:

$$S(t; z) = \exp(-\lambda(z)t^{\gamma(z)}) \qquad (8.16)$$

$$\lambda(t; z) = \gamma(z)\lambda(z)t^{\gamma(z)-1} \qquad (8.17)$$

respectively. One can derive various models by assuming that the shape parameter $\gamma(z)$ does not depend on the covariate set z, i.e., $\gamma(z) = \gamma$. In this case, one can write the hazard function as:

$$\lambda(t; z) = \gamma\lambda(z)t^{\gamma-1} \qquad (8.18)$$

It can easily be proved that the ratio of the hazard functions is independent of failure time t. In other words, if z_1 and z_2 are two different covariate values, then the ratio of the hazard functions is given by:

$$\lambda(t; z_1)/\lambda(t; z_2) = \lambda(z_1)/\lambda(z_2) \qquad (8.19)$$

Hence, the above model is also a proportional hazards model. Intuitively, it means that if the risk of failing at some time t_1 is for one subsample, say, 2 times the risk of failing at t_2 for another subsample, then this relation holds at any time t. Essentially, it implies that the relative risk of failure is constant in time. As stated earlier, the Weibull model can be seen as a generalization of the exponential model in the sense that an exponential model can be obtained by constraining the parameter $\gamma(z) = \gamma = 1$ in the Weibull density. It is often desirable to test the suitability of the Weibull model for the application under consideration. This testing can be conveniently accomplished by using graphical techniques. A graphical check of the Weibull assumption can be made by a plot of $\ln[-\ln S(t)]$ versus $\ln t$, where $S(t)$ is a survival estimate obtained from the Kaplan–Meier method. Also a number of techniques are in use for testing model assumptions based on the concept of regression with order statistics and details of these methods can be found elsewhere (Gross and Clark, 1975).

8.4. THE LOGNORMAL REGRESSION MODEL

The lognormal distribution can be defined as the distribution of a variable whose logarithm follows the normal distribution. The lognormal has been used in reliability applications under the assumption that the failure or death process is due to accumulated wear. The lognormal distribution is known by a variety of names. In some disciplines, it is known as the antilognormal distribution, and in others, it is referred to as the Galton–McAlister distribution. The famous Cobb–Douglas distribution in econometric theory for the study of production data is in fact a lognormal distribution. If the hazard function of interest increases steadily to a maximum value and then decreases as t tends to infinity, then the lognormal is expected to provide a good fit to the data. Our interest in considering the lognormal as a suitable distribution stems from the fact that marriage frequency is known to increase steadily to a maximum during the age span 20–30 and then to decline. The sociological model developed by Hernes (1972) was based on two basic assumptions, one of which is that the chances of marriage drop considerably as the cohort ages. Also, the Coale–McNeil (1972) model considers the initial entry into the marriage process as normally distributed. These empirical observations provide theoretical justification for examining the lognormal model as a means of studying patterns of marriage and first birth timing. The lognormal distribution has also been applied to the study of nonnegative quantitative phenomena in the medical and engineering sciences (Derman *et al.*, 1973). The lognormal probability density function is given by:

$$f(t) = \frac{\exp[-(\ln(t) - \mu)^2/2\sigma^2]}{(\sqrt{(2\Pi)}\sigma t)} \tag{8.20}$$

where μ and σ^2 are scale and shape parameters, respectively, and not the location and dispersion parameters as in the case of the normal distribution. The lognormal hazard function is characterized by an initial rise to a maximum and then a decrease (almost as soon as the median is passed) to zero as time approaches infinity (Watson and Wells, 1961; Goldthwaite, 1961). In other words, one can characterize the hazard function of the lognormal as hump-shaped. The survival function of the lognormal model is given by

$$S(t) = 1 - \phi((\ln(t) - \mu)/\sigma) \tag{8.21}$$

where ϕ is the cumulative distribution function for the normal distribution. The mean and variance of the lognormal distribution are given by $\exp(\mu + \sigma^2/2)$ and $\exp(2\mu + \sigma^2)(\exp(\sigma^2)-1)$, respectively. The estimation of the two parameters of the model with and without censored observations has been discussed in several textbooks and so is not presented here (see Lee, 1980). In general, the shape parameter σ^2 controls the shape of the distributional form, and a greater value of this parameter is an indication of greater skewness. Unlike earlier failure models, the lognormal distribution is not an extension of the exponential model, or in other words, the exponential model is not a special case of the lognormal distribution. Further, the lognormal density defined by $f(t)$ is skewed to the right and has a long tail. A practical example of the lognormal model may be the waiting time to conception or waiting time to first marriage. Formulation of the regression model by incorporating covariates into the model is similar to that of the exponential model discussed earlier. Estimation of parameters with censored data is complicated without powerful computer software, and in such cases the loglogistic distribution is a good approximation for the lognormal model. But the availability of computer programs enables one to apply the lognormal distribution with ease.

8.5. THE LOGLOGISTIC REGRESSION MODEL

The loglogistic model is yet another parametric model that has attracted the attention of biostatisticians and system analysts interested in the study of failure times of various processes. The use of the Weibull model is limited due to the nature of its hazard function. The Weibull hazard function may increase or decrease, but must be monotonic irrespective of its parameter values. This may not be a desirable property for many applications. The loglogistic survival model is similar in shape to the lognormal distribution, but is more suitable for use in the analysis of survival data for the following reasons: (1) its greater mathematical tractability when dealing with censored observations which occur frequently in survival studies and (2) the contribution made by the right censored observations to the likelihood of survival is equal to the value of the survivor function at the time of censoring and can be evaluated explicitly for the loglogistic model, but not for the lognormal model (Bennett, 1983).

The probability density function of the loglogistic survival model is given by:

$$f(t) = \frac{\lambda \gamma t^{\gamma - 1}}{[1 + \lambda t^\gamma]^2} \tag{8.22}$$

where $\gamma = 1/\sigma$ and $\lambda = \exp(-\alpha)$. The survival and hazard functions of the loglogistic model are given by:

$$S(t) = 1/[1 + \lambda t^\gamma] \tag{8.23}$$
$$\lambda(t) = \lambda \gamma t^{\gamma - 1}/[1 + \lambda t^\gamma]$$

respectively. The nonmonotonic nature of its hazard function makes it a unique model for describing some sets of survival data such as cancer (Bennett, 1983). Extending the basic model by incorporating a set of covariates can be achieved by defining the covariate set as a linear function of one of the model's parameters. It has been shown that in such a regression model, the hazard functions for different samples arising from different covariate values are not proportional through time as in the exponential and Weibull models, but their ratio tends to unity. This is a desirable property when initial effects of treatment, or the differences along the time axis tend to diminish with time, and the survival probabilities of different groups of a sample become more similar. Thus, the loglogistic distribution postulates proportionality on a different scale, namely, that of the odds on failure before time t (Gore *et al.,* 1984). It entails the convergence of hazard functions for different concomitant groups and accommodates variable times to peak hazard. The loglogistic regression model can be expressed as:

$$f(t) = \frac{\gamma \exp(\beta \cdot z)\{t \exp(\beta \cdot z)\}^{\gamma-1}}{[1 + \{t \exp(\beta \cdot z)\}^{\gamma}]^2} \qquad (8.24)$$

where β is a vector of unknown parameters. The probability of failure by time t for an individual with the ith covariate group or the ln{odds on death by time t} can be conveniently written as:

$$\gamma[\ln t + \beta \cdot z] \qquad (8.25)$$

The basic difference between the Weibull model and the loglogistic regression model is in terms of proportionality on different scales (cumulative odds versus hazard scale). Some graphical tests can be performed to check the loglogistic assumption. One such test involves the calculation of a non-parametric estimate of the log odds function for each sample using the Kaplan–Meier estimate and the plotting of this against log time. A resulting straight line would show support of the loglogistic regression model. Recently, Keeley (1979) considered using the loglogistic distribution in the analysis of first marriage patterns in the United States. Keeley adopted a two-stage estimation procedure. In the first stage, data on the distribution function of first marriage were used to estimate the parameters of the loglogistic curve, and in the second stage, regression analysis was used to explain variation in the logistic parameters in terms of variation in a set of socioeconomic variables. Further, Keeley attempted to interpret the model parameters as related to entry into the marriage market, search for a spouse, and the equilibrium percentage of ever married. However, Keeley suggests using a maximum likelihood procedure to simultaneously estimate both the model parameters and the covariate effects on the parameters as an efficient way to handle the problem. In our example, we estimate simultaneously both the parameters of the loglogistic model and the covariate effects on the parameters. In the following section, we apply each of the four parametric models to marriage dissolution in Canada.

8.6. APPLICATION OF PARAMETRIC MODELS

Survival probabilities of first marriages in the sample calculated by the Kaplan–Meier method and the four selected parametric models are presented in Table 8.1 for various durations. The hazard rate is the monthly rate of marriage dissolution at time t. Thus, assuming exponential distribution the rate is a constant at 0.0012612. The Weibull distribution fitted is monotonic decreasing, but with a scale parameter g very close to 1 at 0.990. Hence, the hazards are not too different from the exponential. The hazard rate in the lognormal distribution increases from 0.0003208 at month 1 to 0.001528 by the 36th month and decreases thereafter to 0.000879 at 25 years. A pattern similar to the lognormal but less pronounced is found for the loglogistic.

Given the fact that the hazard rates do not vary greatly by duration, it is not surprising to find that the survival probabilities are very close to each other in all of the models at the various durations. Though differences are quite small, it still seems that the loglogistic probably comes closer to the Kaplan–Meier survival estimates than the others, supporting the general findings in social research that the probability of marriage dissolution increases from the date of marriage to a modal duration and decreases afterwards. At the end of 10 years, 84.9% are found to be surviving by the Kaplan–Meier method, compared to 85.5% by the loglogistic. At the longer duration of 25 years, the Kaplan–Meier estimate is 69.1% against 69.0% by the loglogistic. No one model consistently fits the data better than others at all durations. This may more likely be due to two effects:

Table 8.1. Hazard Rates (Monthly Probability of Marriage Dissolution) at Various Durations Implied by the Four Fitted Survival Distributions[a]

Time (months)	Exponential	Weibull	Lognormal	Loglogistic
0	0.0012612			
1	0.0012612	0.0013158	0.0003208	0.0010936
36	0.0012612	0.0012695	0.0015277	0.0013266
60	0.0012612	0.0012630	0.0014535	0.0013280
120	0.0012612	0.0012543	0.0012388	0.0012852
180	0.0012612	0.0012492	0.0010825	0.0012244
240	0.0012612	0.0012456	0.0009672	0.0011617
300	0.0012612	0.0012428	0.0008785	0.0011016
μ	6.67566	6.69047	6.70282	6.45427
σ	1.00000	1.01015	1.85816	0.93796

[a] Source: Balakrishnan *et al.* (1988).

1. Secular rise in divorce means that we are blending largely historical experience at short duration with rather different current patterns at long durations.
2. The data need not follow any of the parametric forms either when blended or when separated by cohort or period.

For the exponential and Weibull distributions, simple empirical tests are available to examine their fit. A linear relationship between time t and $\ln F(t)$, where $F(t)$ is the sample (Kaplan–Meier) estimate, would indicate the appropriateness of the exponential model, and a linear relationship between $\ln t$ and $\ln[-\ln F(t)]$, the Weibull model. If we plot these two curves (not shown here), they reveal that both the exponential and the Weibull model fit the sample data equally well, which is not surprising as the scale parameter for Weibull is very close to unity. One can also use the Durbin–Watson statistic to examine the fit.

Though we are aware that the exponential model with constant hazard, and the Weibull model with monotonic hazard are less suitable to describe the patterns of first marriage dissolution, we have fit these two models for illustrative purposes. The exponential model being the most basic survival model, like the normal distribution in statistical estimation, it is extensively used as a waiting time model. In fact, the Coale–McNeil marriage model can be seen as a convolution of a normal distribution and three exponential delays. There is no reason to believe that any of the three waiting times hypothesized should be exponential. The readers should note that the convolution need not hold and what Coale and McNeil really wanted was an S-shaped curve, and not a theory of marriage. The loglogistic and lognormal models have the functional form that is expected of the timing of first marriage dissolution. In the past, fitting the lognormal distribution involved complicated mathematics requiring special programs and effort. However, in recent times, the availability of computer software has removed this constraint.

To check the suitability of the exponential, one can plot log survival (Kaplan–Meier estimate) versus failure time t. If the lines are not straight, this indicates that the pattern is not likely to conform to the exponential form. Similarly, one can plot log minus log survival versus $\ln t$ to test the suitability of the Weibull model and if the resulting plot is approximately a straight line one can assume that the Weibull model is applicable. Also a plot of log odds* versus $\ln t$ is a test of the suitability of the loglogistic model. The resulting plots are approximately a straight line for all of the birth cohorts. This empirical

---

* Log odds is defined as $\ln[\text{survival}/(1-\text{survival})]$ and is also called the logit transformation of the survival function.

test indicates that the loglogistic, and therefore the lognormal, provides a reasonable fit for marriage dissolution in Canada.

8.6.1. Survival Models with Covariates

In this section, we apply the models with covariates present and compare the derived coefficients for their stability across the different models. The coefficients for the various models along with those derived by Cox's proportional hazards model are presented in Table 8.2. Cox's model is not parametric, but extends the Kaplan–Meier method to include covariates. The computer programs used for the parametric models came from the SAS package while the program for Cox's model came from the BMDP package (BMDP, 1985; SAS, 1986). Since the program specifications were slightly different in the two packages, the coefficients derived for Cox's model are of opposite sign to that of other models. In making comparisons, their signs therefore should be changed. Negative coefficients in the four parametric models denote an earlier dissolution of marriage and positive coefficients, a later dissolution of marriage. In Cox's model it is the other way around. The categories not included in the table form the reference groups with a coefficient of zero.

The coefficients for the different categories across the models show considerable similarity. Noticeable variations can be found only in the Catholic, farm residence, and less than grade 11 education categories. In addition, the difference among the coefficients for categories within any covariate is essentially the same in all of the survival models, indicating that the conclusions derived about relative risks would have been basically the same no matter which parametric model was used. The overall log likelihoods were not too

Table 8.2. Survival Probabilities of First Marriage at Selected Marital Durations Estimated by Various Models and by Kaplan–Meier Method[a]

Time (years)	Kaplan–Meier	Exponential	Weibull	Lognormal	Loglogistic
0	1.000	1.000	1.000	1.000	1.000
3	0.955	0.956	0.955	0.954	0.955
5	0.921	0.927	0.926	0.919	0.925
10	0.849	0.860	0.859	0.849	0.855
15	0.796	0.797	0.797	0.792	0.793
20	0.739	0.739	0.739	0.745	0.738
25	0.691	0.685	0.686	0.705	0.690
μ		6.67566	6.69047	6.70282	6.45427
σ		1.00000	1.01015	1.85816	0.93796

[a] Source: Balakrishnan *et al.* (1988).

different for the parametric models, though Cox's proportional hazards model seems to perform better.

The relative risks implied by the coefficients in Table 8.3 are mostly in the direction one would expect. For example, women married before the age of 20 have a higher probability of divorce compared to the reference group, namely those marrying at ages 20–21. Women who get married at age 25 or after have substantially lower risks of divorce. Similarly, recent marriage cohorts have a higher risk of divorce. A rather surprising finding was that women who cohabited before marriage had a higher risk of marriage breakdown than

Table 8.3. Coefficients for Cox's Model and the Four Parametric Models of Survival of First Marriages[a,b]

Covariates[c]	Cox's	Exponential	Weibull	Lognormal	Loglogistic
Age at marriage					
<20	−0.3249	−0.3159	−0.2664	−0.3416	−0.2875
22–24	0.4050	0.4019	0.3353	0.3845	0.3625
25+	0.8836	0.8831	0.7345	0.6801	0.7365
Year of marriage					
<1965	0.7489	0.6159	0.6040	0.6244	0.6188
1975+	−0.4767	−0.3718	−0.4491	−0.4263	−0.4408
Cohabited before marriage					
Yes	−0.3905	−0.3592	−0.3264	−0.3312	−0.3297
Birth status					
Premarital birth	−0.8494	−0.8327	−0.7077	−0.8857	−0.7746
Premarital conception	−0.3988	−0.3903	−0.3332	−0.3869	−0.3521
Religion					
Catholic	0.1311	0.1313	0.1080	0.1606	0.1407
Religiosity					
Weekly	0.4887	0.4849	0.4083	0.4419	0.4152
Rarely	−0.5708	−0.562	−0.4741	−0.5342	−0.4932
Place of residence					
Urban	−0.4093	−0.4009	−0.3389	−0.3792	−0.3477
Farm	0.6426	0.6373	0.5348	0.4506	0.5195
Education					
<Grade 12	−0.1232	−0.1217	−0.1007	−0.1411	−0.1111
Grade 14+	−0.1786	−0.1751	−0.1492	−0.1952	−0.1625
Intercept		6.9930	6.6742	6.7496	6.4626
σ		1.0000	0.8285	1.5221	0.7563
$-\ln L$	2,614	2238	2224	2232	2220

[a] Signs reversed for consistency with other procedures.
[b] Source: Balakrishnan *et al.* (1988).
[c] Reference categories are age at marriage 20–21; year of marriage 1965–1974; did not cohabit before marriage; no premarital birth or conception; non-Catholic; sometimes church attendance; small urban residence; and grade 12–13 education.

those who did not. As one would expect, Catholic marriages and those where the women are more religious as measured by their frequency of church attendance are longer lasting than those in other religious categories. Farm women have a much lower probability of marriage dissolution than urban dwellers. Another unexpected finding was that educational differences in survival probabilities were minimal. The absence of an education effect may be due to the higher stability of French than English marriages and historically lower educational level of the French. The high stability of French marriages at low education balances the lower stability of English marriages at lower education and other variables are also picking up the non-French dissolution rates at low education. Similarly, note the possible relevance of ethnicity and language.

The coefficients in Table 8.3 enable one to calculate the survival probabilities of first marriage for women with a particular set of covariates. If we denote by β a column vector of coefficients and by z a row vector of covariates, the factor $\beta \cdot z$ will be proportional to relative risks and can be used for deriving survival probabilities. Though these formulas are available in many references (SAS, 1986; BMDP, 1985; Kalbfleisch and Prentice, 1980), they are given below for ready reference with an example of an actual calculation.

For the proportional hazards model

$$F(t; z) = [F_0(t)]\exp^{(\beta \cdot z)} \qquad (8.26)$$

where $F_0(t)$ is the survivorship function for the baseline or reference group. $F(t)$ is calculated by setting the values for the covariates at their means in the above equation and solving

$$F_0(t) = F(t, z)\exp^{(-\beta \cdot z)} \qquad (8.27)$$

The group (A) with the highest risk of marital dissolution are those with the highest positive coefficients in Cox's model. $\beta \cdot z$ for this group works out to 3.20 (sum of the coefficients) and when raised to the power of e is 24.5. In other words, this group has a 24.5 times greater relative risk of marital dissolution than the reference group at every duration. Since the survival probability for the reference group $F_0 (36) = 0.977$, for the high-risk group the probability will be

$$F_A(36)0.977^{24.5} = 0.565$$

For the exponential model, $\beta \cdot z$ for the same highest-risk group A is the sum of the coefficients including the intercept, which amounts to 3.9748. At a duration t, this can be used to calculate the survival probability by the formula:

$$F(t) = \exp(-\alpha t) \tag{8.28}$$

where $\exp(-\mu) = \alpha$ and $\mu = \beta \cdot z$.

Thus, for Group A at time $t = 36$ months, survival probability $F_A(36) = 0.509$, etc.

For the Weibull distribution, $\beta \cdot z$ for the same risk group is 3.9624. The survival probability at time t is given by:

$$F(t) = \exp(-\alpha \tau \gamma) \tag{8.29}$$

where $\alpha = \exp(-\mu/\sigma)$, $\mu = \beta \cdot z$, and $\gamma = 1/\sigma$.

For Group A at time $t = 36$ months, survival probability $F_A(36) = 0.531$.

For the lognormal distribution, $\beta \cdot z$ for Group A is similarly 3.6562. The survival probability at time t is given by:

$$F(t) = 1 - f((\ln(t) - \mu)/\sigma) \tag{8.30}$$

where f is the cumulative distribution function for the normal distribution, and $\mu = \beta \cdot z$.

At time $t = 36$ months, $F_A(36) = 1 - f(-0.04775) = 1 - 0.481 = 0.519$.

For the loglogistic distribution, $\beta \cdot z$ for Group A is 3.6266.

The survival probability at time t is given by:

$$F(t) = 1/(1 + \alpha \tau \gamma) \tag{8.31}$$

where $\gamma = 1/\sigma$, $\alpha = e^{-\mu/\sigma}$, and $\mu = \beta \cdot z$.

At time $t = 36$ months, $F_A(36) = 0.525$.

Survival probabilities were calculated for the highest- and lowest-risk groups (A and C) and the reference group in Cox's model (B) by using the different survival models at various durations. These are presented in Table 8.4. They are shown as illustrations only, as in real situations most groups will fall between the extremes. Using the coefficients, one can easily estimate the survival probabilities for any combination of covariates of interest. It can be seen from Table 8.4 that survival probabilities can vary a great deal depending on the set of covariates.

Various parametric models were tested for their suitability to survival analysis of first marriage in Canada, using Kaplan–Meier estimates as a standard. Model estimates are not very different from each other, but there seems to be a slightly better fit with loglogistic. When eight covariates were used in the analysis, it was found that the coefficients were similar in all of the models and the overall conclusions about the relative risks would not have been different. The findings reveal that in marriage dissolution the differences according to demographic and socioeconomic characteristics may be far more

Table 8.4. Survival Probabilities of First Marriage Dissolution for the Highest-Risk, Reference, and Lowest-Risk Groups of Women by Different Models[a]

Time (years)	Cox	Exponential	Weibull	Lognormal	Loglogistic
		Highest-risk group (Group A)[b]			
0	1.000	1.000	1.000	1.000	1.000
3	0.565	0.509	0.531	0.519	0.514
5	0.315	0.324	0.310	0.387	0.380
10	0.074	0.105	0.067	0.229	0.177
15	0.018	0.034	0.012	0.156	0.112
20	—	0.011	—	0.115	0.079
25	—	—	—	0.089	0.060
$\beta \cdot z$	3.2002	3.9748	3.9624	3.6562	3.6266
		Reference group (Group B)[c]			
0	1.000	1.000	1.000	1.000	1.000
3	0.977	0.967	0.976	0.981	0.978
5	0.954	0.946	0.957	0.959	0.958
10	0.899	0.896	0.903	0.902	0.902
15	0.849	0.848	0.846	0.847	0.843
20	0.782	0.802	0.789	0.798	0.786
25	0.721	0.759	0.733	0.755	0.732
$\beta \cdot z$	0.0	6.9930	6.6742	6.7496	6.4626
		Lowest-risk group (Group C)[d]			
0	1.000	1.000	1.000	1.000	1.000
3	0.999	0.998	0.999	0.999	0.999
5	0.997	0.996	0.998	0.999	0.998
10	0.994	0.993	0.994	0.998	0.996
15	0.991	0.989	0.991	0.995	0.992
20	0.986	0.986	0.987	0.991	0.989
25	0.982	0.983	0.983	0.987	0.985
$\beta \cdot z$	−2.8949	9.7455	9.0638	9.1072	8.8933

[a] Source: Balakrishnan *et al.* (1988).
[b] Group A: <20 age at marriage; 1975 year of marriage; cohabited before marriage; had a premarital birth; non-Catholic; rarely or never goes to church; large urban residence; education 14 years.
[c] Group B: age at marriage 20–21; year of marriage 1965–1974; did not cohabit before marriage; no premarital birth or conception; Catholic; sometimes attends church; small urban residence; grade 12–13 education.
[d] Group C: 25+ age at marriage; <1965 year of marriage; did not cohabit before marriage; had no premarital birth or conception; Catholic; weekly church attendance; farm residence; education grade 12–13.

important than say in fertility or mortality generally found in many studies. Therefore, one should not treat the population as homogeneous in analyzing survival probabilities of marriages, other than for cursory analysis of overall trends.

The last model in the series considered is the loglogistic regression model. In the past the loglogistic model was employed by Keeley (1979) to study the age pattern of first marriage. The Coale–McNeil model is one functional form of the distribution function of first marriage. However, one can specify this functional form as lognormal or loglogistic or something else. Keeley (1979) points out that the choice of the functional form of first marriage distribution function is an empirical matter. The empirical check for the loglogistic model (plotting log odds versus ln$t$) confirms the suitability of the model for the study of first marriage behavior in Canada. The log likelihood for the null models indicates that the loglogistic distribution has maximum value for all birth cohorts except 1955–59 and 1960–64 where the lognormal has maximum value. The model with maximum value for likelihood is said to be the preferred model compared to other models. On the basis of this criterion, the loglogistic is the best model for the four older birth cohorts, and the lognormal is the best model for the two younger cohorts compared to Weibull and exponential models.

8.7. SUMMARY

The chapter began with an introduction to the nature of parametric models and their comparison to nonparametric models. The importance of exponential distribution in failure time analysis was discussed. Details into the nature of the exponential distribution and the shape of its hazard function were provided. Besides exponential distribution, we considered Weibull, lognormal, and loglogistic models for illustration. After discussing the general properties of each of these models, we formulated regression models to incorporate covariates that are expected to influence the survival times. The maximum likelihood procedure to estimate the one-parameter exponential model was discussed in detail. A general likelihood in the presence of censored data was derived and presented in terms of a probability density function and the survival function. This can be used to derive the likelihood for other models. One of the major concerns with parametric models is the selection of a suitable functional form to describe the given process. We fitted all four models with and without covariates to marriage dissolution in Canada. The patterns across cohorts and the relative risks for various groups of women were substantively unaffected by the choice of functional form. It is difficult to decide finally about their role in demographic modeling without further testing with other data sets and other phenomena. However, the present exercise does provide the necessary logistics for the fitting of these models and their application to other relevant processes should be straightforward.

CHAPTER 9

Multiregional Demographic Models

9.1. INTRODUCTION

Conventional demographic analysis has a built-in constraint arising from the assumption of a "closed" population, which implies that there is no migration. The interdependence of demographic processes such as fertility, mortality, and migration in determining the growth and structure of human populations in a multiregional framework cannot be undermined. Further, subnational population analysis has been gaining momentum in recent years as an integral part of population policy studies, where a multiregional perspective is imperative because of interregional migration. In order to circumvent the aforementioned limitation of conventional demographic analysis, a plethora of techniques were developed by Andrei Rogers and his associates during the last decade. The area has grown as a subfield of demography, namely, multiregional demography. Our aim in this chapter is to introduce the reader to this specialty of demographic analysis. Interested readers should consult specific texts or monographs for more details. In this chapter, we will attempt to present a synthesis of the core methodology, allied techniques, algorithms, and related problems.

Multiregional demographic analysis is basically an extension of the single region analysis where the deterministic role of spatial mobility is also studied. More specifically, the approach entails the decomposition of demographic events according to "where" they occur. It focuses on an integrated study of the impact of migration on regional population growth and composition and regional differentials in fertility and mortality. Instead of being treated in isolation, each region is considered as a part of a larger system of interdependent units. The regional demographic linkages consist of two components:

(1) a direct linkage due to migration, and (2) an indirect linkage due to differing patterns of fertility and mortality. Both components are captured and represented in the multiregional analytical perspective. Regional differentials are represented by region-specific measures of fertility, mortality, and migration levels. Interregional migration is modeled by destination-specific outmigration measures. The essential feature of the multiregional approach is therefore the simultaneous treatment of the demographic processes in all regions.

The powerful tool of matrix algebra is useful for dealing with the elaborate and complicated data systems in multiregional analysis. Expressions for probabilities, expectancies, rates, and so forth are treated as elements of matrices rather than as scalars in the conventional or single region system of analysis. With the advent of standard computer software, the treatment of a larger and comprehensive data set has become easy. Andrei Rogers made it possible to express complex relations in simple form, so that even a nonspecialist in mathematical demography could comprehend them (Rogers, 1966, 1968, 1973a, 1975). In subsequent developments, Rogers (1973a, 1975) successfully combined the Markov models of interregional population change with cohort-survival and cohort component projection models.

Rogers's earlier developments in multiregional demography gave rise to an accounting system for multiregional demographic analysis (Wilson and Rees, 1974; Rees and Wilson, 1975). This system is useful for marrying in a single framework all the missing figures and hence for ensuring an internally consistent data base (Willekens and Drewe, 1984). Using the accounting system, Rees and Wilson (1975) suggested ways of deriving multiregional analogs. Multiregional life tables, multiregional stable population analysis, multiregional population projection models, and fertility analysis incorporating internal migration are of special significance in multiregional demography. It is also useful to simplify the estimation of transition rates using the accounting equation.

The underlying logic of multiregional analysis is fruitfully exploited and extended to multidimensional analysis. While in multiregional analysis, the dimensions are at present primarily age and region (place) of residence, it is being extended to age and marital status, age and labor force status, and so forth. For each dimension, several states or demographic categories may be distinguished; e.g., age groups of 5 years, marital status categories (never married, married, divorced, widowed), and so forth. This requires the estimation of transition probabilities for all categories. The same applies for multiregional models. In it, the transition probabilities are derived from a probabilistic model, postulated to describe the underlying continuous stochastic process of which the data are realizations. The model parameters are derived from those data. The underlying probability structure is taken to be that of a Markov process (Willekens, 1984).

Research on the demographic consequences of a set of transition rates and probabilities led to the multistate life table and to multistate projection and stable population models. Needless to say, the life table is a description of a fictitious cohort which experiences the same event during a given period of time (life history perspective); a projection model refers to an actual group of people present at a given point in time and describes the evolution of this group. Detailed documentation of the development of multistate models is found in Willekens and Rogers (1978) and Rogers and Willekens (1986).

In sum, multiregional demography deals with the evolution of spatially interdependent regional populations. At a regional level, population changes are due to fertility, mortality, interregional and international migration. Multiregional demography focuses on population size, composition, and geographic distribution as well as on the changes of these characteristics over a period of time. This approach allows us to evaluate the demographic interactions between the regions that shape national patterns.

Models of multiregional demography have been useful tools to study the growth and structure of regional populations, but wider applications of these models are seriously limited by the quality and quantity of input data available, especially in the developing countries but also to some extent in developed countries. Hence, development of multiregional demography is hindered by the gap between data availability and requirements. It is relevant to discuss briefly the developments of important data estimation techniques before looking into some of the components of multiregional demography.

9.2. DATA REQUIREMENTS

The data problem is particularly acute in the case of interregional migration flows disaggregated by migrant categories. Willekens *et al.* (1981) present a particular class of estimation techniques which demonstrate the great potential for dealing with migration data. These techniques may be used in disaggregating the data into various migrant categories when initially only aggregate data on migration patterns are available. For instance, how may one disaggregate a total origin destination migration flow matrix into age-specific flows where the only information available is a national estimate of the age composition of migrants? Does additional information improve the estimates significantly? Questions of this nature will be dealt with in discussing those techniques. Willekens *et al.* (1981) identify the common feature of these techniques as the fact that the aggregate data appear as sums (referred to as "marginal sums" hereafter) of different groups of elements of two- or n-dimensional arrays. The elements of those matrices are unknown and must be estimated. There are two main approaches to estimation and these are described below: (1) the entropy maximization approach and (2) the quadratic or multiproportional adjustment approach.

9.2.1. Entropy Maximization Approach

The concept of entropy is borrowed from the realm of physics. Let us examine here its adaptation in the field of migration. A thorough discussion of this approach can be found in Willekens (1977a). The illustration and explanation of this technique in the case of migration is heavily based on Willekens (1977a). We will use the same notation as Willekens, and similar examples.

Suppose that we know the migration flow matrix of the total population but not the migration patterns of the subsets of population such as age, sex, nationality, region, and occupation. Also we have the marginal totals of those subset categories, i.e., total number of arrivals and departures. With this information, the problem is to estimate the migration patterns of subsets of the population. To illustrate the philosophy of the technique, let us start with a simple example similar to Willekens (1977a). Let us say we have a two-region system. The only information given is the total departures and arrivals for each region. Let us make an assumption that the system is a closed one, meaning that the total number of arrivals equals the total number of departures. The system can then be represented in a two-dimensional form as shown in Table 9.1, where m_{ij} is the number of migrants going from region i to region j. For example m_{12} is the number of people migrating from region 1 to 2 in the unit time interval; $m_{.1}$ is the total number of arrivals in region 1. Thus,

$$m_{.2} = m_{11} + m_{21} = \sum_i m_{i1}$$

$m_{.2}$ is the total number of arrivals in region 2

$$m_{.2} = m_{12} + m_{22} = \sum_i m_{i2}$$

$m_{1.}$ is the total number of departures from region 1

$$m_{1.} = m_{11} + m_{12} = \sum_j m_{1j}$$

$m_{2.}$ is the total number of departures from region 2

$$m_{2.} = m_{21} + m_{22} = \sum_j m_{2j}$$

Table 9.1. Origin–Destination Table

	Origin		
	Region 1	Region 2	Arrivals
Destination			
Region 1	m_{11}	m_{21}	$m_{.1} = 4$
Region 2	m_{12}	m_{22}	$m_{.2} = 2$
Departures	$m_{1.} = 3$	$m_{2.} = 3$	$m_{..} = 6$

$m_{..}$ is the total number of migrants

$$m_{..} = \sum_j m_{1.} = \sum_j m_{.j} = \sum_i \cdot \sum_j m_{ij}$$

Based on the row totals and column totals that we know, our task is to find the cell values m_{11}, m_{12}, m_{21}, m_{22}, such that they add up to the known totals. The problem can be written in a mathematical language as follows, to estimate the unknown cells:

$$\sum_j m_{ij} = m_{i.} \qquad \text{for} \qquad i = 1, 2 \tag{9.1}$$

$$\sum_i m_{ij} = m_{.j} \qquad \text{for} \qquad j = 1, 2 \tag{9.2}$$

Based on satisfaction of the constraints (9.1) and (9.2), there are three combinations of cell entries of M as given below:

$$M_a = \begin{bmatrix} 3 & 1 \\ 0 & 2 \end{bmatrix} \qquad M_b = \begin{bmatrix} 2 & 2 \\ 1 & 1 \end{bmatrix} \qquad M_c = \begin{bmatrix} 1 & 3 \\ 2 & 0 \end{bmatrix} \tag{9.3}$$

Willekens calls each arrangement of the entires of M a *macrostate* of the system. Since all three macrostates satisfied the constraints (9.1) and (9.2), which macrostate is the true one? This question can be answered with the help of the entropy method. This method selects the true macrostate as the one based on the highest probability of occurrence. It should be noted that each macrostate is generated by an assignment of *individual* migrants (microstates) to the origin–destination table. For instance, the first macrostate (M_a) involves a total of six migrants and there are three individual migrants from region 1 to 1 (i.e., m_{11} indicating movement within the region). To select the three individuals from six migrants, there are 20 possible ways. Mathematically, it is written as

$$\frac{6!}{3!(6-3)!}$$

After making a selection of three people to represent m_{11}, we must select one person out of the remaining three to constitute m_{21}. The analog to the above formula for this is: $3!/1!(3-1)! = 3$.

Since $m_{12} = 0$, the only remaining cell to be selected is m_{22}, which would constitute the remaining two. In summary, we can state that the total number of ways of selecting three out of six, and one out of the remaining three, and two out of the remaining two is:

$$\frac{6!}{3!(6-3)!} \times \frac{3!}{1!(3-1)!} \times \frac{2!}{2!} = 20 \times 3 \times 1 = 60$$

In other words, there are 60 ways of assigning individuals for this particular macrostate. Willekens (1977a) provides a general formula to select a *particular* macrostate from the total number of migrants $m_{..}$ as follows:

$$W = \frac{m_{..}!}{m_{11}!m_{12}!m_{21}!m_{22}!} = \frac{m_{..}!}{\prod_{i,j} m_{ij}!} \tag{9.4}$$

If we apply this general formula, for each macrostate of Eq. (9.3), we will get $W = 60$ for M_a, $W = 180$ for M_b, and $W = 60$ for M_c. The value W is the number of ways in which individuals can be assigned in a particular macrostate, and is called the *entropy* of the macrostate.

To answer the earlier question which macrostate to choose as the best estimate of the true migration flow out of the three presented in Eq. (9.3), we choose the macrostate with the highest entropy value. In our case, M_b is the appropriate one. However, the choice of this rests on two critical assumptions:

1. The probability that a macrostate represents the true migration flow matrix is proportional to the number of microstates of the system which give rise to this macrostate (entropy) and which satisfy the constraints (9.1) and (9.2).
2. Each microstate is equally probable (Willekens, 1977a, p. 7).

Willekens (1977a) extends the above example for more than two dimensions and he states the problem as well as the solution in general terms. For instance, in Willekens's notation, $m_{ij}(.)$ represents the total migration from region i to region j, the number of departures from region i by category x is $m_{i.}(x)$, and the number of arrivals in region j is $m_{.j}(x)$. Now the problem is to estimate $m_{ij}(x)$, the most probable flow matrix, given the total departures and arrivals of each category. The problem can be stated in the familiar mathematical programming problem as the entropy maximizing model in the form:

$$\max \hat{W} = -\sum_i \cdot \sum_j \cdot \sum_x [m_{ij}(x)\ln m_{ij}(x) - m_{ij}(x)] \qquad (9.5)$$

subject to the constraints

$$\sum_i m_{ij}(x) = m_{.j}(x) \qquad \text{for all } j \qquad (9.6)$$

$$\sum_j m_{ij}(x) = m_{i.}(x) \qquad \text{for all } i \qquad (9.7)$$

$$\sum_x m_{ij}(x) = m_{ij}() \qquad \text{for all } i \text{ and } j \qquad (9.8)$$

Equation (9.5) is also called an "objective function" and the solution of this function is found by the method of Lagrange multipliers. The Lagrangean is:

$$L = \ln\hat{W} + \sum_i \cdot \sum_x \{\lambda_i(x)[m_{i.}(x) - \sum_j m_{ij}(x_j)]\}$$
$$+ \sum_j \cdot \sum_x \mu_{jx}\{m_{.j}(x) - \sum_i m_{ij}(x)\} + \sum_i \cdot \sum_j \gamma_{ij}\{m_{ij}() - \sum_x m_{ij}(x)\}$$

Application of the Lagrangean multiplier technique leads to the following result:

$$m_{ij}(x) = A_i(x)B_j(x)m_{i.}(x)m_{.j}(x)T_{ij} \qquad (9.9)$$

where $A_i(x)$, $B_j(x)$, and T_{ij} are parameters or balancing factors related to the Lagrange multipliers. In the context of this problem, to find the solution for the parameters, we substitute Eq. (9.9) in the constraints (9.6) to (9.8) and the resulting equations are (9.10), (9.11), and (9.12), respectively:

$$\sum_i A_i(x)B_j(x)m_{i.}(x)m_{.j}(x)T_{ij} = m_{.j}(x)$$

$$B_j(x)m_j(x) \sum_i A_i(x)m_{i.}(x)T_{ij} = m_j(x) \qquad (9.10)$$

$$B_j(x) = [\sum_i A_i(x)m_{i.}(x)T_{ij}]^{-1}$$

$$\sum_j A_i(x)B_j(x)m_{i.}(x)m_j(x)T_{ij} = m_{i.}(x)$$

$$A_i(x)m_{i.}(x) \sum_i B_j(x)m_j(x)T_{ij} = m_{i.}(x) \qquad (9.11)$$

$$A_i(x) = [\sum_j B_j(x)m_j(x)T_{ij}]^{-1}$$

$$\sum_x A_i(x)B_j(x)m_{i.}(x)m_j(x)T_{ij} = m_{ij}(.)$$
$$T_{ij} = m(.)[\sum_x A_i(x)B_j(x)m_{i.}(x)m_j(x)]^{-1} \qquad (9.12)$$

The above equations belong to the system of nonlinear equations. The system does not have an analytical solution and it must be solved by iterative procedures.

9.2.2. Quadratic Adjustment Approach

Another method for estimating the complete origin–destination migration flow matrix M with elements m_{ij} is the quadratic adjustment approach. For this procedure also we need the total number of migrants arriving in each region I_j, and departing from each region, O_i, in a two-region system. The problem is then to estimate the complete origin–destination migration flow matrix M with elements m_{ij}. The only difference between the entropy method and this method is that unlike the entropy method, the present method requires initial estimates of the elements m_{ij}.

Let us consider the matrix to be estimated as

$$\dot{M} = \begin{bmatrix} m_{11} & m_{21} \\ m_{12} & m_{22} \end{bmatrix}$$

where $I_1 = m_{.1}$, $O_1 = m_{1.}$, $I_2 = m_{.2}$, and $O_2 = m_{2.}$.

Suppose we also have a matrix M^0 of initial estimates, with elements m_{ij}^0, i.e.,

$$\dot{M} = \begin{bmatrix} \dot{m}_{11} & \dot{m}_{21} \\ \dot{m}_{12} & \dot{m}_{22} \end{bmatrix}$$

The initial estimates may be obtained from a variety of sources such as expert opinions, migration tables of earlier years, and so forth. Note that the column sums $m_{i.}$ and the row sums m_{j} of M need not be equal to the predefined number of departures $O_i = m_{i.}$, and arrivals $I_j = m_{.j}$. We have to adjust the elements of M so as to add up to the required totals. The sum constrained quadratic adjustment problem is as follows:

$$\sum_j m_{ij} = O_i \qquad \text{for all } i$$

$$\sum_j m_{ij} = I_j \qquad \text{for all } j$$

Based on these constraints, the task now is to adjust matrix $\dot{M}$ so that elements of $\dot{M}$ are as close as possible to the elements of M and the row sums and column sums add up to the predefined number of arrivals and departures. One such method that was recently used in the case of India is a biproportional adjustment approach (Nair, 1985). This method assumes that the elements of matrix M are biproportional to the elements of a guess matrix M. Then the elements (m_{ij}) of a matrix M can be as follows:

$$m_{ij} = r_{i.}s_{j.}M_{ij} \qquad (9.13)$$

where m_{ij} and M_{ij} are elements of matrix $\dot{M}$ and M respectively; r_i and s_j are the row and column balancing factors. The values of r_i and s_j are estimated based on the constraints as follows:

$$\sum_i m_{ij} = m_{.j} \qquad \text{for all } j$$

$$\sum_j m_{ij} = m_{i.} \qquad \text{for all } i$$

$$\sum_i m_{i.} = \sum_j m_{.j} = m_{..} \qquad \text{for all } i \text{ and } j$$

where $m_{i.}$ and $m_{.j}$ are the known row and column totals of the matrix M, and $M_{..}$ is the overall total of M. By summing (9.13) over all i, we get

$$\sum_j m_{ij} = m_{.j} = s_j \sum_i r_i m_{ij}$$

or   (9.14)

$$s_j = m_{ij}/(\sum_i r_{i.}m_{ij})$$

or summing (9.13) over all j, we get

$$\sum_i m_{ij} = m_{i.} = r_i \sum_i s_j.m_{ij}$$

or (9.15)

$$r_i = m_{i.}/(\sum_j s_j.m_{ij})$$

To solve Eqs. (9.14) and (9.15), Stone (1962) suggested an iterative procedure which was stated by Nair (1985, p. 134) as follows:

Step 0: $K = 0$

$$r_i^0 = 1 \quad \text{fixed arbitrarily}$$

Step 1: $K = K + 1$
Calculate s_j:

$$s_j^{(k)} = \frac{m_j}{(\sum_i r_i^{(k-1)} \dot{m}_{ij}^0)}$$

Step 2: Calculate r_i

$$r_i^{(k)} = \frac{m_{i.}}{(\sum_j s_j^{(k)} \dot{m}_{ij})}$$

Go to step 1 until convergence is reached for r_i and s_j values, or a stopping criterion is reached. For an empirical application and computer programming, see Nair (1985).

Apart from the aforementioned generalized estimation procedures and algorithms, there have been several notable developments specific to the field of multiregional demography. We shall focus on some of these in the following sections.

9.3. MODEL MIGRATION SCHEDULES

As indicated in Chapters 1 and 2, by and large, demographic phenomena exhibit regularities. The regularities observed in mortality schedules prompted Coale and Demeny (1966) to develop model life tables, Brass (1971) to develop simple models relating the survival probabilities of a population to a standard survival function, and Heligman and Pollard (1980) to give a parameterized description of the mortality curve. Similarly, the regularity of fertility curves stimulated research on their graduation (Coale and McNeil, 1972; Hoem *et al.,* 1981). Finally, regularities in migration schedules led Rogers and Castro (1981) to develop model migration schedules.

The development of model migration schedules, like model life tables in mortality studies, has been a useful exercise, especially in the developing countries where migration data are either not available or often inadequate. Most of the time available data are only at an aggregate level such as in- and out-migrants without detailed regional migration flows by age and sex. In this context, one could use model migration schedules to generate estimates. This in turn can be used as input data for other multiregional analysis such as population projections. Hence, we felt that it is appropriate to discuss briefly the development of model migration schedules. Our discussion is heavily based on the work of Rogers and Castro (1984).

Age-specific schedule is characterized by two parameters: (1) pertaining to the level or intensity and (2) its age pattern. The area under the curve of the schedule—the sum of the age-specific rates times the width of the age interval—is the level variable. This is meaningful for renewable events such as birth and migration. If μ_x denotes the age-specific intensity of the schedule considered, and dx represents an infinitely small age interval, then the set of all μ_x values forms a function, and the area under the curve, which is a gross rate, is given by:

$$GR = \int_0^\omega \mu_x dx$$

with ω being the highest attainable age.

The pattern variable is the mean age of the schedule,

$$\bar{x} = \frac{\int_0^\omega x\mu_x dx}{\int_0^\omega \mu_x dx} \tag{9.16}$$

Note that the level and pattern variables are independent of the age–region composition. The inclusion of age–region composition in these variables gives rise to many useful measures in multiregional demography. For example, the migration analog of the gross reproduction rate in fertility is calculated by first computing migration rates for each single year of age and then summing these over all ages of life. This is known as the gross migration rate (GMR).

As mentioned earlier, age-specific migration schedules exhibit remarkable regularity. This was expressed by Rogers and Castro (1984) in mathematical form as a model migration schedule defined by a total of 11 parameters. Figure 9.1 illustrates a typical observed age-specific migration schedule (the jagged outline) and its graduation by a model schedule (the superimposed smooth outline) defined by the sum of four components (Rogers and Castro, 1984, pp. 45–46):

1. A single negative exponential curve of the pre-labor force ages, with its rate of descent α
2. A left-skewed unimodal curve of the labor force ages positioned at mean age μ_2 on the age axis and exhibiting rates of ascent λ_2 and descent $-\alpha_2$
3. An almost bell-shaped curve of the post-labor force ages positioned at μ_3 on the age axis and exhibiting rates of ascent λ_3 and descent α_3
4. A constant curve C, the inclusion of which improves the fit of the mathematical expression to the observed schedule

In mathematical equations, the sum of four components suggests the sum of four curves as follows:

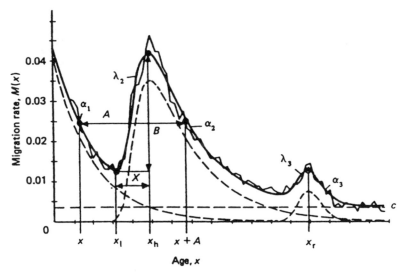

Figure 9.1. The model migration schedule.

α_1 = rate of descent of pre-labor force component
λ_2 = rate of ascent of labor force component
α_2 = rate of descent of labor force component
γ_3 = rate of ascent of post-labor force component
α_3 = rate of descent of post-labor force component
c = constant

x_l = low point
x_h = high peak
x_r = retirement peak
X = labor force shift
A = parental shift
B = jump

$$M(x) = a_1 \exp(-\alpha_1 x)$$
$$+ \, a_2 \exp\{-\alpha_2(x - \mu_2) - \exp[-\lambda_2(x - \mu_2)]\}$$
$$+ \, a_3 \exp\{-\alpha_3(x - \mu_3) - \exp[-\lambda_3(x - \mu_3)]\} \qquad x = 0, 1, 2, \ldots, z$$
$$+ \, c$$

where

$M(x)$ = migration rate
α_1 = rate of descent of pre-labor force component
x_1 = low point
λ_2 = rate of ascent of labor force component
x_h = high peak
α_2 = rate of descent of labor force component
x_r = retirement peak
λ_3 = rate of ascent of post-labor force component
t_x = labor force shift
α_3 = rate of descent of post-labor force component
c = constant

Rogers and Castro (1984) explain that the model schedule equation provided above in four components has 11 parameters. The parameters α_1, μ_1, α_2, λ_2, α_3, μ_3, and λ_3 define the profile of the full model schedule and the remaining four parameters, a_1, a_2, a_3, and c, determine its level. The migration rate $M(x)$ presented above can be reduced to a 7-parameter model if there is no retirement peak.

9.4. MULTIREGIONAL MORTALITY ANALYSIS

Termote (1986) suggests a method known as the "shift-share," used in regional economic analysis, to analyze the regional differences in mortality. This method decomposes a region's population growth into two main components: the growth resulting from population composition (structural effect) and the growth resulting from regional dynamics (the competitive effect). The first expresses the number of deaths in the region, if one applies national (standard) age-specific death rates to the given age structure of the region. That is, it provides the number of deaths expected in the region if there are no regional mortality differentials. The second component gives the number of deaths that would occur in a region at the region's age-specific rates. Termote provides the computational formula as follows:

$$K_.^{id} = \sum_x K_x^i m_x^d + \sum_x K_x^i (m_x^{id} - m_x^d) \tag{9.17}$$

where

K_x^i = the number of inhabitants of age x in region i
m_x^{id} = the death rate at age x in region i
m_x^d = the national death rate at age x
$K_.^{id}$ = the total (all ages) number of deaths in region i

Termote explains three important features of the regional mortality differential.

> First, it is the sum of age-specific differentials, weighted by the relative importance of the corresponding age group. This process of weighting curtails the influence of the level of regional disaggregation. With most indicators of regional disparity, the finer the disaggregation, "the larger the national measure of disparity." This is because, explicitly (as when the mean absolute deviation is used) or implicitly (as when comparing, for instance, the results of regional parameterization), one gives the same weight to each regional observation. Here, however, because each of the m regional observations is actually the weighted sum of a finite number n of subregional observations, the national measure of regional disparity, being itself regionally weighted, will be the same with m or with mn, thus eliminating one of the main obstacles to international comparisons (Termote, 1986, p. 81).

The second feature of the regional component is related to the first. Combining age and mortality differentials may create its own problems, of segregating effects. In order to take this into account, Termote suggests the further decomposition of the regional component (R) into two parts:

$$R^i = \sum_x K_x^i (m_x^{id} - m_x^d) \tag{9.18}$$

$$= \sum_x \left[\frac{K_x^i}{K_.} K_. \right] (m_x^{id} - m_x^d) + \sum_x \left[K_x^i \frac{K_.}{K_.} K_. \right] (m_x^{id} - m_x^d) \tag{9.19}$$

where the first term on the right-hand side of the above equation expresses the number of deaths due to regional mortality differentials, and the second term represents the effect of interaction between differences in age structure and mortality conditions. The equation provides a measure of absolute numbers. To obtain a measure of above- or below-average mortality, a nonstandardized index of mortality differential (IMD) is proposed for a given region i by Termote (1986):

$$\text{IMD}^i = \frac{\sum_x K_x^i (m_x^{id} - m_x^d)}{\sum_x K_m^i m_x^d} \tag{9.20}$$

Similarly, the index for standardized differences in age structure is:

$$*\text{IMD} = \frac{\sum_x [(K_x/K_{\cdot})K_{\cdot}^i](m_x^{id} - m_x^{d})}{\sum_x K_x^i m_x^d}$$ (9.21)

The sign of the index would indicate how the region compares with the national average. A positive index indicates that the region has an above-average mortality and a negative index indicates that the region has a below-average mortality.

In addition to a measure of above-/below-average mortality, one may need a national measure that will express the degree of regional disparity. Hence, a third feature of the IMD is that it can be used to express the regional mortality differential component by a mathematical property of the regional component. If X is an age group in a given region i, then as in Eq. (9.18),

$$R = \sum_x K_x^i(m_x^{id} - m_x^{d}) = K_x^i m_x^{id} - K_x^i m_x^d$$ (9.18)

After summing over all regions of a country, one gets

$$\sum_i R_x^i = \sum_i K_x^i m_x^{id} - \sum_i K_x^i m_x^d = 0$$ (9.22)

This implies that the total number of expected deaths necessarily equals the total number of observed deaths for a given age group, so that the sum over all regions of the regional differential component necessarily equals zero (Termote, 1986, p. 83).

When the sum of the regional differential components is zero, it leads to a balancing of the number of excess deaths in the region of above-average mortality with the number of missing deaths in the below-average region. By relating this total of deaths—excess and missing—by age, Termote, obtains an index of regional mortality disparity for age group X in a country j:

$$^j\text{IMD}_x = \frac{\sum_i |K_x(m_x^{id} - m_x^{d})|}{^jK_x^d}$$

$$^j\text{IMD} = 2 \sum_i [K_x(m_x^{id} - m_x^{d})]/^jK_x^d \quad \text{for} \quad (m_x^{id} - m_x^{d}) > 0$$ (9.23)

Now the following relationship holds:

$$\sum_x \sum_i R_x^i = \sum_x [\sum_i K_x^i(m_x^{id} - m_x^{d})] = 0$$ (9.24)

Similarly,

$$\sum_x \sum_i R_x^i = \sum_i [\sum_x K_x^i (m_x^{id} - m_x^d)] = 0 \qquad (9.25)$$

By adding all these total numbers of excess and missing deaths, the result will be total number of deaths, irrespective of age, which have to be transferred between regions in order to obtain uniform regional mortality conditions:

$$^j IMD = \frac{\sum_i |\sum_x K_x^i (m_x^{id} - m_x^d)|}{^j K^d} \qquad (9.26)$$

or

$$^j IMD = \frac{2 \sum_i [\sum_x K_x^i (m_x^{id} - m_x^d)]}{^j K^d} \qquad \text{for} \qquad (m_x^{id} - m_x^d) > 0 \quad (9.27)$$

This index is not greatly affected by the level of regional disaggregation, as long as the aggregated areas have homogeneous above- or below-average mortality. A detailed description of all of these indices and their application is found in Termote (1986).

9.5. MULTIREGIONAL FERTILITY ANALYSIS

In order to examine the level of fertility not only by age but also by region, Kim (1986) suggests a concept of a two-way table of responses, with ages of mothers along the columns and regions along the rows. A linear model is fitted to this table using the "median polish" technique developed by Tukey (1977). In this procedure, the response in each cell of a two-way table is expressed as the sum of the best fit and residual, i.e.,

$$\text{Response} = \text{fit} + \text{residual}$$

where fit = common value + row effect + column effect. The rationale for this model is that age cannot bear the same relation to fertility experience in all regions, because of the regional differences with respect to socioeconomic, cultural, and contraceptive practices. This procedure is used by Page (1977) in different circumstances. Her model takes into account age and marital duration, instead of region. One can easily translate Page's (1977) model of age and duration into age and regions. The equation of the model is:

$$m(a, r, t) = L(t) \cdot V(a, t) \cdot U(r, t) \qquad (9.28)$$

where $m(a, r, t)$ is the fertility rate for women at age a, region r, and time t. $L(t)$ is the general level of fertility at time t, averaged over all ages and regions. $V(a, t)$ is a factor characteristic of age a at time t, and $U(r, t)$ is a factor characteristic of region r at time t.

The vector $V(a, t)$ represents an age pattern shared by all regions at time t, and the vector $U(r, t)$ is a regional pattern shared by all age groups. Note that the model is multiplicative in nature, meaning that "the extreme situation would arise if fertility varied exponentially with age and region . . . all the regional effects would automatically be included in both the $V(a, t)$ and the $U(r, t)$ estimates and there would be no distinctive pattern of residuals left to indicate its existence. If a regional effect exists, but is not completely exponential then any exponential element will be included in the $V(a, t)$ and $U(r, t)$ estimates, but the remainder will appear as a concentration of residuals in certain age and region combinations" (Page, 1977, p. 90).

The data need to be presented in a two-way table for an estimate of overall average value, $L(t)$, and row and column effects, $V(a, t)$ and $U(r, t)$, to be made. Then one can use procedures suggested by Tukey (1977) such as "trimmed mean polish," to calculate a mean that is unaffected by extreme values. It may be mentioned that since the model is multiplicative, for the sake of convenience, logarithmic transformations can be made to the observed ratios and the mean then calculated for each row. For each row, residuals from their mean can also be calculated. A mean for the whole table needs to be calculated and this is nothing but the mean of all row means. If we subtract the row means from the total mean we get row effects, and after converting these back from logarithms we get the regional effects or the region vector $U(r, t)$. Similarly, to calculate the age vector $V(a, t)$, the mean of the residuals within each column is extracted as the column effect. By converting these column effects back from logarithms, we get the age effects. The only difference between this method and that of Kim (1986) is that Kim uses medians instead of means.

In order to see the fit of the data, Kim suggests that the average size of the residuals be compared with the average deviation of the original data from their median values. She defines this measure of goodness of fit as:

$$G = 1 - \frac{\text{sum of absolute values of residuals}}{\text{sum of absolute values of deviations of the data from median}}$$

$$(9.29)$$

The value of G represents the proportion of the variation in the data accounted for by the row-plus-column model. McNeil (1977) has developed a FORTRAN program that can be used to compute G with one modification, that is, by adjusting the row effects and column effects to sum to zero as in the case of analysis of variance.

Other important measures of reproduction used in fertility analysis are the total fertility rate (TFR), which represents the mean parity of a cohort of women at the end of its childbearing age, assuming that the childbearing years are unaffected by mortality. A slight modification of this measure called the gross reproduction rate (GRR) includes only female births. The GRR is a measure of replacement under the assumption of no mortality. Yet another refinement, which accounts for mortality as well, is known as the net reproduction rate (NRR). The multiregional analog of the NRR is the net reproduction rate matrix, where fertility, mortality, and migration effects are accounted for. When the NRRs are added over all regions of residence for a given region of birth, the resulting total NRR may not be equal to the conventional single region NRR, because the spatial NRR includes the impact of migration on fertility. The high NRR value of a region may be a reflection of higher fertility, lower mortality, and higher migration rates. The decomposition of NRR values, in terms of "where" the offspring would be born, offers a special feature of multiregional analysis. Moreover, in addition to fertility and mortality, the level of interregional migration of parents is also implicit. For a thorough discussion and computer programs, we refer the reader to Willekens and Rogers (1977).

9.6. MULTIREGIONAL STABLE POPULATION ANALYSIS

With fixed age-specific schedules of birth and death rates over a period of time, a closed population ultimately evolves into a stable population. A stable population that exactly maintains itself is known as a stationary population. Extending this phenomenon from the single region case, Rogers (1975) has developed a model of multiregional population dynamics in which migration schedules also play an integral part in addition to fertility and mortality schedules. The multiregional analog states that if regional age-specific schedules of fertility, mortality, and migration are fixed for a long time, the population evolves into a multiregional stable population with fixed regional shares and fixed regional age composition.

If the population evolves into a multiregional stable population, then the stable growth ratio and distribution are independent of the current growth rate and population distribution. Willekens and Rogers (1978) provide a mathematical formula for constant growth matrices in the limit as follows:

$$\{K^{(\infty)}\} = \lim_{t \to \infty} G^t \{K^{(0)}\} \tag{9.30}$$

where $\{K^{(\infty)}\}$ represents the stable population distribution by age and region and G^t is the growth matrix. The age and region composition of this population will be constant, i.e., all regions grow at the same constant ratio, λ. In the case of large values of t, say n, the above equation is expressed as:

$$\lim_{n \to \infty} \{K^{(n)}\} = G^n\{K^{(0)}\} = G^n y\{x\} = \lambda^n y\{x\} = \lambda^n\{y\} \tag{9.31}$$

This equation implies that the concept of stable population would help to separate the population change into two components:

1. That part of the change due to the fundamental demographic parameters (schedules)
2. That part of the change due to the age and regional structure of the base year population (Willekens and Rogers, 1978, p. 69)

The stable growth rate r ($r = \ln\lambda$) can be considered as a rate of discounting. The notion of discounting has relevance to the theory of the *spatial reproductive value*. This concept was developed in multiregional demography by Rogers (1975), Rogers and Willekens (1976), and Willekens (1977b). In the following section we will provide a brief introduction to this concept. The discussion is summarized from Willekens and Rogers (1978).

9.6.1. The Concept of the Spatial Reproductive Value

The concept was originally developed by Fisher (1930). He conceived of life as a debt one incurs at birth, and the production of a child as the repayment of this debt. By assuming the debt at birth to be equivalent to unity, under the stability condition, then the present value of the subsequent repayment will be the characteristic equation of a single-region population system and is given as:

$$1 = \int_0^\infty e^{-ra} m(a)l(a)da = \psi(r) \tag{9.32}$$

The multiregional analogue of (9.32) is

$$\{Q^s\} = \psi(r)\{Q^s\} \tag{9.33}$$

An alternative generalization of (9.33) is

$$\{v^{\langle 0 \rangle}\} = \{v^{\langle 0 \rangle}\}'\psi(r) \tag{9.34}$$

where $\{v^{\langle 0 \rangle}\}$ is the corresponding left eigenvector of $\psi(r)$ and where the prime denotes transposition. If one considers the investment approach to life and childbearing, the new definition of $\{Q^s\}$ is the spatial distribution of the investments (i.e., births) with the intrinsic rate of return of each investment equal to r. Equation (9.33), as a whole, represents births in one generation as a function of the number of births in previous generations. In other words, it implies the number of daughters by which a woman will be replaced in the stable population. With this background, Willekens and Rogers (1978, p. 121) define the reproductive value as follows: "The regional distribution of births is consistent with the given fertility, mortality and migration schedules and with the growth rate or rate of discount, r. Since these schedules differ from one region to another, whereas r is unique, a birth in a less fertile region contributes less to the sustainment of the overall r than a birth in a highly fertile area. The value of a birth for sustaining r depends on the capacity of the 0-year old to produce new lives. This capacity is measured by the '*reproductive value.*' " A detailed discussion on this issue and its empirical application is found in Willekens and Rogers (1978).

9.7. MULTIREGIONAL POPULATION PROJECTION

The problem of multiregional population projection was addressed by Rogers (1966, 1968, 1973a, 1975). The earlier model of Rogers, based on two assumptions to deal with multiregional population growth, is: (1) individuals migrate independently of one another, and (2) migration rates are known (or can be estimated) for all time intervals of the projection period. As far as the first assumption is concerned, it follows the traditional concept of demographic rates by age group of individuals. Rogers's second assumption, that of knowledge of future migration rates, has not been fully examined. But recent research on multiregional projection methodology replaces the use of migration rates by qualitative indicators of past trends in migration. This methodology allows for dynamic changes in the population's redistribution among the various regions. In short, this methodology is a modified form of Rogers's cohort component model of multiregional population growth (Akkerman, 1984).

The most recent and comprehensive model for the multiregional projection of regional populations is one developed by Willekens and Drewe (1990). The important features of this model are as follows:

1. It is a purely demographic model.
2. It is a two-sex, female-dominant model.
3. Lengths of age intervals are free, but equal to the unit length of the projection periods.

4. The number of regions is free (an upper limit of 12 regions is introduced for reasons of data processing).
5. External migration is taken into account.
6. It is a deterministic model.
7. It is a time discrete model.
8. The model parameters are occurrence/exposure (or central) rates of regional fertility, mortality, emigration, and interregional migration.
9. The model structure and estimators of the parameters are derived from a set of accounting equations.

Willekens and Drewe (1990) provide a thorough description of the model including the features of the data requirement and collection procedures. In this section, we will provide a summary of the basic structure of the model. The presentation is directly taken from Willekens and Drewe (1990) and Ramachandran (1990).

Let $_sK_i(x, t)$ be the number of persons in region i at time t, who belong to age x and sex s. The vector $K(t)$ can be partitioned as follows:

$$
K(t) = \begin{bmatrix} K(0, t) \\ K(1, t) \\ \vdots \\ K(x, t) \\ \vdots \\ K(z, t) \end{bmatrix} \quad K(x, t) = \begin{bmatrix} K_1(0, t) \\ K_2(1, t) \\ \vdots \\ K_i(x, t) \\ \vdots \\ K_N(z, t) \end{bmatrix} \quad (9.35)
$$

The model is expressed in the following matrix form:

$$K(t + 1) = G(t)K(t) + F(t)I(t) \quad (9.36)$$

where $K(t)$ is the population vector at time t and $G(t)$ is the coefficient matrix of transition probabilities. $I(t)$ is the vector of the number of immigrants in the interval $(t, t + 1)$ and $F(t)$ is the coefficient matrix indicating the contribution of the immigrants to the population stock at time $t + 1$. Equation (9.35) gives only the general form of the model; Willekens and Drewe (1990) also provide the accounting equations for the initial age group, end age group, and intermediate ages. The accounting equation for the intermediate ages X with $0 < X < (Z - 1)$ for region i is as follows:

Population at time $t + 1$ aged $x + 1$ is

$$K(x + 1, t + 1) = [I + \tfrac{1}{2}M(x, t)]^{-1}[I - \tfrac{1}{2}M(x, t)]K(x, t)$$
$$+ [I + \tfrac{1}{2}M(x, t)]^{-1}O_o(x, t) \qquad (9.37)$$

where $M(x, t)$ is the matrix of occurrence/exposure rates in the interval $(t, t + 1)$, I is the identity matrix, and $O_o(x, t)$ is a vector of x-year-old "immigrants" (i.e., the absolute number of persons) according to region in the interval $(t, t + 1)$.

The matrix $M(x, t)$ is of the form

$$M(x, t) = \begin{bmatrix} m_{11}(x, t) & -m_{21}(x, t) & \cdots & m_{N1}(x, t) \\ -m_{12}(x, t) & m_{22}(x, t) & \cdots & -m_{N2}(x, t) \\ \cdot & \cdot & \cdots & \cdot \\ \cdot & \cdot & \cdots & \cdot \\ \cdot & \cdot & \cdots & \cdot \\ -m_{1N}(x, t) & -m_{2N}(x, t) & \cdots & m_{NN}(x, t) \end{bmatrix} \qquad (9.38)$$

where

$m_{ii}(x, t) = m_{id}(x, t) + \sum_{j \neq i} m_{ij}(x, t) + m_{io}(x, t)$
$m_{id}(x, t) =$ age-specific mortality rate in region i
$m_{ij}(x, t) =$ age-specific internal migration rate from region i to j
$m_{io}(x, t) =$ emigration rate from region i

Equation (9.37) may be expressed as

$$K(x + 1, t + 1) = S(x, t)K(x, t) + F(x, t)O_o(x, t) \qquad (9.39)$$

with

$$S(x, t) = [I + \tfrac{1}{2}M(x, t)]^{-1}[I - \tfrac{1}{2}M(x, t)]$$

and

$$F(x, t) = [I + \tfrac{1}{2}M(x, t)]^{-1}$$

The matrix $S(x, t)$ contains the transition probabilities. An element $S_{ij}(x, t)$ represents the probability that a person aged x to $x + 1$ at moment t and residing in region i survives till $t + 1$ and is in region j. An element $F_{ij}(x, t)$ of $F(x, t)$ denotes the probability that an x-year-old immigrant of region i will be in region j at the end of the interval.

The accounting equation for the last open-ended age group $(z+)$ consists of two groups. The first group, $K(z, t + 1)$, consists of survivors of $(z - 1, z)$-year-old persons at times t. They are between z and $z + 1$ years of age at time $t + 1$. The second group $K(z + 1, t + 1)$ consists of persons who already belong to the highest age group at moment t. Hence, the equation for the last group is:

$$
\begin{aligned}
K(z+, t + 1) &= [I + \tfrac{1}{2}M(z - 1, t)]^{-1}[I - \tfrac{1}{2}M(z - 1, t)]K(z - 1, t) \\
&\quad + [I + \tfrac{1}{2}M(z+, t)]^{-1}[I - \tfrac{1}{2}M(z+, t)]K(z+, t) \\
&\quad + [I + \tfrac{1}{2}M(z - 1, t)]^{-1}O_o(z - 1, t) \\
&\quad + [I + \tfrac{1}{2}M(z+, t)]^{-1}O_o(z+, t) \\
&= S(z - 1, t)K(z - 1, t) + S(z+, t)K(z+, t) \\
&\quad + F(z - 1, t)O_o(z - 1, t) + F(z+, t)O_o(z+, t)
\end{aligned}
\tag{9.40}
$$

The accounting equation for the first age group is derived by considering babies born during the project interval from the population of the first age group 0 at time $t + 1$. First, the number of births during the time interval $(t, t + 1)$ is derived. Next, the number of children in the first age group is expressed.

Number of births during the interval of time $(t, t + 1)$

Let $m_{ib}(x, t)$ denote the age-specific fertility rate of females in the age group x to $x + 1$ in region i at time t. Here the assumption is that the babies born in the unit time interval $(t, t + 1)$ are born in the region of residence to the mothers of age x to $x + 1$. The number of births in region i during t and $t + 1$ in terms of female population of age x is:

$$
B_i(x, t) = \tfrac{1}{2}[m_{ib}(x, t)_f K_i(x, t) + m_{ib}(x + 1, t + 1)_f K_i(x + 1, t + 1)] \tag{9.41}
$$

Note that the immigrant female population is contained in $[_f K_i(x + 1, t + 1)]$.

The equation can be expressed in a matrix form for all of the regions as:

$$
\begin{aligned}
B(x, t) = \tfrac{1}{2}\{&[M_b(x, t) + M_b(x + 1, t + 1)][I + _f S(x, t)]_f K(x, t) \\
&+ \tfrac{1}{2}[M_b(x + 1, t + 1)][_f F(x, t)_f O_o(x, t)]\}
\end{aligned}
\tag{9.42}
$$

where

$B(x, t)$ is a vector of births according to region and age of the mother
$M_b(x, t)$ is a diagonal matrix of age- and region-specific fertility rates

$_fS(x, t)$ is a matrix of transition probabilities of x-year-old women
$_fF(x, t)$ is a matrix of transition probabilities of immigrant women
$_fO_o(x, t)$ is the vector of female immigrants

The total number of births according to region in the interval t to $t + 1$ is:

$$B(t) = \sum_x B(x, t) \qquad (9.43)$$

Number of zero-year-old children at time $t + 1$

All of the babies born during t to $t + 1$ may not survive and be in the same region of birth to become the population of the first age group. These total births contain male and female births. As we do not know the proportion of births of each sex, they can be divided according to the sex ratio at birth. As the survival and migration probabilities are different for each sex, we introduce those probabilities in the equation.

Let g be the sex ratio at birth, i.e., the number of male to female births. The sex ratio is assumed to be independent of age and region of residence of the mother.

The proportion of female births is $_fC = 1/1 + g$ and the proportion of male births is $1 - _fC$.

Assuming uniform distribution of events in the observation interval, the person years lived from birth to first age group in the interval $(t, t + 1)$ is

$$L_i(oo, t) = \tfrac{1}{2}[B_i(t) + K_i(0, t + 1)]$$

The occurrence/exposure rate of dying in the interval $(t, t + 1)$ for newly born children is:

$$m_{id}(00, t) = \frac{2O_{id}(00, t)}{[B_i(t) + K_i(0, t + 1)]}$$

The migration rates are obtained analogously. Now we can obtain the first age group by sex using the respective survival and migration probabilities. We can express it for all regions in the matrix form. The female population in the first age group is

$$_fK(0, t + 1) = [I + \tfrac{1}{2}_fM(oo, t)]^{-1}[_fCB(t) + _fO_o(oo, t)] \qquad (9.44)$$
$$= _fF(oo, t)[_fCB(t) + _fO_o(oo, t)]$$

and the male population is

$$_mK(0, t + 1) = [I + \tfrac{1}{2m}M(oo, t)]^{-1}[(1 - _fC)B(t) + _mO_o(oo, t)] \quad (9.45)$$
$$= _mF(oo, t)[(1 - _fC)B(t) + _mO_o(oo, t)]$$

where $M(oo, t)$ is a matrix of the form (9.38) with the occurrence/exposure rates for newly born children as elements. The $F(oo, t)$ contains the probabilities of the survival and migration of these children.

9.7.1. Two-Sex Open Multiregional Projection Model

The projection model can be expressed in a single matrix expression by integrating Eqs. (9.39), (9.40), (9.42), (9.44), and (9.45) as follows:

$$K(t + 1) = \begin{bmatrix} _fK(t + 1) \\ _mK(t + 1) \end{bmatrix} = \begin{bmatrix} _fH(t) & O \\ _{mf}R(t) & _mH(t) \end{bmatrix} \begin{bmatrix} _fK(t) \\ _mK(t) \end{bmatrix} + F(t) \begin{bmatrix} _fO_o(t) \\ _mO_o(t) \end{bmatrix} \quad (9.46)$$

where

$_sK(t)$ = a vector of the number of people according to sex, age, and region of residence at time t

$_mH(t)$ = a matrix with the transition probability matrices $_mS(x, t)$ on the N subdiagonals

$_fH(t)$ = a matrix with the transition probability matrices $_fS(x, t)$ on the N subdiagonals

$_{mf}R(t)$ = a matrix with the matrices $_mb(x, t)$ on the first N rows

$_sO_o(t)$ = a vector of the number of immigrants in the interval $(t, t + 1)$ according to sex, age at time t, and region of destination; for each sex, the first element refers to the immigration of children born during the interval

$F(t)$ = a matrix of transition probability matrices $_sF(x, t)$

Equation (9.46) is of the form of Eq. (9.36) which will be useful for analyzing and projecting the regional population by sex, age, and region by incorporating international migration.

9.8. SUMMARY

Demography deals with the transition of people from one state at a particular time to another state after a period of time (Keyfitz, 1980). These states can be from nursery to school, school to job, job to retirement; from single to married, married to divorced, divorced to married, married to widowhood; able to disabled, disabled to dead. In the past, these transitions have been calculated in various forms such as constructing an ordinary life table to study the mortality conditions, a nuptiality table, a working life table, and a school going life table, as separate problems. This does not depict the reality where the movements between states occur simultaneously. The multiregional demography that is introduced in this chapter shows that combinations of movements can be handled. This is because formulas that are presented and/ or can be developed based on this approach are multidimensional analogs of the ordinary life table. As Keyfitz (1980) states, this approach unifies a large part of the great complexity, taking account simultaneously of death, migration, working and nonworking, and other movements.

In a simplistic way, in this chapter we have attempted to introduce important developments in the area of multiregional demography. These include model migration schedules, multiregional mortality and fertility analysis, extension of stable population theory to the multiregional analysis, and multiregional population projection.

References

Abdelrahman, A. I., and P. S. Morgan. "Socioeconomic and institutional correlates of family formation: Khartoum, Sudan, 1945–75." *J. Marriage Fam.* **49**:401–412, 1987.

Akkerman, A. "The household composition matrix as a notion in multiregional forecasting of population and households." Unpublished paper, 1984.

Alba, R. D. "Interpreting the parameters of log-linear models." *Sociol. Methods Res.* **16**(1):45–77, 1987.

Aldrich, J., and F. D. Nelson. *Linear Probability, Logit, and Probit Models.* Sage, Beverly Hills, 1984.

Arjas, A., and P. Kangas. "A discrete time method for longitudinal analysis in demography: A comparative study of the data on third births in Sweden by B. and J. Hoern." In James Trussell (Ed.), *Demographic Applications of Event History Analysis.* Oxford University Press, Oxford in press.

Bagozzi, R. P., and M. F. Van Loo. "Toward a general theory of fertility behavior: A causal modeling approach." *Demography* **15**:301–319, 1978.

Balakrishnan, T. R., J. F. Kantner, and J. D. Allingham. *Fertility and Family Planning in a Canadian Metropolis.* McGill–Queen's University Press, Montreal and London, 1975.

Balakrishnan, T. R., K. V. Rao, K. J. Krotki, and E. Lapierre-Adamcyk. "A hazard model analysis of the covariates of marriage dissolution in Canada." *Demography* **24**:395–406, 1987.

Balakrishnan, T. R., K. V. Rao, K. J. Krotki, and E. Lapierre-Adamcyk. "Parametric versus Cox's model: An illustrative analysis of divorce in Canada." *Janasamkhya,* **6**(1):13–27, 1988.

Barclay, G. W. *Techniques of Population Analysis.* Wiley, New York, 1958.

Basavarajappa, K. G., and M. V. George. "An analysis of change in the labour force participation rate, 1961–1976, 1976–1991." Paper presented at the Federation of Canadian Demographers Conference, Montreal, 1979.

Basavarajappa, K. G., and D. Nagnur. "Is the divorce rate in Canada 10% or 40%? Pitfalls in measurement and interpretation." Paper presented at the Canadian Population Society Meetings, Windsor, 1988.

Beckman, L. L., R. Aizenberg, A. B. Forsythe, and T. Day. "A theoretical analysis of antecedents of young couples' fertility decisions and outcomes." *Demography* **20**:519–533, 1983.

Bennett, S. "Loglogistic regression models for survival data." *Appl. Stat.* **32**:165–171, 1983.

Berkson, J. "Application of the logistic function to bio-assay." *J. Am. Stat. Assoc.* **39**:357–365, 1944.

Berkson, J. "Why I prefer logits to probits." *Biometrics* **December**:327–339, 1951.

Berkson, J. "A statistically precise and relatively simple method of estimating the bio-assay with quantal response based upon the logistical function." *J. Amer. Stat. Assoc.* **48**:565–599, 1953.

Bhat, P. N. M. "Estimation of vital rates and age distribution under quasi-stability: Case of India, 1961, re-examined." *Popul. Index* **43**(2):187–205, 1977.

Bilsborrow, R., T. McDevitt, S. Kossoudji, and R. Fuller. "The impact of origin community characteristics on rural–urban out-migration in a developing country." *Demography* **24**:191–210, 1987.

Bishop, Y. M. M., S. E. Fienberg, and P. W. Holland. *Discrete Multivariate Analysis: Theory and Practice.* MIT Press, Cambridge, Mass., 1975.

BMDP. *BMDP Statistical Software Manual.* University of California Press, Berkeley, 1985.

Bock, R. D. *Multivariate Statistical Methods.* Wiley, New York, 1975.

Brass, W. "On the scale of mortality." In W. Brass (Ed.), *Biological Aspects of Demography.* Taylor & Francis, London, 1971.

Brass, W. "Perspectives in population prediction: Illustrated by the statistics of England and Wales (with discussion)." *J. R. Stat. Soc. Ser. A Gen.* **137**(4):532–583, 1974.

Brass, W. *Methods for Estimating Fertility and Mortality from Limited or Defective Data.* Population Research Laboratory, North Carolina University, Chapel Hill, 1975.

Breslow, N. E. "Covariance analysis of censored survival data." *Biometrics* **30**:89–99, 1974.

Burch, T. K. "The index of overall headship: A simple measure of household complexity standardized for age and sex." *Demography* **17**:15–37, 1980.

Burch, T. K., and A. Madan. "A note on the components of Coale's Ig and other indirectly standardized indices." *Can. Stud. Popul.* **13**:151–166, 1986.

Burch, T. K., S. S. Halli, A. Madan, K. Thomas, and L. Wai. "Measures of household composition and headship based on aggregate routine census data." In J. Bongaarts, T. Burch, and K. Wachter (Eds.), *Family Demography: Methods and Their Applications.* Clarendon Press, Oxford, 1987.

Bynner, J. M., and D. M. Romney. "LISREL for beginners." *Can. Psychol.* **26**(1):43–49, 1985.

Carrier, N. H., and J. N. Hobcraft. *Demographic Estimation for Developing Societies.* London, 1971.

Clogg, C. C. "Cohort analysis of recent trends in labor force participation." *Demography* **19**:459–479, 1982.

Coale, A. J. "The decline of fertility in Europe from the French Revolution to World War II." In S. J. Behrman, L. Corsa, Jr., and R. Freedman (Eds.), *Fertility and Family Planning: A World View.* University of Michigan Press, Ann Arbor, 1969.

Coale, A. J. "Constructing the age distribution of a population recently subject to declining mortality." *Popul. Index* **37**(2):75–82, 1971a.

Coale, A. J. "Age patterns of marriage." *Popul. Stud.* **25**(2):193–214, 1971b.

Coale, A. J. *The Growth and Structure of Human Populations: A Mathematical Investigation.* Princeton University Press, Princeton, N.J., 1972.

Coale, A. J. "The development of new models of nuptiality and fertility." Special Issue of *Population* (Sept.):131–154, 1977.

Coale, A. J. "Lecture on demographic models." Office of Population Research, Princeton University, 1988.

Coale, A. J., and P. Demeny. *Regional Model Life Tables and Stable Populations,* 2nd ed. (with B. Vaughan). Academic Press, New York, 1983.

Coale, A. J., and D. R. McNeil. "The distribution by age of the frequency of first marriage in a female cohort." *J. Am. Stat. Assoc.* **67**(340):743–749, 1972.

Coale, A. J., and T. J. Trussell. "Model fertility schedules: Variations in the age structure of childbearing in human populations." *Popul. Index* **40**(2):185–258, 1974.

Cook, N. R., and J. H. Ware. "Design and analysis methods for longitudinal research." *Annu. Rev. Public Health* **4**:1–23, 1983.

Cox, D. R. *The Analysis of Binary Data*. Methuen, London, 1970.

Cox, D. R. "Regression models and life tables (with discussion)." *J. R. Stat. Soc. Ser. B* **34**:184–220, 1972.

Cox, D. R. "Partial likelihood." *Biometrika* **62**:269–276, 1975.

Davis, K., and J. Blake. "Social structure and fertility: An analytic framework." *Econ. Dev. Cultural Change* **4**(3):211–235, 1956.

DeMaris, A. "Interpreting logistic regression results: A critical commentary." *J. Marriage Fam.* **52**:271–277, 1990.

DeMaris, A., and K. V. Rao. "Loglinear models for qualitative dependent variables." Paper presented at the seminar *New Methods for Social and Population Research*. S.V. University, India, 1989.

Derman, C., L. J. Glesen, and I. Olkin. *A Guide to Probability Theory and Applications*. Holt, Rinehart, & Winston, New York, 1973.

Draper, N. R., and H. Smith. *Applied Regression Analysis*. Wiley, New York, 1981.

Duchene, J., and S. Gillet-de Stefano. "Adjustment Analytique des Courbes de Fécondité Generale." *Popul. Fam.* **32**:853–936, 1974.

Enslein, K., A. Ralston, and H. S. Wilf. *Statistical Methods for Digital Computers*, Vol. III. Wiley, New York, 1977.

Ewbank, D. C., J. C. Gomez De Leon, and M. A. Stoto. "A reducible four-parameter system of model life tables." *Popul. Stud.* **37**(1):105–128, 1983.

Farkas, G. "Cohort, age, and period effects upon the employment of white females: Evidence for 1957–1968." *Demography* **14**:33–42, 1977.

Feinberg, S. E., and W. M. Mason. "Identification and estimation of age–period–cohort models in the analysis of discrete archival data." In K. F. Schuessler (Ed.), *Sociological Methodology*. Jossey–Bass, San Francisco, 1978.

Fienberg, S. E. *The Analysis of Cross-Classified Categorical Data*. MIT Press, Cambridge, Mass., 1977.

Feller, W. *An Introduction to Probability Theory and Its Applications*. Vol. 1. Wiley, New York, 1957.

Finney, D. J. *Probit Analysis*. Cambridge University Press, Cambridge, 1971.

Frost, W. H. "The age selection of mortality from tuberculosis in successive decades." *Am. J. Hyg.* **30**(3A):91–96, 1939.

Gehan, E. A. "Estimating survival functions from the life table." *J. Chronic Dis.* **21**:629–644, 1969.

Glenn, N. D. "Cohort analysts' futile quest: Statistical attempts to separate age, period, and cohort effects." *Am. Sociol. Rev.* **41**(Oct.):900–904, 1976.

Gokhale, D. V., and N. S. Johnson. "A class of alternatives to independence in contingency tables." *J. Am. Stat. Assoc.* **73**:800–804, 1978.

Goldscheider, C. *Population, Modernization, and Social Structure*. Little, Brown, Boston, 1971.

Goldthwaite, L. "Failure rate study for the lognormal life time model." *Proceedings of the Seventh National Symposium on Reliability and Quality Control* pp. 208–213, 1961.

Goodman, L. "The analysis of multi-dimensional contingency tables: Stepwise procedures and direct estimation methods for building models with multiple classifications." *Technometrics* **13**:33–61, 1971.

Goodman, L. "A modified multiple regression approach to the analysis of dichotomous variables." *Am. Sociol. Rev.* **37**(Feb.):28–46, 1972.

Gore, S. M., S. J. Pocock, and G. R. Kerr. "Regression models and non-proportional hazards in the analysis of breast cancer survival." *Appl. Stat.* **33**:176–195, 1984.

Graunt, J. *Natural and Political Observations Mentioned in a Following Index, and Made Upon the Bills of Mortality*, London, England, 1662.

Greenhalgh, S., and J. Bongaarts. "Fertility policy in China: Future options." *Science* **235**:1167–1172, 1987.

Grenier, G., D. E. Bloom, and D. J. Howland. "An analysis of the first marriage patterns of Canadian women." *Can. Stud. Popul.* **14**(1):47–68, 1987.

Grindstaff, C. F. "The baby bust: Changes in fertility patterns in Canada." *Can. Stud. Popul.* **2**:15–22, 1975.

Grizzle, J. E., C. F. Starmer, and G. G. Koch. "Analysis of categorical data by linear models." *Biometrics* **25**:489–504, 1969.

Gross, A., and V. Clark. *Survival Distributions: Reliability Applications in Biomedical Sciences.* Wiley, New York, 1975.

Haberman, S. J. *The Analysis of Frequency Data.* University of Chicago Press, Chicago, 1974.

Haberman, S. J. *Analysis of Qualitative Data,* Vol. 1. Academic Press, New York, 1978.

Halpern, M., W. C. Blackwelder, and J. I. Verter. "Estimation of the multivariate logistic risk function: A comparison of the discriminant function and maxim likelihood approaches." *J. Chronic Dis.* **24**:125–158, 1971.

Hanson, S. L., D. E. Myers, and A. L. Ginsburg. "The role of responsibility and knowledge in reducing teenage out-of-wedlock childbearing." *J. Marriage Fam.* **49**:241–256, 1987.

Hanushek, E. A., and J. E. Jackson. *Statistical Methods for Social Scientists.* Academic Press, New York, 1977.

Hayduk, L. A., and T. Wonnacott. "Effect equations' or 'effect coefficients': A note on the visual and verbal presentation of multiple regression interactions." *Can. J. Sociol.* **5**:399–404, 1980.

Heckman, J., and B. Singer. "A method for minimizing the impact of distributional assumptions in econometric models for duration data." *Econometrica* **52**:271–320, 1984a.

Heckman, J., and B. Singer. "The identifiability of the proportional hazard model." *Rev. Econ. Stud.* **51**:231–241, 1984b.

Heligman, J., and J. H. Pollard. "The age pattern of mortality." *J. Inst. Actuaries* **107**:49–80, 1980.

Henry, L. "Some data on natural fertility." *Eugen. Q.* **8**(2):81–91, 1961.

Hernes, G. "The process of entry into first marriage." *Am. Sociol. Rev.* **37**:173–182, 1972.

Hobcraft, J., J. Menken, and S. Preston. "Age, period, and cohort effects in demography; A review." *Popul. Index* **48**(spring):4–43, 1982.

Hoem, J. M., D. Madsen, J. L. Nielsen, E. M. Ohlsen, H. O. Hansen, and B. Rennerman. "Experiments in modelling recent Danish fertility curves." *Demography* **18**:231–244, 1981.

Hogan, H. R., and D. R. McNeil. "On fitting statistical relations to age-specific mortality data." Unpublished paper, Princeton University, Princeton, N.J., 1979.

Holford, T. R. "Life tables with concomitant information." *Biometrics* **32**:587–597, 1976.

Jayachandran, J. "Determinants of fertility in two Canadian populations: A causal modeling approach." *Can. Stud. Popul.* **13**:57–82, 1986.

John, M., J. Menken, and J. Trussell. "Estimating the distribution of interval length: Current status and retrospective history data." *Popul. Stud.* **42**:115–127, 1988.

Johnston, R. J. *Multivariate Statistical Analysis in Geography: A Primer on the General Linear Model.* Longman Group Limited, London, 1978.

Joreskog, K. G. "A general method for estimating a linear structural equation system." In A. S. Goldberger and O. D. Duncan (Eds.), *Structural Equation Models in the Social Sciences.* Seminar Press, New York, 1973.

Joreskog, K. G., and A. S. Goldberger. "Factor analysis by generalized least squares." *Psychometrica* **37**:243–260, 1972.

Kachigan, S. K. *Statistical Analysis: An Interdisciplinary Introduction to Univariate and Multivariate Methods.* Radius Press, New York, 1986.

Kalbfleisch, J., and R. Prentice. *The Statistical Analysis of Failure Time Data.* Wiley, New York, 1980.

Kalmuss, D., and J. A. Seltzer. "Continuity of marital behavior in remarriage: The case of spouse abuse." *J. Marriage Fam.* **48**:113–120, 1986.

Kaplan, E., and P. Meier. "Nonparametric estimation from incomplete observations." *J. Am. Stat. Assoc.* **53**:457–481, 1958.

Kay, R. "Proportional hazard regression models and the analysis of censored survival data." *Appl. Stat.* **26**(3):227–237, 1977.

Keeley, M. C. "An analysis of the age pattern of first marriage." *Int. Econ. Rev.* **20**(2):527–544, 1979.

Kerlinger, F., and E. Pedhazuer. *Multiple Regression in Behavioural Research.* Holt, Rinehart, & Winston, New York, 1973.

Keyfitz, N. "Multidimensionality in population analysis." In K. F. Schuessler (Ed.), *Sociological Methodology.* Jossey–Bass, San Francisco, 1980.

Kim, J. O., and C. W. Mueller. *Factor Analysis: Statistical Methods and Practical Issues.* Sage, Beverly Hills, 1978.

Kim, Y. J. "Fertility." In A. Rogers and F. J. Willekens (Eds.), *Migration and Settlement: A Multiregional Comparative Study.* Reidel, Dordrecht, 1986.

Kitagawa, E. M. "Components of a difference between two rates." *J. Am. Stat. Assoc.* **50**(272): 1168–1194, 1955.

Kleinbaum, D. G., L. L. Kupper, and K. E. Muller. *Applied Regression Analysis and Other Multivariable Methods* (2nd ed.). PWS-Kent, Boston, Mass., 1988.

Knoke, D., and P. J. Burke. *Log-linear Models.* Sage, Beverly Hills, 1980.

Knoke, D., and M. Hout. "Social and demographic factors in American political party affiliations, 1952–72." *Am. Sociol. Rev.* **39**(Oct.):700–713, 1974.

Knoke, D., and M. Hout. "Reply to Glenn." *Am. Sociol. Rev.* **41**(Oct.):905–908, 1976.

Lagakos, S. "The graphical evaluation of explanatory variables in the proportional hazard regression models." *Biometrika* **68**:93–98, 1981.

Land, K., and A. Rogers (Eds.). *Multidimensional Mathematical Demography.* Academic Press, New York, 1982.

Larzelere, R. E., and S. A. Mulaik. "Single-sample tests for many correlations." *Psychol. Bull.* **84**(3):557–569, 1977.

Lavee, Y. "Linear structural relationships (LISREL) in family research." *J. Marriage Fam.* **50**: 937–948, 1988.

Le Bras, H. (Translated by J. Hobcraft.) *Model Life Tables.* Unpublished manuscript, United Nations, 1979.

Lee, R. D. "Aiming at a moving target: Period fertility and changing reproductive goals." *Popul. Stud.* **34**:205–226, 1980.

McDonald, J. *A New Methodological Approach for the Analysis of World Fertility Survey Current Status Breast Feeding Data.* World Fertility Survey Technical Report No. 1732, World Fertility Survey, London, 1981.

McNeil, D. R. *Interactive Data Analysis.* Wiley, New York, 1977.

Magidson, J. "Some common pitfalls in causal analysis of categorical data." *J. Marketing Res.* **19**:461–471, 1982.

Mann, N. R., R. D. Schafer, and N. D. Singpurwalla. *Methods for Statistical Analysis of Reliability and Life Data.* Wiley, New York, 1974.

Mason, K. O., W. M. Mason, H. H. Winsborough, and W. K. Poole. "Some methodological issues in cohort analysis of archival data." *Am. Sociol. Rev.* **38**(April):242–258, 1973.

Maxim, P. "Cohort size and juvenile delinquency: A test of the Easterlin hypothesis." *Social Forces* **63**(3):661–681, 1984.

Menzies, H. *Women and the Chip: Case Studies of the Effects of Informatics on Employment in Canada.* Institute for Research on Public Policy, Montreal, 1981.

Miller, M. D. *Elements of Graduation, Actuarial Monographs No. 1,* The Actuarial Society of America, American Institute of Actuaries, Chicago, 1946.

Miller, R. G., Jr. *Survival Analysis.* Wiley, New York, 1981.

Morgan, P., and R. Rindfuss. "Marital disruption: Structural and temporal dimensions." *Am. J. Sociol.* **90**:1055–1077, 1985.

Mukherjee, B. N. "A factor analysis of some qualitative attributes of coffee." *J. Advertising Res.* **March:**35–38, 1965.

Murphy, E. M., and D. N. Nagnur. "A Gompertz fit that fits: Applications to Canadian fertility patterns." *Demography* **9:**35–50, 1972.

Nair, P. S. "Estimation of period-specific gross migration flows from limited data: Bi-proportional adjustment approach." *Demography* **22**(1):133–142, 1985.

Namboodiri, K., and C. M. Suchindran. *Life Table Techniques and Their Applications.* Academic Press, New York, 1987.

Neter, J., and W. Wasserman. *Applied Linear Statistical Models.* Richard D. Irwin, Inc., Homewood, Ill., 1974.

Newcomer, S., and R. J. Udry. "Parental marital status effects on adolescent sexual behavior." *J. Marriage Fam.* **49:**235–240, 1987.

Nie, N., H. C. Hadlai Hull, J. G. Jenkins, K. Steinbrenner, and D. H. Beut. *Statistical Package for the Social Sciences,* 2nd ed. McGraw–Hill, New York, 1975.

Norusis, M. J. *SPSS Introductory Guide: Basic Statistics and Operations.* McGraw–Hill, New York, 1982.

Page, H. J. "Patterns underlying fertility schedules: A decomposition by both age and marriage duration." *Popul. Stud.* **31**(1):85–106, 1977.

Palmore, E. "When can age, period, and cohort be separated?" *Social Forces* **57**(Sept.):282–295, 1978.

Parnes, H. S. *Unemployment Experience of Individuals Over a Decade: Variations by Sex, Race, and Age.* The W. E. Upjohn Institute for Employment Research, Kalamazoo, Mich., 1982.

Pearl, R. *The Natural History of Population.* Oxford University Press, New York, 1939.

Phillips, P., and E. Phillips. *Women and Work: Inequality in the Labour Market.* Lorimer, Toronto, 1983.

Poppel, F. V., and F. Willekens. *The Decrease in the Age at First Marriage in the Netherlands After the Second World War: A Log-linear Analysis.* Working Paper No. 31, Netherlands Interuniversity Demographic Institute, Voorburg, 1982.

Preston, S. H. "Estimating the proportion of American marriages that end in divorce." *Sociol. Methods Res.* **3**(4):435–460, 1975.

Preston, S. H., and N. G. Bennett. "A census based method for estimating adult mortality." *Popul. Stud.* **37**(1):91–104, 1983.

Preston, S. H., and A. J. Coale. "A generalization of stable population relations." *Popul. Index* **48:**217–259, 1982.

Preston, S. H., N. Keyfitz, and R. Schoen. *Causes of Death Life Tables for National Populations.* Seminar Press, New York, 1972.

Pullum, T. W. "Parameterizing age, period, and cohort effects: An application to U.S. delinquency rates, 1964–1973." In K. F. Schuessler (Ed.), *Sociological Methodology, 1978.* Jossey–Bass, San Francisco, 1977.

Pullum, T. W. "Separating age, period, and cohort effects in white U.S. fertility, 1920–1970." *Soc. Sci. Res.* **9**(Sept.):225–244, 1980.

Ramachandran, P. "Two-sex open multiregional projection model." Paper presented at the North American Applied Demography Conference, Bowling Green, Ohio, Oct. 1990.

Rao, K. V. "Childlessness in Ontario and Quebec: Results from 1971 and 1981 census data." *Can. Stud. Popul.* **14:**27–46, 1987a.

Rao, K. V. *Demographic models of age at first marriage and first birth: An application to Canadian data.* Unpublished Ph.D. dissertation, University of Western Ontario, London, Canada, 1987b.

Rao, K. V. "Analysis of first marriage patterns in Canada." Proceedings of a colloquium Family in Crisis: A Population Crisis? by the Royal Society of Canada and the Canadian Federation of Demographers, pp. 287–302, 1989b.

Rao, K. V. "A note on life table measures from survey data." *Janasamkhya* **6**(2):127–135, 1988a.

Rao, K. V. "Recent trends and sociodemographic covariates of childlessness in Canada." *Can. Stud. Popul.* **15**(2):181–200, 1988b.

Rao, K. V. "Age at first birth in Canada: A hazards model analysis." *Genus* **44**(1, 2):53–72, 1988c.

Rao, K. V., and T. R. Balakrishnan. "Timing of first birth and second birth spacing in Canada." *J. Biosoc. Sci.* **2**:293–300.

Rees, P. H., and A. G. Wilson. "Accounts and models for spatial demographic analysis: Rates and life tables." *Environ. Planning* **A**(7):199–231, 1975.

Robbins, C., H. B. Kaplan, and S. S. Martin. "Antecedents of pregnancy among unmarried adolescents." *J. Marriage Fam.* **47**:567–583, 1985.

Rodgers, W. L. "Estimable functions of age, period, and cohort effects." *Am. Sociol. Rev.* **47**(Dec.): 774–787, 1982.

Rodriguez, G., and J. Hobcraft. *Illustrative Analysis: Life Table Analysis of Birth Intervals in Columbia.* World Fertility Survey Scientific Report No. 16. International Statistical Institute, Voorburg, 1980.

Rogers, A. "The multiregional matrix growth operator and the stable interregional age structure." *Demography* **3**:537–544, 1966.

Rogers, A. *Matrix Analysis of Interregional Population Growth and Distribution.* University of California Press, Berkeley, 1968.

Rogers, A. "The mathematics of multiregional demographic growth." *Environ. Planning* **5**:3–29, 1973a.

Rogers, A. "The multiregional life table." *J. Math. Sociol.* **3**:127–137, 1973b.

Rogers, A. "The multiregional net maternity function and multiregional stable growth." *Demography* **11**:473–481, 1974.

Rogers, A. *Introduction to Multiregional Mathematical Demography.* Wiley, New York, 1975.

Rogers, A., and L. J. Castro. *Model Migration Schedules.* Research Report RR-81-30. International Institute for Applied Systems Analysis, Laxenberg, Austria, 1981.

Rogers, A., and L. J. Castro. "Age patterns of migration: Cause-specific profiles." In A. Rogers and Associates (Eds.), *Migration, Urbanization, and Spatial Population Dynamics.* Westview Press, Boulder, 1984.

Rogers, A., and F. Willekens. "Spatial population dynamics." *Pap. Reg. Sci. Assoc.* **36**:3–34, 1976.

Rogers, A., and F. Willekens. "A short course on multiregional mathematical demography." In A. Rogers and F. J. Willekens (Eds.), *Migration and Settlement: A Multiregional Comparative Study.* Reidel, Dordrecht, 1986.

Rogers, A., R. Raquillet, and L. J. Castro. "Model migration schedules and their applications." *Environ. Planning A* **10**(5):475–502, 1978.

Rousseeuw, P. J., and A. M. Leroy. *Robust Regression and Outlier Detection.* Wiley, New York, 1987.

Roy, T. K., and N. U. Nair. "Marriage and marital fertility: A further decomposition of their effects in the study of levels and changes in the birth rate." *Can. Stud. Popul.* **10**:15–30, 1983.

Rozeboom, W. W. "Ridge regression: Bonanza or beguilement?" *Psychol. Bull.* **86**(2):242–249, 1979.

Ryder, N. B. "La Mesure des Variations de la Fecondite au Cours du Temps." *Population* 7(1): 29–46, 1956.

Ryder, N. B. "The cohort as a concept in the study of social change." *Am. Sociol. Rev.* 30(6): 843–861, 1965.

Ryder, N. B. "Cohort analysis." In D. E. Sills (Ed.), *International Encyclopaedia of the Social Sciences.* Macmillan Co., New York, Vol. 2, pp. 546–550, 1968.

Ryder, N. B. "The future of American fertility." *Soc. Probl.* 26(Feb.):359–370, 1979.

Ryder, N. B. *Progressive Fertility Analysis.* World Fertility Survey Technical Bulletin No. 8. London, England, 1982.

Ryder, N. B. "Observations on the history of cohort fertility in the United States." *Popul. Dev. Rev.* 12(4):617–643, 1986.

SAS Institute Inc. *SUGI Supplemental Library User's Guide* (Version 5 ed.). SAS Institute Inc., Cary, N.C., 1986.

Schoen, R. *Modeling Multigroup Populations.* Plenum Press, New York, 1988.

Schoenfeld, D. "Goodness-of-fit tests for the proportional hazards regression model." *Biometrika* 67:145–154, 1980.

Sheps, M. C., and Menken, J. A. *Mathematical Models of Conception and Birth.* University of Chicago Press, Chicago, 1973.

Shryock, H. S., J. S. Siegel, and Associates (Condensed Edition by E. G. Stockwell) *The Methods and Materials of Demography.* Academic Press, New York, 1976.

Smith, D. P. *Life Table Analysis.* World Fertility Survey Technical Bulletin No. 6, International Statistical Institute, Voorburg, 1980.

Smith, D. P. "A reconsideration of Easterlin cycles." *Popul. Stud.* 35(2):247–264, 1981.

Smith, D. P. *Formal Demography.* Plenum Press, New York, 1991.

Smith, H. L., W. M. Mason, and S. E. Fienberg. "More chimeras of the age–period–cohort accounting framework: Comment on Rodgers." *Am. Sociol. Rev.* 47(Dec.):787–793, 1982.

SPSS Inc. *SPSS User's Guide* (4th ed.). SPSS Inc., Chicago, 1990.

Srinivasan, K. *Birth Interval Analysis in Fertility Surveys.* World Fertility Survey Scientific Report No. 7, International Statistical Institute, Voorburg, 1980.

Statistics Canada. *Revised Annual Estimates of Population, by Sex and Age, Canada and the Provinces, Catalogue 91-512.* Ottawa, 1973.

Statistics, Canada. *Guide to Federal Government Labour Statistics, Catalogue 72-512.* Ottawa, 1979a.

Statistics Canada. *Revised Annual Estimates of Population, by Sex and Age, Canada and the Provinces, Catalogue 91-518.* Ottawa, 1979b.

Statistics Canada. *Post-Censal Estimates of Population, by Sex and Age, Canada and the Provinces, Catalogue, 91-518.* Ottawa, 1982.

Statistics Canada. *Inter-censal Annual Estimates of Population, by Sex and Age, Canada and the Provinces, Catalogue 91-518.* Ottawa, 1983.

Stix, R. E., and F. W. Notestein. *Controlled Fertility: An Evaluation of Clinic Services.* Williams & Wilkins, Baltimore, 1940.

Stone, L. O. *The Frequency of Geographic Mobility in the Population of Canada.* Statistics Canada, Ottawa, 1978.

Studer, M., and A. Thornton. "Adolescent religiosity and contraceptive usage." *J. Marriage Fam.* 49(1):117–128, 1987.

Swafford, M. "Three parametric techniques for contingency table analysis: A nontechnical commentary." *Am. Sociol. Rev.* 45:664–690, 1980.

Tabachnick, B. G., and L. S. Fidell. *Using Multivariate Statistics* (2nd ed.). Harper & Row, New York, 1989.

Taylor, K. W., and N. L. Chappell. "Multivariate analysis of qualitative data." *Can. Rev. Sociol. Anthropol.* 17(2):93–108, 1980.

Teachman, J. D. "Analyzing social processes: Life tables and proportional hazards models." *Soc. Sci. Res.* **12**:263–301, 1983.

Termote, M. "Canada." In A. Rogers and F. J. Willekens (Eds.), *Migration and Settlement: A Multiregional Comparative Study.* Reidel, Dordrecht, 1986.

Thurstone, L. L. *Multiple Factor Analysis.* University of Chicago Press, Chicago, 1947.

Truett, J., J. Cornfield, and W. Kannel. "A multivariate analysis of the risk of coronary heart disease in Framingham." *J. Chronic Dis.* **20**:511–524, 1967.

Trussell, J. "Estimating the determinants of birth interval length." In John Hobcraft (Ed.), *The Measurement of Fertility: Incorporating the Proximate Determinants.* Oxford University Press, Oxford, in press.

Trussell, J., and D. Bloom. "Estimating the covariates of age at marriage and first birth." *Popul. Stud.* **37**:403–416, 1983.

Trussell, J., and K. V. Rao. "Premarital cohabitation and marital stability: A reassessment of the Canadian experience." *J. Marriage Fam.* **51**:535–544, 1989.

Trussell, J., and S. Preston. "Estimating the covariates of childhood mortality from retrospective reports of mothers." *Health Policy Educ.* **3**:31–36, 1982.

Trussell, J., and T. Richards. "Correcting for unobserved heterogeneity in the hazard models: An application of the Heckman–Singer model to demographic data." In N. Tuma (Ed.), *Sociological Methodology.* Jossey–Bass, San Francisco, 1985.

Tucker, L., and C. Lewis. "A reliability coefficient for maximum likelihood factor analysis." *Psychometrica* **38**:1–10, 1973.

Tukey, J. W. *Exploratory Data Analysis.* Addison–Wesley, Reading, Mass., 1977.

Tuma, N. B., M. T. Hannan, and L. P. Groeneveld. "Dynamic analysis of event histories." *Am. J. Sociol.* **84**:820–854, 1979.

United Nations. *Age and Sex Patterns of Mortality: Model Life Tables for Underdeveloped Countries.* ST/SOA/SEX A/22, New York, 1955.

United Nations. *Manual IV: Methods of Estimating Basic Demographic Measures from Incomplete Data.* Population Studies No. 42. ST/SOA/SEX A/42, New York, 1967.

United Nations. *Manual X: Indirect Techniques for Demographic Estimation.* Population Studies No. 81. ST/ESA/SER A/81, New York, 1983.

Watson, G. S., and W. T. Wells. "On the possibility of improving the mean useful life of items by eliminating those with short lives." *Technometrics* **3**:281–298, 1961.

Whelpton, P. K. "Reproduction rates adjusted for age, parity, fecundity, and marriage." *J. Am. Stat. Assoc.* **23**(6):501–516, 1946.

White, J. "Premarital cohabitation and marital stability in Canada." *J. Marriage Fam.* **49**:641–647, 1987.

Willekens, F. *The Recovery of Detailed Migration Patterns from Aggregate Data: An Entropy Maximizing Approach.* Research Report RR-77-58. International Institute for Applied Systems Analysis, Laxenberg, Austria, 1977a.

Willekens, F. "Sensitivity analysis in multiregional demographic models." *Environ. Planning A* **9**:653–674, 1977b.

Willekens, F. "Approaches and innovations in policy-oriented migration and population distribution research." In H. T. Heide and F. J. Willekens (Eds.), *Demographic Research and Spatial Policy: The Dutch Experience.* Academic Press, New York, 1984.

Willekens, F. *Multiregional Demography.* Working Paper No. 59. Netherlands Interuniversity Demographic Institute, Voorburg, 1985.

Willekens, F., and N. Baydar. *Hybrid Log-linear Models.* Working Paper No. 41. Netherlands Interuniversity Demographic Institute, Voorburg, 1983.

Willekens, F., and J. Drewe. "A multiregional model for regional demographic projection." In H. T. Heide and F. J. Willekens (Eds.), *Demographic Research and Spatial Policy: The Dutch Experience.* Academic Press, New York, 1984.

Willekens, F., and J. Drewe. "A multiregional model for regional demographic projection." In F. Willekens (Ed.), *Multistate Demography: New Methods and Applications.* Reidel, Amsterdam, 1990.

Willekens, F., and A. Rogers. *Normative Modeling in Demo-Economics.* Research Report RR-77-23. International Institute for Applied Systems Analysis, Laxenberg, Austria, 1977.

Willekens, F., and A. Rogers. *Spatial Population Analysis: Methods and Programs.* Research Report RR-78-18. International Institute for Applied Systems Analysis, Laxenberg, Austria, 1978.

Willekens, F., A. Por, and R. Raquillet. "Entropy, multiproportional, and quadratic techniques for inferring patterns of migration from aggregate data." In A. Rogers (Ed.), *Advances in Multiregional Demography.* Research Report RR-81-6. International Institute for Applied Systems Analysis, Laxenberg, Austria, 1981.

Willekens, F. J., I. Shah, J. M. Shah, and P. Ramachandran. "Multi-state analysis of marital status life tables: Theory and applications." *Popul. Stud.* **36**:129–144, 1982.

Wilson, A. G., and P. Rees. "Accounts and models for spatial demographic analysis: Age–sex disaggregated populations." *Environ. Planning A* **6**:101–116, 1974.

Wunsch, G. J., and M. C. Termote. *Introduction to Demographic Analysis: Principles and Methods.* Plenum Press, New York, 1978.

Zaba, B. "The four-parameter logit life table system." *Popul. Stud.* **33**(1):79–100, 1979.

Index